Dark Continent
My Black Arse

Dark Continent
My Black Arse

by bus, boksie, matola … from Cape to Cairo

SIHLE KHUMALO

UMUZI

The author is indebted to http://en.wikipedia.org for much of the information contained in the 'Father of the Nation' boxes at the start of each chapter in this book.

Some names of persons encountered on this trip have been altered for their protection.

Published by Umuzi
P.O. Box 6810, Roggebaai 8012
umuzi@randomhouse.co.za
an imprint of
Random House (Pty) Ltd,
Isle of Houghton, Corner Boundary Road &
Carse O'Gowrie, Houghton 2198, South Africa

First edition, first printing 2007
Second printing 2007
Third printing 2007
Fourth printing 2008
ISBN: 978-1-4152-0036-0

Cover and text design by mr design
Cover image based on an old etching from David and Charles Livingstone's
Zambesi Expedition, 1865, and a photograph supplied by Sihle Khumalo
Set in Palatino
Printed and bound by Paarl Print, Oosterland Street, Paarl, South Africa

For Nonkululeko 'Lulu' Khumalo (née Matiwane) –
the wind beneath my wings

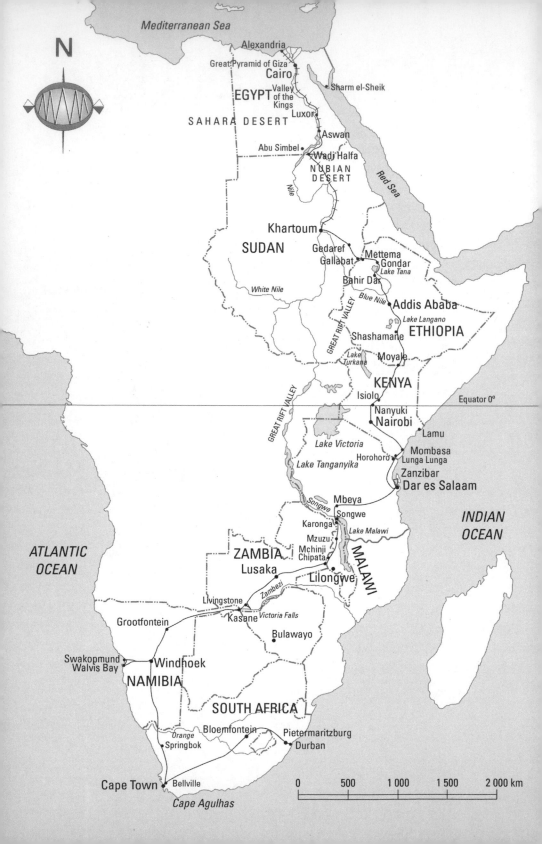

Contents

The rest of Africa is calling

It is said that, when Colonel Ewart S Grogan wanted to marry the woman of his dreams, the father of the bride-to-be thought Grogan was not man enough. 'Will travelling from Cape to Cairo make me man enough to marry your daughter?' the colonel-to-be asked.

The rest, as they say, is history. Ewart S Grogan became the first European to undertake the Cape to Cairo – on foot. It took the 22-year-old Cambridge undergraduate three years. He arrived in Cairo in the year 1900 and returned to London to marry his loved one.

More recently, Peter Moore, author of *Swahili for the Broken Hearted*, did the Cape to Cairo because he had been dumped by the Girl Next Door (GND). Legend has it that Dr Livingstone explored Africa for 33 years because he wanted to escape from his wife, Mary, the daughter of the missionary Robert Moffat.

For me, however, things could not have been better on the love front. I did not have to prove myself to a future father-in-law or to cure a broken heart or to get away from a wife. I had been engaged for six months to the woman of my dreams and we had a 16-month-old baby. (It's a black thing: darkies have a baby first and only then get engaged or married.) But I – like Mike Copeland, author of *Cape to Cairo* and one of the most recent followers in the footsteps of Colonel Grogan – wanted to do the trip to celebrate something. Mike was celebrating his 50th birthday; I wanted to celebrate having turned 30.

As expected, not everyone thought it was a great idea. For instance, my future father-in-law's response was: 'I always thought you were a psychopath but now, over and above that, I think you are a serial killer.' To this day I am not sure what doing the Cape to Cairo has to do with being a serial killer, but I have learned the wisdom of agreeing with my now-for-real father-in-law.

My dream of travelling up Africa started when I was a young boy and learned about an imperialist named Cecil John Rhodes who wanted to link Cape Town and Cairo through railway infrastructure. From that moment on I was obsessed with the idea of travelling from the Cape to Cairo. My occasional travels through southern Africa in my twenties further ignited my childhood dream of 'conquering' Africa.

Six months before my 30th birthday, I began to seriously consider resigning from the company for which I had been working for almost ten years. In retrospect I can see that I started working, relatively speaking, at too young an age. I think that, for a boy who was raised by a single mother in the rural areas, things happened too quickly for me.

From Grade 1 (in township schools we called it *u-festiya* – 'first year') until my last year at a tertiary institution I was always the youngest in my class, notwithstanding the fact that after matric (Grade 12) I spent a whole year loitering at home because my mother could not afford to send me to Natal Technikon, in Durban. I joined the corporate world at 20 and already had my own car and apartment by the sea by the age of 22 (no sea views, though); at 24, I was a middle manager. Two local return air tickets per annum were part of my package, as well as a 75 per cent discount on an international flight every five years. My other perks included a car and cellphone allowance, and the usual fringe benefits associated with a large progressive company.

By resigning I would be giving up all of this and, as if that were not enough, I would have no form of income for approximately one year, which was the time I had allocated for travelling and for attempting to write a book based on my travels.

I knew that if I did not do the Cape to Cairo trip when I was 30, I would not do it at all. Even as a young boy I had felt that 32 was the right age to get married, especially if you are a male. So I was working towards getting officially settled round about that time. Therefore it made perfect sense, to me at least, to do all the 'stupid' things I could before legally giving my woman a chain and padlock.

In his book *When Everything You Ever Wanted Is Not Enough*, Harold Kushner talks about something called the imposter phenomenon– having everything you've ever dreamt of yet getting bored with life because you have nothing to look forward to. Although I was indeed at times bored with life, I was not exactly suffering from the imposter phenomenon. I was, rather, at a point in my life where money on its own was no longer enough of a motivator. I wanted to do something more fulfilling and meaningful with my life than just accumulating material things and having a big fat bank balance. I did not have loads of money, mind you, but if you, like me, grew up just below the poverty line, middle class looks and feels like you have arrived.

A month before my birthday, I took the plunge and resigned. A few days later there were rumours going around at work that I had won the Lotto. Understandably so, since people normally resign because they are either venturing into business or migrating to greener pastures. Hence, most people did not understand how I could leave a good job in such a good company with such good colleagues to 'do something so stupid and dangerous'.

What they did not know was that I was leaving the corporate world and normal life because I was sick and tired of

> routine
> being stuck in the comfort zone
> being stuck in a rut
> being stuck in traffic every morning and every afternoon
> driving on the same road to the same office every weekday to
>   do pretty much the same thing
> dealing with the same things daily, weekly, monthly, yearly
> sweating the small stuff
> trying to solve imaginary problems
> being a manager
> dealing with systems, guidelines, policies and procedures
> attending meetings, workshops and conferences
> sending reports to Head Office
> worrying about how to make more money
> looking at life from a strictly financial perspective
> worrying about tomorrow and the day after and the day after
> being a statistic

being in limbo
wasting golden opportunities
wasting God's precious time and my own
voting in all the general elections but, somehow, still feeling
    oppressed
sleeping with beautiful women and thinking that would make
    me happy
drinking beer and watching soccer on TV every weekend
being bored with life and doing nothing about it
not living the life I suspected I was meant to live
feeling life was passing me by
feeling like I was missing out on something
In short: enduring the pain of a dying soul crying out to be free.

Instead I wanted to:

take the bull by the horns
give life my all
give life my best shot
live in the present
find myself
find peace of mind
be who I wanted to be
do the things I genuinely wanted to do
do challenging and out-of-this-world things
create my own beautiful, yet simple, life
live my own life, in my own way, on my own terms
leave a difficult act to follow when I die
In short: be me – just me, nobody else but me.

As much as I knew that from a financial perspective it was almost impossible to live without some type of income, I did not want to carry
on doing things I didn't want to do. I wanted to wake up in the morning – for at least a year – and not have to worry about deadlines to
meet, reports to submit and meetings to attend. I wanted a break from

it all, where I could live a life with no responsibilities and worries. I wanted to, as the Indians in Durban say, 'Do my own thing and carry on – one time.'

I'm still not sure how people work for years, especially in the corporate world, without taking a proper break. Let's face it, even when you are on leave you are constantly thinking about work. After ten years of corporate bullshit, I wanted to take a breather or, as we say in Zulu, *bengifuna ukukhokh'umoya*.

Not least among my reasons for taking myself on the Cape to Cairo was a burning desire to see with my own eyes the present state of Africa – a bit like Paul Theroux, who did the trip in reverse overland and then wrote *Dark Star Safari*. This motive, which seems political but was in fact deeply personal, inspired the brief 'Father of the Nation' note at the beginning of each chapter in this book – i.e., for each country I travelled through.

The Father of the Nation of the country I come from, South Africa, is none other than Nelson Mandela, the man who spent 27 years in prison because of his convictions and came out of prison with no recriminations. Ironically, when he became the first democratically elected president of the Republic of South Africa in 1994, he was more willing to forgive and let bygones be bygones than many black South Africans who had suffered much less. He led from the front as far as nation-building and creating a racially-inclusive society are concerned, and he is one of the best leaders this planet has seen in recent times. With someone like that from whom to learn a few lessons in humanity, I thought I could handle whatever the rest of Africa could throw at me.

On my first weekend as an unemployed person, I felt an excruciating pain while playing soccer, just above my right heel. Suddenly, I could not even walk, leave alone finish the game. The following day my doctor referred me to an orthopaedic surgeon.

After examining my foot and asking me a few basic questions, the man told me the bad news: 'Mr Khumalo, you have snapped your Achilles tendon. You have to undergo an operation and will have your leg in a cast for six to eight weeks.' When I told him about my travel plans he, without thinking twice, said, 'Cancel the trip. You will damage your tendon further and it might never fully recover.'

He gave me a day to decide – operation or not?

For me, there was really nothing to decide. I had given up my job and there was no way I was going to cancel or even postpone the trip. An option, he told me when I saw him again, was to wear a built-up shoe to help the tendon heal naturally. That sounded more reasonable and I was referred to another specialist to help me obtain the orthopaedic shoe.

The second surgeon suggested that my shoe be elevated by four centimetres and that a centimetre be taken off every week so that, under normal circumstances, I would be wearing normal shoes after just four weeks. I was soon in high spirits again. However, when I went to see the second surgeon for the second time he discovered that my tendon was healing more slowly than anticipated. It was going to take two months, if not more, for it to heal completely.

When I had two centimetres still left on the shoe I realised that the whole process was taking far too long for my liking and decided that I would start the journey with an elevated shoe. My official version for the specialist was that I was going on a two-week trip. He said it was fine but it was important that I see him as soon as possible after my return.

Just in case, I made sure I had good travel insurance, and – armed with five vaccinations from the travel doctor – I was more than ready to paint Africa red.

But it was not the end of being tried and tested. Two days before I left, two completely unrelated events almost made me cancel my trip.

The first was the bombing at the Red Sea resort town of Sharm el-Sheik in Egypt, in which more than 88 people were killed, mostly tourists. According to the route I had planned (you don't have an itinerary when you do a trip like this), I would be going through this Red Sea resort on my way to Cairo.

The second was a burglary. While my fiancée and I were asleep, an unknown person (persons?) broke into my car and stole the sound system. It is amazing that they left untouched five bottles of whisky in the boot, which were going to be consumed the following day at my bon voyage party. What made me really scared, though, was the well-known fact that criminals do their homework very well before breaking in. It was clear to me that some person(s) had been monitoring our movements.

What was even more worrying for me was what would happen if our monitor(s) continued to monitor us and, realising that I had left, tried something more sinister than breaking into the car while my fiancée was alone with our daughter. White people in our country tend to think that they are the prime targets of crime. Not so. South African criminals must be one of the most non-racist sectors of our society. As long as you have what the criminal wants, he does not care about your colour. That is why, contrary to popular belief, more criminal activities actually take place in the townships than in the suburbs. That's just how it is.

Angry as I was that my sound system had been stolen, I could not let such a small event in the bigger scheme of things deter me from going on a once-in-a-lifetime expedition. I resigned myself to the fact that as long as unemployment remained high and the majority of people in our country continue to live below the poverty line thugs would have an excuse to take my state-of-the-art sound system from the parking area of a secure residential complex without asking my permission. Despite some reservations – even after a boisterous bon voyage party at my brother's place in Westville where family members and close friends bid me *uhambo oluhle* – it was all systems go.

My plan was to take an early flight from Durban to Cape Town, pick up a car and drive to the southernmost tip of the continent, Cape Agulhas, to start the journey there. The following morning I would drive back to Cape Town in time to catch a bus to Windhoek, Namibia.

It seemed like a reasonable plan.

On the appointed day, 25 July 2005, my fiancée and I woke up very early in order to make it to the airport on time. I kissed my 17-month-old daughter goodbye, making sure that I did not wake her up. She looked so peaceful, innocent and vulnerable. I knew it would be

15

months before I saw her again and at that moment I felt like a selfish and irresponsible father. But there was no turning back. With a wave of the hand to u-Anti (the nanny), I was off.

On our way to the airport, the situation was, somehow, tense. My fiancée had been feeling very unsafe after the car break-in and, on top of that, she was very concerned about my safety in other African countries. While preparing for the trip I had planned that on our way to the airport I would play two classic hits full blast: 'Africa' by Toto and 'Africa' by Salif Keita. Like me, both had the continent on their mind. With the car's sound system gone, my plan came to nothing. We drove down the N2 in deathly silence.

At the airport, there was a small glitch: employees of the national airline were on strike and most SAA flights departing from Durban were cancelled. I had seen on the news the previous night that there was a strike on and thought that, at worst, flights would be delayed but not cancelled indefinitely, as now appeared to be the case. Using another airline was not an alternative because all flights were already fully booked.

Since I had booked a ticket on the Cape Town–Namibia bus for the following day, it was imperative that I got to Cape Town without much further ado. While other passengers were cursing and shouting at the airline's senior managers, who were at pains to try to explain and to apologise for the inconvenience caused, I reasoned that the logical thing to do was to take a bus.

My fiancée and I left a chaotic and packed airport terminal and rushed to Durban station to see if there was still a bus leaving for Cape Town that morning. With people who live in the southern part of Durban motoring to work on a Monday morning, traffic had started to accumulate on the M4 freeway (recently renamed Inkosi Albert Luthuli Highway after Chief Luthuli, once president of the African National Congress and the first African to receive the Nobel Prize). It took us 30 minutes to negotiate the traffic on Luthuli Highway and arrive at Durban station.

Once there, I was very relieved to be able to book a seat and purchase a bus ticket. Which meant that, instead of a two-hour flight,

I was going to spend 22 hours travelling by road to Cape Town. I knew that the Cape to Cairo was not always going to be easy, but I had not anticipated that getting to the starting point was going to be this difficult.

The bus was going to leave Durban only in four hours' time. Since my fiancée was working in the city centre we decided to go to her office to kill time. One thing led to another and before I knew it we were having sex in her office (she, like other women, prefers to call it 'making love'). There is something exciting about having sex in the office. The possibility of files falling from the table/somebody walking in/accidental bumping of the head on the computer screen/trying to suppress any noises in case someone is walking past, etc., etc., heightens the pleasure.

Back at Durban station, rejuvenated and in high spirits, we hugged and kissed, my fiancée very much aware that this was one of the biggest risks I would ever take. I promised that I was going to be safe and that I was going to keep in touch. By then she was in tears and the other passengers were giving her the 'what-is-wrong-with-you' look. Close as I was to crying myself, I had to be strong for her sake and quickly stepped into the Greyhound bus, my backpack stowed in the belly of the bus but my sleeping bag with me.

As the bus joined the main freeway, just past the Berea Centre, I spotted my fiancée driving next to us, waving and blowing kisses. I reciprocated while fighting back the tears, and looked steadfastly at the office parks and the Musgrave Centre flashing by.

An hour later we arrived at Pietermaritzburg, KwaZulu-Natal's capital city, now sometimes also called by the original Zulu name uMgungundlovu and not by the name of the Voortrekker leader Piet Retief. Here I was joined in the bus by Nkosinathi Mtshali, who I learned was a student in Cape Town who had come up for his older brother's funeral. Lying back in the seat next to me, Nathi told me his late brother, a teacher, loved two things: babes and booze. He had been sick for more than 18 months. I could see that Nathi was still hurting.

Being an introvert I normally find it very hard to console someone I know, leave alone a stranger. So, instead of trying to comfort Nathi I changed the subject. I started talking about beautiful women.

That seemed to work. Nathi confessed that he, too, could not resist beautiful women. By the time we stopped in Montrose – the unofficial halfway point between Durban and Johannesburg – he had relaxed and we were talking about cars, politics, sports and stuff like that. Because the bus was not full, I was able to move, towards evening, to an empty seat and sleep comfortably. My sleeping bag ensured that I survived the freezing Free State night.

It was a comfortable trip, except that roadworks and fog between Laingsburg and Worcester caused the bus to run about 60 minutes late. We were still about an hour and a half from Cape Town when I realised I was going to miss the bus to Namibia. I thought of forfeiting the ticket I had bought for the Cape Town–Windhoek leg of the journey but, since buses to Namibia travel only on certain days, this meant I would be forced to spend at least three days in Cape Town. Apart from Mpucuko, a friend who was a medical student at the University of Cape Town, and Nathi, blissfully asleep sprawled over two seats, I knew no one there. Also, I had not budgeted for three days in a city that caters mainly for overseas tourists with deep pockets.

I had, again, to think proactively. I decided to jump off the bus at Bellville, the second-to-last stop before Cape Town and the first stop out of Cape Town for buses en route to Namibia, in the hope that my seat would not have been sold to standby passengers at Cape Town station, the starting point.

The implication for my trip was of course that it would not begin at the southern tip of the continent. In fact, I was not even going to be able to start from Cape Town, leave alone Cape Agulhas, the south-ernmost point of the continent. I had always wanted to visit Cape Agulhas ('Cape of Needles'), so named by the seafaring Portuguese explorers of the 15th century because of the sharp rocks and reefs that wrecked so many of their ships. It looked as if I was not going to be able to see the meeting place of the Atlantic and Indian oceans, the great oceanic divide where two currents – the cold Agulhas and the warm Benguela – merge.

Since I had been to Cape Town a number of times, I was not too disappointed about this change of plan and about not visiting one of the most beautiful cities on the continent, if not on earth. However, there are four Cape Town trips that I want to include in this Cape to Cairo account:

I made my first trip to Cape Town when I was a third-year student at the then Natal Technikon (now Durban University of Technology). I remember only one thing well about that trip – drinking cheap brandy in the backseat of the bus. It was 1995 – a year after South Africa's first democratic elections – and, once in Cape Town, we headed for Parliament where we were addressed by a female MP. As a highly ignorant student I did not understand the significance of sitting in a hall which, until the previous year, was a no-go area for black people – not to mention the significance of being addressed by a black female parliamentarian. Pity I was too drunk to care or understand what she was talking about.

The one thing I remember about that speech is the phrase 'the new dispensation', which the MP kept repeating. At the time I was too inebriated to appreciate that after 46 years of official racial segregation and white domination our lives would no longer be determined by the colour of our skin. It did not strike me then that, precisely because of the new dispensation the woman was talking about, I stood a better chance in life than my parents when they were my age.

My second trip to the fairest Cape was the most enjoyable and best organised. It was my first year in the corporate world and, together with two colleagues, I attended a week-long course there. One of my colleagues, Stephanie, had studied in the Cape, so she took us around to all the hip-and-happening bars and some of the exclusive and sought-after strip clubs Cape Town had on offer. It was on that trip that I came to the conclusion that, although I had never been outside South Africa, Cape Town had to be one of the most beautiful cities in the world.

My third and most enriching trip to Cape Town was when I took my mother to the Mother City. It was just before South Africa's second general election in 1999 and it was the first time she had been in an airplane. For her everything was fascinating and mind-blowing. She did not eat during the flight because she thought she might throw up. She prayed every time we hit a bit of turbulence.

The show-stopper on that trip was a visit to Robben Island. My mother was deeply moved by what Nelson Mandela and the other political prisoners went through during their incarceration. On our way back from the island I noticed that she was uncharacteristically quiet and absorbed in very deep thought. As the ferry entered the Cape Town harbour she said, out of the blue, *'Hhayi ngeke, ngizovotela i-ANC.'* Loosely translated this means: 'Hell no, I will vote for the ANC!' To appreciate the extent of this life-changing experience it must be remembered that my mother, although educated, had spent almost all her life in rural northern KwaZulu-Natal, where the Inkatha Freedom Party was the only party anyone ever voted for.

My fourth and most recent trip to the Mother City was when I went down with the Top Dogs, my friends, to listen to the likes of Beyonce Knowles, Peter Gabriel, Anastasia, Bob Geldof, Eurhythmics, Angelina Kidjo and Youssou N'dour at the first 46664 Concert at Greenpoint Stadium on 29 November 2003. The concert was part of a series of charity shows to honour Nelson Rholihlahla Mandela, former Robben Island polical prisoner number 46664 – the 466th prisoner to arrive, in 1964. The trip was fun although we were in the company of our girlfriends and could not manoeuvre, as most guys would love to do when visiting another city, because our madams kept a very close eye on us.

While I was offloading my bags from the Durban bus in Bellville, the Namibia-bound bus pulled in. I realised that if I had stayed on the Durban bus until it reached Cape Town station I would most definitely have missed the Namibia bus. It was literally a case of getting off one bus and climbing into the other. It was certainly not the ideal way of starting a long overland trip. I had already spent a long night on a bus and I was tired. Naturally, my Cape to Cairo expedition started with a very big yawn.

'Are you related to Doctor Khumalo, the soccer player?'

This was the first question the hostess on the bus asked me, in typical Cape Coloured English, peppered with Afrikaans words and sounds, after checking my ticket.

'The question should be "Is Doctor Khumalo related to me?"' I replied. 'And the answer to that question will be: "No he is not."' While she was giving me that 'who-do-you-think-you-are' look, I used the opportunity to peer at Table Mountain, looking unimpressive from a distance but clearly visible on this cold Cape winter's morning.

On the upper deck I found a seat next to a slightly overweight girl at the back of the bus. Her name was Laura and she had been visiting her boyfriend in Cape Town for three days. She looked tired and exhausted. I understood why.

We passed Tygervalley shopping mall, drove through Durbanville and took the R302 to the N7, which runs in a northerly direction from Cape Town through Namibia, where it is called the B1, all the way to the Angolan border. This was the fourth time I had been on the West Coast. The other three times I had to go to the port of Saldanha for work reasons. Whenever I travel in the Wes-Kaap, as the locals call it, I cannot help but think of my retirement days. I would love to retire to a place like the West Coast, with little traffic, white sand, laid-back culture and open spaces. I like the dry look of the coast with its short and sparse vegetation – the exact opposite of my home town Durban where lush sub-tropical shrubs and trees compete for space with thousands of human beings living all over the place.

Apart from a nervous feeling that our bus was having a problem with gear selection and transmission, it was pleasant and relaxing to go through the small towns along the N7: Piketberg, Clanwilliam, Klawer, Vanrhynsdorp, Bitterfontein, Garies, Kamieskroon. Throughout the journey I kept asking myself: what do people do with themselves in these small towns in the middle of nowhere? I knew that in spring tourists flocked there to view the thousands of desert flowers that turn most of Namaqualand into a colourful garden, but at this time of year, besides the occasional sheep, there were few signs of human activity on those grey and dusty plains.

One thing for sure, though, is that people there have a far better quality of life than we city dwellers. Living in a small town makes you stop living life as if it is one big emergency. You stop chasing your own tail because you are not thinking that more money will make you happy

You do not have to accept the concrete jungle, which is what a big city is, with noise, fake/shallow people, air pollution and traffic as part of your daily life.

People who live in small towns tend to be more relaxed and calm and their lives far simpler and more stress-free than those of their big-city brothers and sisters. That is why I know that it is unlikely that I will ever meet a happy billionaire.

Laura spent most of her time sleeping. Now and then she would rest her head on my shoulder, without my permission of course. I did not mind. Not at all.

At dusk, we finally arrived at the small, attractive town of Springbok, strung out along one long street. I wondered, firstly, why most of the buildings were white and, secondly, whether South Africa's (or should I say Mzansi's) rugby team, the Springboks – the Amabokoboko as they are called by black South Africans – had ever played a game in Springbok in the town's 114-year history. As far I was concerned this town should be their spiritual home.

Passing through Springbok made me think that rugby remained one of the least transformed sports in our country because not only was the Springbok coach (at the time) white, but his surname, too, was White. It was obvious to me that the SA Rugby Union could appoint a coach of any race as long as his surname was Swart (Black). With such a move rugby's transformation problems would be solved once and for all.

I was disappointed not to see any springboks in Springbok although I have no particular attachment to these athletic antelope. I suppose it was a quite irrational feeling. After all, Baptists do not have to baptise, or Protestants to protest, or Methodists to be methodical.

It was already dark when we got to our last stop in South Africa: a very small and sleepy town called Steinkopf. Even though we were just over 500 kilometres from Cape Town, we were not yet halfway to Namibia's capital city, Windhoek.

For the record, I wish to state that throughout this stretch of the trip we were within 90 kilometres of the coast and the cold waters of the Atlantic. I had already covered more than 2 200 kilometres since leaving

Durban, and was within an hour of crossing the first of the many borders I was going to have to go through on my journey.

In Steinkopf, I made two big mistakes: First, I decided to phone my fiancée from the only public phone in town. When I phoned I could hear our daughter, Nala, crying in the background. I enquired and the answer was simple: 'I think she is missing you.' We had a brief chat and after the call, although I had only been away for just over a day, I started feeling terribly homesick.

My second mistake was that for one reason or another I decided to buy a litre of fresh milk from a general dealer who stocked all the basic necessities – to judge from the bending shelves.

It was already pitch-dark when we got to the Vioolsdrif/Noordoewer border. As a result, I could not see the mighty Orange River, which separates South Africa from Namibia, but I was stamped out of South Africa without a glitch. So far so good.

Each time I go through a border I cannot help but think that working at a border post in the middle of nowhere, stamping people in or out of a country, has to be one of the most boring jobs. No wonder immigration officials hardly ever smile and always make a big fuss about nothing.

Nujoma's Namibia

Father of the Nation

When the European powers were scrambling for Africa in the 1880s, Germany grabbed the area between the Orange River and the Kunene River and, in 1884, declared it a protectorate named Deutsch-Südwestafrika. Only Walvis Bay was excluded because Great Britain had already laid claim to it. Germany, it seems, found it difficult to manage the territory and its brutal policies towards the 'natives' caused many uprisings.

Deutsch-Südwestafrika became South West Africa at the end of World War I, when the League of Nations gave South Africa a mandate to administrate the territory. When South Africa later became reluctant to let go of her gains, despite a 1978 UN resolution to recall the mandate, a new hero emerged: Samuel Daniel Shafiishuna Nujoma, the first president of the South West African People's Organisation (SWAPO). Nujoma had co-founded SWAPO's forerunner, the Ovamboland People's Organisation, in the late 1950s. In 1966 he authorised SWAPO to turn to armed resistance. During the struggle for independence he took the combat name Shafiishuna – 'lightning'.

Namibia became Namibia on 21 March 1990. As head of SWAPO, Sam Nujoma was unanimously declared president after the party was victorious in UN-supervised elections. Nujoma was elected president three times (the constitution was changed in 1999 to allow him to become president for the third time). When, after 15 years in office, he could no longer be president, Hifikepunye Pohamba – described by some as Nujoma's 'hand-picked successor' – was elected with a large majority. Nujoma stayed on as president of the ruling SWAPO party, a position he still holds. Just before relinquishing his position as head of state in March 2005, he was given the official title of 'Founding Father of the Namibian Nation'.

Namibia is the 34th largest country in the world and, after Mongolia, the least densely populated, with fewer than two million people, i.e., only two inhabitants per square kilometre.

I realised that I was in another country when I registered that most of the notices hanging in the immigration offices were in German and Afrikaans, although English was made the official language of Namibia in 1990. The Namibian immigration official asked me, 'Why are you only visiting Namibia for the first time when we are neighbours?'

I had no answer, really. Otherwise, getting into Namibia, which takes its name from the 1 600-kilometre stretch of desert along the Atlantic coast known as the Namib, was no problem at all.

My second consecutive night on a bus proved to be much more difficult than I had expected. You know what it's like when you're dog tired and yet keep waking up every half-hour. The fact that I had drunk all that milk and had to visit the toilet three times did not help either.

While trying to sleep I made the first of the many resolutions I was to make on the trip: I resolved that I would return one day to Namibia to do the five-day hike in the Fish River Canyon, the world's second largest canyon after Colorado's Grand Canyon. That was my Resolution No. 1. Zooming, exhausted, through the south of our northwestern neighbour in the middle of the night was not good enough.

The only thing that helped me to keep going was Laura's suggestion that we share my sleeping bag and her blanket. Otherwise, I am not sure how I would have survived that cold night. Laura seemed a genuinely nice person, but a Eugène Terre'Blanche look-alike seated opposite us did not appear to approve of our getting so cosy. As the minutes passed, I could see from the way he was looking at us that he was turning greener and greener with envy.

My first glimpse of Namibia, at dawn, was of a vast nothingness: few plants, huge open spaces – uninhabitable semi-desert under a big sky with no people anywhere to be seen, the towns very few and very far between. On the 786-kilometre stretch between the Orange River and Windhoek there were only two sizeable towns: Keetmanshoop and Mariental. There were no mines visible either along the route – as with many African countries, Namibia's main exports are minerals, mainly diamonds and uranium.

It was still early in the morning when we arrived in the spread-out, uncluttered city of Windhoek. The bus stop was right in front of the modern Supreme Court building. I was struck by the multi-storey modern buildings that could be anywhere in the world, the wide but, at this early hour, deserted streets. Except for a few stragglers.

It was a cloudless day and I could literally smell clean, very cold, air. While we were waiting for our backpacks to emerge from the bus, Laura introduced me to a guy who had come to pick her up.

'Meet Robert, my boyfriend,' she said with a straight face.

Hey Laura, what about the boyfriend you were visiting in Cape Town? I felt like asking, thinking to myself as I firmly shook Robert's hand, I hope you are using a condom, my brother.

I had to wait for almost an hour for the bus to Swakopmund. We left Windhoek along one of the main streets – Sam Nujoma Drive – before heading through the northern industrial area, stopping at Okahanja only three-quarters of an hour later. It was strange that we should be stopping so soon after leaving Windhoek, but the hostess explained that this was our first and last opportunity to buy something to eat as we would stop only to pick up and drop passengers from now on. Although I was hungry, I could not buy anything because I had not yet had the opportunity to change currency.

In no time we turned in a westerly direction, heading for the sea through a featureless landscape.

After 48 hours of non-stop bus travel since leaving Durban, I found myself in the very clean and compact town of Swakopmund with its bright old-world German architecture. The bus dropped us off in one of the small streets running parallel to Sam Nujoma Drive, by way of which we had entered town.

As to be expected, Swakopmund's skyline is dominated by its light-house; despite the town's popularity, no skyscrapers have as yet been erected. Swakopmund was built at the end of the 19th century as Deutsch-Südwestafrika's main harbour, after the discovery of uranium 70 kilometres away made a harbour a necessity. Three-quarters of the town, with its grid-like layout, is surrounded by desert; the fourth quarter borders on the Atlantic. Most restaurants are on the beachfront, and most of the buildings that line the streets are painted unusual colours – bright yellow, orange, blue – the general impression a brilliant mix of colours.

For me it was love at first sight.

North of the town, the Skeleton Coast stretched all the way to the mouth of the Kunene River and, beyond it, Angola. The skeletons commemorated in the name were what remained of those who were shipwrecked off the coast in the dense Atlantic fog and on offshore rocks and then died of exposure, hunger and thirst in the desert.

Later that afternoon I spent a good two hours in the town's museum trying to put Namibia's history into perspective, especially the remnants of the German era. Before venturing into the museum, however, hunger and thirst forced me to go to a bureau de change. At a small office, next to a bank, a stunning fair-haired, blue-eyed girl said to me in a strong German accent, 'There is no need to change your South African rands because the Namibian dollar is fixed to the rand. Therefore, paying with Namibian dollars or South African rands is the same thing.'

I was dumbfounded. I could not help but wonder what would have happened if the Zimbabwean dollar were also linked to the rand.

Another thing I did not know was that you can 'hibernate' for an hour longer in winter in Namibia – according to one local 'people do not have to wake up early'. A little confused, I turned my watch back one hour. Later, someone else told me that Namibia's standard time is, in fact, GMT+1 and that in summer they have daylight-saving time. Hence they move to GMT+2 on the first Sunday in April each year, and back to GMT+1 in September.

I could not believe that Namibia has a daylight-saving programme. It was on that note that I decided that once my trip was over I would spearhead the introduction of such a programme in South Africa. Just imagine trying to explain to a 60-year-old rural Zulu man (a generation well known to get heavily confused at the slightest change in the environment) that time must be changed forwards or backwards on a specific day. It should be great fun. However, it was not so serious a decision as to make it Resolution No. 2.

One of the advantages of travelling alone is that you can do almost anything without worrying too much about other people judging you because, quite frankly, they do not really know you.

It's mostly people that know you, or think they know you, who are judgemental.

With that in mind, I decided to get myself a hairstyle that I had always wanted but had not gone for because of corporate culture, as well as the 'what are people going to say' mentality. I decided to have my hair plaited. Since I did not know any reputable hair salons in Swakop I decided to use the very first one I spotted, two blocks from the beachfront. I was drawn by the ad that made it clear that my request would not be out of the ordinary.

The lady (there were three) who was plaiting my hair had never heard of customer service. While working on my hair she would happily abandon me to chat to her two friends or other girls passing by, or to sell braids to other customers. During the intervals, when she *did* plait my hair, we chatted about her ambition to come to South Africa because to her it seemed to offer more opportunities. We also talked about what music she and her friends listened to. Besides their local artists, whom I had never heard of, they loved our Brenda Fassie and Yvonne Chaka Chaka. Of course we also discussed soccer. When I asked her which was the coolest night spot around, her response was: *'Ek weet nie, ek is van die lokasie af'* – I don't know, I'm from the township.

Later that night, sporting my new hairdo, I had to find my own way through Swakop's nightlife. The first place that caught my eye was the Rafter Action Pub. Within minutes of my walking into the bar, a man who must have been in his early fifties came up to me and volunteered to buy me a shot of whisky. Although I was a little anxious, I thought what the hell. We started chatting about music and he quickly invited me to his car to listen to his new Meatloaf CD.

His bakkie was parked right outside the bar. He got in behind the steering wheel and I sat in the passenger seat. Both front doors were open. I told him that the only Meatloaf song I knew was 'I could do anything for love but I will not do that'.

At that he turned around. 'What is it that you will not do for love?'

I was speechless.

After listening to bits of his Meatloaf CD, we went back into the bar and he bought another round of double whiskies. By this time I was feeling really uncomfortable. My mind was already in overdrive. I was thinking along gay lines. I could not understand how a white man who had just met me could offer to pay for my drinks without looking for anything in return.

After another round he said he was about to leave. When I volunteered to pay for my drinks, his response was: 'I'm a pissed old man with loads of cash.' Those were his parting words as he staggered towards the door.

After a final round on my own, just after midnight, I walked – none too steady myself – back to my budget hotel. It had two dormitories on the first floor – one for males, the other for females. The bathroom was a bit grubby. No one told me so, but I was sure that if I did not wear slip-slops in the shower I would walk away with athlete's foot.

With its relaxed atmosphere, Swakopmund has maintained its reputation as Namibia's premier beach resort. But it is also its adventure capital. Naturally, the three adventurous activities that it is renowned for – quadbiking, skydiving and sandboarding – have to do with the Namib desert. The previous day, within an hour of being in town, I had booked myself on a quadbiking trip. As I am addicted to adventure, I didn't really have a choice.

Four years earlier, as part of my 26th birthday celebrations, I did some parachuting at Oribi airport in Pietermaritzburg. Although I had already done more than ten parachute jumps (all on static line), I had not progressed to the free-fall level because I was not jumping regularly enough. Unlike many of my white co-adventurers, who enjoyed sponsorships and could jump as often as the weather permitted, I had to pay for my jumps out of my own pocket – the reason why my parachuting adventures came to an abrupt end.

Back in Swakopmund, my lack of expertise meant that if I wanted to parachute jump I had to do the tandem jump – jumping while attached to a qualified tandem master. Jumping with another man on my back was not really my idea of fun, so I decided against skydiving altogether. And, owing to my leg injury, sandboarding was out of the question.

When I awoke in the morning in the male dormitory of my budget hotel, I discovered I had a dormitory mate, Steve, who told me that he had just resigned from his job as a lawyer in Windhoek. His father, he said, was a well-known advocate in Windhoek and, as firstborn, he had been manipulated into following the legal profession so that he could take over from his dad one day. He hated the law with all his heart. So, after three years of 'selling my soul', he had decided to quit. Obviously, Steve's father was not impressed and Steve was in Swakop to gather his thoughts and decide what he was going to do next. He had started working as a barman in one of the local bars 'just to kill time'.

After listening to Steve's story it was time to go quadbiking. Along with a German couple, I was picked up from the adventure company's offices and driven to the launch site about a kilometre outside the town. Our instructor, Willie, a tall, thin, clean-shaven black Namibian, explained everything in great detail, from starting, accelerating, turning and stopping to the signs he was going to use while leading us on a 50-kilometre trip through the most ancient (at least 80 million years old) desert in the world.

Thank goodness the bikes were automatic and, although the first few seconds were jittery, I was soon cruising and feeding the German couple loads of dust. Willie was really showing off on his manual quadbike – revving and changing gears and standing up, sometimes riding on the rear wheels only or, even more impressive, on only the two left wheels. After a few minutes, I tried copying Willie by standing while the quad was in motion. It was not as bad as I thought it would be. Although I could not ride the bike on its rear wheels, I was really surprised at my natural bike-handling skills.

Meanwhile, the German woman was struggling to keep pace with the three of us. Now and then we would stop and wait for her. I could see that her husband was not impressed. The entire trip basically consisted of driving up and down the dunes. I discovered that the dunes were getting bigger and more thrilling (read 'dangerous' if you're a woman).

Twice we took a break just to enjoy looking around and to take photographs. The views of the desert were amazing: countless rolling sand dunes on one side and the desert running straight into the Atlantic Ocean on the other. Before going on that quadbike trip I had never thought that the Namib desert was so immense. In fact, if Willie had decided to leave us behind we might still be looking for our way back to Swakop.

We drove back to the launch site along the Swakop–Walvis Bay road. Overall, the trip took about two hours. As I disembarked from the quadbike I resolved (Resolution No. 2) that one day, when I own a farm in the KwaZulu-Natal Midlands Meander area, I will get myself a quadbike or two just to ride around the lush rolling lawns. It was awesome stuff. I made a note on my writing pad: *Do it again sometime soon.*

Because the harbour built at Swakopmund in 1892 was too shallow and too unprotected, most of its activities were transferred within a quarter of a century to Walvis Bay, which is only 30 kilometres to the south. After Willie dropped us off in town it was time to hitch there. I was eager to see the over-the-border territory that had been part of South Africa for almost two hundred years – from when the British flag was first hoisted there in 1795 to 28 February 1994, when the small enclave was handed back to Namibia by South Africa.

Within five minutes I was in a minibus to Walvis Bay on a road that runs right on the edge of the desert, with the sea on your right. Midway, I noticed beautiful penthouses being built at Long Beach, which has to be one of the most sought-after places on the Namibian coast. A year later I learned that Brad Pitt and Angelina Jolie – Brangelina – would spend a few weeks there while waiting for the birth of their child, Shiloh Nouvel Jolie-Pitt. The couple did go there and, being the celebrities that they are, helped to put Namibia on the world map.

To my amazement, the minibus dropped passengers right in front of their houses. We started off in a small township called Narraville and as we went down the main street – Sam Nujoma Drive – people would give directions to their houses. After all the Narravillers were safely deposited at their front doors, it was time to go to Kuisebmond, another township, and down its main street – Sam Nujoma Drive.

And that is as far as the minibus taxi went. From Kuisebmond I had to take a cab to the town itself.

My main aim in Walvis Bay was to visit the waterfront. The problem was the cab driver did not understand any English and, being the product of Bantu Education, my Afrikaans is almost non-existent. There are only two things I can say in Afrikaans: *groete* (greetings) and *Die hout word deur die man gekap*, which is the *lydende vorm* (passive form) of *Die man kap die hout* – The man chops the wood. I was therefore ill-equipped to explain where I wanted to go. Somehow I remembered, though, that the beach is a *strand*. So I said confidently to the taxi driver, *'Ek gaan na die strand af.'*

He looked at me and frowned and dropped me in front of the restaurant on the main road (yes, you guessed it, Sam Nujoma Drive), right in the middle of town. After asking a few locals I gathered that there was no waterfront, so I had lunch at the Fish & Chipper restaurant.

Walvis Bay's deep-water port is its economic hub and everything revolves around the harbour. I had worked in a port all my life. In fact, the reason I stayed in Durban for such a long time was because every time I felt the corporate bullshit was getting too much – especially the people from Head Office who constantly wanted their egos stroked – I would leave the office to be soothed by a beautiful view of Africa's biggest and busiest port, literally within a few steps from the entrance to the building where I worked. Water tends to have a calming effect on me.

It was natural, therefore, that I wanted to visit the port at Walvis. The security guards at the main gate did not think that that was a good idea, however. They would not allow me in.

Legend has it that Walvis Bay was named 'Whale Bay' because of its abundance of whales and other marine creatures way back when Bartholomeu Diaz, the Portuguese navigator who was looking for a sea route to the East, entered the bay in 1487. Smaller fish must have been abundant then too since the Portuguese named the coast Praia dos Sardinha – Coast of Sardines.

After about three hours of not spotting any whales – obviously because I was not allowed on the waterside – it was time to head back to Swakop.

B ack in Swakop, I decided to go for a sunset stroll on the beach. The beach reminded me of Durban's 'golden mile', except that in Swakop they should consider calling it 'rocky half mile'. I wondered how people could swim in such rock-infested waters. Needless to say, there were no surfers. There were quite a few couples, however, sauntering hand in hand and enjoying the sunset.

After a 20-minute walk I decided to sit on one of the benches and just feast my eyes on the ocean view. I noticed an attractive woman walking on the sand right at the water's edge. She looked as if her man had disappointed her. She would walk, stop and stare at the sea for a moment and then continue walking very slowly. Although she was not beautiful, she had curves in all the right places. I saw that she could do with some comforting.

So I decided to join her for a walk. I took off my shoes, rolled up the legs of my trousers and headed for the water. After I had introduced myself, she, ironically, was the one who was full of pity.

'Oh you poor thing. You are travelling alone,' she said. I was surprised since she had looked like the lonely one.

'So, what are your plans for tonight?'

'Nothing in particular,' I replied, honestly.

'Why don't we go out for a drink or two?' she suggested as she jumped back from a big wave.

I have always been attracted by women who know what they want and are not shy of going out and getting it. It seemed and looked as if my trip was going to start with a very big bang.

She jotted down her number for me and we agreed that I would phone her in about two hours' time. We continued walking on the sand, chatting about this and that. As she bent down to put on her shoes I naturally had to check out her backside. To say I was disappointed is an understatement. In a flash I knew that my diagnosis that she had been disappointed by her man was right. This realisation came from the fact that she was wearing full panties. It was a real turn-off. At her age, she should have been wearing a G-string. I decided that I was not going to call her later.

As we said goodbye to each other she suggested a few good places that we could visit that night. By then it was getting dark and I headed towards my backpackers past people having drinks on the terraces of the wonderful cafés that line Swakopmund's clean streets. Right next to the backpackers was the Cape to Cairo restaurant where, since I was doing the Cape to Cairo trip, I thought it would be fitting to have dinner. After all, as its motto suggested, I could let my 'tongue to do the travelling' ahead of my feet.

I had mussels for starters and a Somali spiced-lamb stew as a main course, all the while sipping Windhoek lager. The stew was slightly pungent but very tender and delicious. I had never thought Somalis could come up with such a scrumptious dish.

After dinner I went upstairs to the Cool Bananas bar for more beers. After about five beers, despite my earlier resolution, I thought it would not be a bad idea to call the curvaceous lady I had met earlier on the beachfront.

There was a small problem, however. I had torn up the piece of paper with her phone number and thrown the pieces into a dustbin just outside the restaurant. I set about looking for it. However, rather than having to explain to everyone entering the restaurant that I was not a drunk hobo but had thrown a small yet very important piece of paper in the bin, I decided to go to bed.

The following day, I had a good breakfast in one of the attractive little restaurants in Swakop. This time a typical English breakfast in a small restaurant overlooking the sea. I loved the easy lifestyle and brightly coloured colonial buildings in Swakop, not to mention the adrenalin-raising activities in the dunes, but it was time to head north to Livingstone in Zambia – another 26-hour trip.

Earlier that morning I had met a new guest who had installed himself in the dormitory. I could not miss him because he was so tall that his feet stuck out over the slats at the bottom of the bed. Peter, a 28-year-old from Ireland, had been travelling for 18 months and had been to 42 countries. His goal was to travel to 50 countries before turning 30. He was in Africa to do the Cape to Nairobi.

One of the many pleasures of travelling is that you meet so many interesting people doing things they genuinely want to do. It was very inspiring to talk to Peter. When I expressed my amazement that he had travelled to so many countries at such a young age, he responded modestly, 'There are more than 180 countries in the world. So I have done just more than a quarter.' Although he was into information technology, he also worked as a barman in the different countries he visited in order to finance his trips.

Peter and I had a long talk about the unending war in Northern Ireland. He explained to me, in detail, that the war had nothing to do with religion but was about the independence of Northern Ireland from Britain. 'Just like the ANC ended up resorting to an armed struggle and using its armed wing Umkhonto weSizwe to further its objective of having a free South Africa, Sinn Fein could not achieve its goals just by talking to the guys in London. That is where the Irish Republican Army came in,' my well-travelled companion explained.

Peter had tried to convince me that we should go to Etosha National Park for a few days and then do the Nairobi trip together. Although he looked like a cool dude, I wanted to do this whole thing on my own so as to be as flexible as possible and not have to explain anything to anybody. That was why I was on a bus that was heading not for Etosha but for Livingstone, via Windhoek.

When travelling in Namibia you are bound to go through Windhoek because, although Windhoek is in the middle of nowhere, it is right in the heart of Namibia. On the bus I sat next to a man who I was sure, judging by the size of his tummy, was a farmer. He was wearing a Springbok T-shirt. Just to break the ice, I said, 'I see you are a great rugby supporter.'

He did not respond and the way he looked at me made me wonder why I had asked him the question in the first place. That was a good reminder of how behind the times some people still are.

I was obliged, thus, to spend most of the time looking through the window, trying to enjoy the scenery, which reminded me once again that Namibia is a really vast, dry, sparsely-vegetated and sparsely-populated country. The four-hour trip to Windhoek felt more like 14 hours. After all, I was sitting next to a heavy-breathing, Klipdriftguzzling, white racist pig whose dress sense stretched to khaki shorts and a small black comb held in place by a long grey sock.

At Windhoek bus station I noticed that the bus heading to Cape Town was carrying a number of beautiful young girls. I found myself re-thinking the question I thought I had answered long ago: was it better to do the Cape to Cairo or to start in Cairo and end in Cape Town? At that moment, looking at those fresh, sexy things, I thought maybe I should have started in Cairo and ended in Cape Town. That was such a stupid thought, though, because if I had started in Cairo I would still be in Egypt at that moment.

Those are the kind of ideas men entertain when they start thinking with their second head, which was the case with me right then.

The bus left Windhoek at sunset, heading up Sam Nujoma Drive in a northeasterly direction to Livingstone. I was now seated next to a man who was obsessed with eating peanuts and was using a matchstick as a toothpick. I spent most of the time looking out the window. I was really impressed, in transit, by the small and attractive towns of Otjiwarongo and Tsumeb, the capital city of the Otjikoto region in northern Namibia which is known as the 'Gateway to the North'.

Tsumeb is the town closest to the Etosha National Park, one of the greatest reserves for wildlife in all of Africa and a major tourist attraction. Although Tsumeb was once a thriving mining town, owing to a rich ore pipe that has produced large quantities of copper, zinc, lead, silver and unusual crystals, it is now mainly a transit point for tourists.

When we stopped eventually in Grootfontein, named after its large hot spring, I had no sooner stretched my legs than a man came up to me and greeted me in Zulu, 'Unjani mfowethu?'

Before I could respond, he began to tell me his life story.

'You see, my broer, I was born in Kenya, grew up in Namibia and studied electrical engineering in Cape Town. I am now back and working for the Namibian Electricity Corporation.' As to be expected of a coloured man who had lived in Cape Town, he had no front teeth and smelled of alcohol.

Why can't you coloured guys leave the snoek fish and Black Label alone? I was about to ask, but he did not give me a chance.

'You see, my broer, I can see the difference between Xhosas and Zulus by looking at their eyes. All Zulus have squint eyes. So that is how I knew that you are a Zulu,' he continued, confidently.

That was a first for me. Nobody had ever told me that I have squint eyes. What is a well-known difference between Xhosas and Zulus, acknowledged especially among black South Africans, is that Xhosas are very manipulative, power-hungry people whereas Zulus are stupid, taxi-driving war-mongers who are capable of insulting you until you develop concussion.

After a half-hour break at Grootfontein, which also used to be a thriving mining town, we headed north again. My 'broer' had in the meantime wandered off in search of new companionship.

It was not such a comfortable night because, instead of cuddling with Laura the man-eater as on the Cape Town to Windhoek leg of the journey, this time I was stuck next to a peanut-eating black man who could speak only Afrikaans, his home language. How weird. He clearly did not know of June 16, 1976, when more than 15 000 unarmed school kids in Soweto, on a march to protest against the use of Afrikaans as a medium of instruction, clashed with police and about 700 people were killed in the violence that followed. Because of the peanut eater's monolingualism we could not communicate and there was nothing to do but put my head back and close my eyes. Even while dozing off, I was surprised by how wide and straight the tarred road through Ovamboland was – until I registered this was territory occupied until 1990 by the South African Defence Force.

We got to the rural border town of Kasane at sunrise. The majority of passengers, including the peanut guzzler, disembarked. The rest of us were stamped out of Namibia in a modern immigration office without any problems whatsoever.

To the woman I met on Swakopmund's beachfront: For just one day, I regretted having thrown away your phone number.

Kaunda's Zambia

Father of the Nation

Zambia, formerly Northern Rhodesia, became an independent country under Kenneth Kaunda after the United National Independence Party, which he had led since his release from jail four years earlier, won the general election held in 1964. Born at Lubwa Mission in Northern Rhodesia in 1924, KK, as he is affectionately known, started off as a teacher. He left his teaching career at the age of 27 to work full time for the political liberation of this country.

The 'Rhodesia' part of 'Northern Rhodesia' obviously came from Cecil John Rhodes, whose British South Africa Company (BSAC) pushed the railway line further north of Bulawayo (in what was then Southern Rhodesia), via the town of Livingstone, between 1904 and 1909. In 1911, the BSAC amalgamated North-Western Rhodesia and North-Eastern Rhodesia into Northern Rhodesia and received a charter to administrate it. In 1924 the British government took over the administration of the territory until it achieved independence on 24 October 1964.

KK was president for 27 years. After seven years as head of state, he turned Zambia into a one-party state and declared himself president for life. Frederick Chiluba, leader of the Movement for Multi-Party Democracy (MMD), spearheaded the reintroduction of multiparty democracy in Zambia and succeeded KK in 1991. When things got so bad under Chiluba's leadership that some Zambians wanted KK to stand for re-election, Chiluba amended the constitution to make only Zambian-born Zambians eligible for election as president. The fact that KK's father was born in Malawi was enough to put him out of the running. In 2001 Zambia elected its third president – Levy Mwanawasa, the new MMD leader.

Kenneth Kaunda played an important role in the liberation of South Africa by allowing anti-apartheid freedom fighters who had gone into exile to stay in Zambia, and by permitting South Africa's then banned ANC to locate its head office in Lusaka. For that I am grateful to KK.

The wheels of bureaucracy ground more slowly on the Zambian side of the border. In a corrugated-iron shack masquerading as an immigration office, the queues were longer and more questions were asked, and our bus was inspected in a leisurely fashion by one of the immigration officials. Some passengers, I am not sure why, were taken into a back office. As a result, it took more than an hour to process the 25 passengers on the bus.

Once everyone was back on board and we were on the road to Livingstone, I observed that the landscape was no longer the same. On the Zambian side there was more undergrowth and shrubs and trees, as well as huts and houses, not to mention cattle strolling across the road. The roads, compared with those in Namibia, had deteriorated.

Not long after leaving the border we hit a roadblock. A police officer climbed into the bus and walked halfway up the aisle, turned and got off, without saying a word to anyone, including the driver. Almost the same thing happened at the second roadblock a while later, except that the officer walked all the way to the back of the bus before turning and leaving without breathing a word to either us or the driver.

About 20 kilometres from Livingstone we came across a local bus that was stuck in a ditch. The passengers, mostly women it seemed, were trying to push it out, but to no avail. Our driver stopped to investigate and, in consultation with the hostess on our bus, decided that we must try to help.

The hostess announced to us passengers, 'This is Africa; we have to help them, because tomorrow we might get stuck and then we will expect them to help us.' After those few words everyone was ordered off the bus. Nobody seemed put out and we all obeyed quietly.

The ditch in which the local bus was stuck was much deeper than anticipated and our bus struggled in vain to pull the other bus out with the help of a thick rope. A few minutes later a truck arrived and, naturally, the truck (driver, that is) volunteered to help. In no time the bus was out of the ditch and everyone clapped while some women ululated. We got back on our east-bound bus and the other passengers got into their bus, which headed in the opposite direction.

After about 15 minutes we found ourselves on the outskirts of Livingstone, where our driver had to fork out 100 000 Zambian kwachas at a dilapidated tollgate plaza. It was the first of a number of currency transactions in Zambia and neighbouring Zimbabwe that involved many thousands of kwachas and Zim dollars. (At the time the exchange rate was 770 kwachas to a rand, so the tollgate fee amounted to about R130.)

Twenty-five hours after leaving Swakopmund, I was in Livingstone.

The man after whom Livingstone is named, the missionary and explorer Dr David Livingstone, was the first European to see (on 16 November 1855) the breathtaking falls on the Zambezi River that he named Victoria Falls. At present, the Zambezi River forms the border between Zambia and Zimbabwe. It is strange that the name Victoria Falls remains, considering how much Zimbabwe's Robert Mugabe hates Britain. The original name was Mosi-oa-Tunya, which means 'smoke that thunders'.

The British explorers, including John Hanning Speke, must have esteemed their queen, Victoria, very highly. While looking for the source of the Nile, Speke stumbled onto the largest lake in Africa and promptly named it after her as well. Again, after all these years of Africa's 'independence', that vast body of water, which is of great natural importance to the continent, is still named after Her Royal Highness, Her Majesty Queen Victoria, who died more than a hundred years ago.

Thank goodness, neither Livingstone nor Speke, as far as I know, saw the Sahara. Had they done so, the world's largest desert would no doubt be known today as Victoria Desert. Nobody can blame the explorers, I suppose, because they were mostly sponsored, after all, by the Royal Geographical Society. They had to show their gratitude and appreciation in some way, and naming their 'discoveries' after their Queen was an easy way out.

Unlike the early British explorers, who were looking for fame and fortune and, especially in Livingstone's case, to spread Christianity, I had reasons of a more personal nature for undertaking my journey. Given all the negative things I had read about the African continent, I wanted to experience for myself – by myself – Africa's culture and languages, cuisine, architecture and whatever else she had to offer, and to see the effect outsiders had had on her.

Livingstone, which the locals also refer to as Maramba, is very small for a town that for 24 years was the capital of Northern Rhodesia. What's more, despite its old and run-down buildings, dusty and pot-holed roads and very relaxed atmosphere, thousands of travellers regard it as the African adrenalin capital, with bungee jumping, white-river rafting, canoeing, elephant riding and viewing of wildlife and of the falls all at your doorstep, so to speak. It is little wonder that within an hour of arriving in Livingstone I had booked myself on a Zambezi sunset cruise for later the same day and for a microlight flight over the Vic Falls the following day.

At midday I checked in at the Jolly Boys backpackers in town. My dorm mates were Dave from London, who was in Zambia for four days, and Lizzy, also from London, who was going to spend a week in Zambia before heading for Botswana and on to Namibia. Jollies, as Jolly Boys is called, had a swimming pool, a bar and no garden but a wonderful view over the treetops of the spray rising above the Victoria Falls.

Soon after checking in I decided to have a shower. After all, I had not washed for more than a day. I had rubbed a good lather of soap all over my body when the water from the showerhead suddenly diminished to a trickle, and before I knew it there was no water at all. I was, in a matter of seconds, left with soap all over my body but no water with which to rinse it off. So I had to rub the stinging lather off with my face cloth. As much as I agree that half a loaf of bread is better than nothing, half a shower is definitely worse than nothing. But, as they say, if you pay peanuts, expect monkey service.

With an itchy and sticky body, I headed for the bar, by then the only place that could make me feel better. I spent an hour sippping beer before the transport arrived to take me, along with some other tourists, to the river.

Although it was winter, the volume of water in the falls was impressive, the white mist churned up by the cascading water thundering softly. Our double-decker boat had a motor, but only minimum power was used and, as a result, we just glided gently over the mighty Zambezi. The price of the cruise included food and drinks, so I continued from where I had left off at the bar. I was spoilt for choice as far as alcohol was concerned: there were several brands of local beer, whisky and brandy. I opted to continue drinking Zambia's finest beer – Mosi.

The two-hour cruise was very relaxing, especially after spending more than 24 hours in a bus, and almost everyone was on the upper deck to enjoy the view of the small overgrown islands dotted all over the river and of the banks covered in tall trees in which you could glimpse monkeys swinging from branch to branch. Meanwhile, something was bugging me. After a couple of drinks, I had enough courage to approach the captain. I was convinced that we were drifting downstream and I wanted to know when we were going to turn around to keep us from plummeting down the Victoria Falls.

'No, my friend, we are going upstream. The falls are actually behind us,' he said in a calm and soft voice. Although I was tipsy, I felt very embarrassed. The comforting thing was that nobody had heard our conversation because almost everyone on board was too busy boozing.

Later, I chatted to two young girls whom I had seen at reception at Jollies. They were African-Americans who had just finished a three-week exchange programme in Durban at the University of KwaZulu-Natal. Small world, hey, I thought to myself. Since we were the only black people on board, besides the crew, we talked about a variety of issues of common interest, ranging from why black people don't travel to why some African-Americans look down on Africa when their forefathers come from here. For their age, the girls seemed to be very clued up on world affairs.

Sunset on the Zambezi was surreal, magical, the red sun reflecting off the water as the river continued on its more than 2 500-kilometre journey from its source in the northwestern part of Zambia to where it flows into the ocean, more or less midway up the Mozambican coast. It was one of those moments when I felt like making time stand still so that the moment could linger forever. The tall grass and trees overhanging the banks of the river made me love the place and feel even more peaceful.

I stood on the upper deck of the boat enjoying the fresh breeze and looking at the sun as it disappeared quietly behind the horizon. While most of my fellow tourists were busy taking photographs of hippos, I took time to think about the journey on which I had embarked. I came to the conclusion that for my trip to be successful I would just have to take it a day at a time and not worry about what might be in store for me tomorrow.

Back at Jollies it seemed like a good idea to return to the bar for some more of Zambia's finest before going to bed. At the counter the two African-American students joined me for more chatting. I wasn't really interested in them, though – I may look and act like a young man on the loose, but I do have principles. One is that I don't take advantage of young girls and/or students. I made that decision during my student days when I saw older, working brothers having relationships with young students. It just did not seem right. In fact, I came to the conclusion that older guys who go out with students suffer from low self-esteem. After all, why, if you are working, don't you date people in the same boat as yourself?

However, another principle I have is to be polite. So, my new 'friends' and I continued to talk about things, including relationships. They said all men were dogs and could not be trusted. Michelle, the sexier of the two, told us how she had had a relationship with a married pastor for 18 months and nobody had suspected anything.

I was not surprised about that. I have always known that pastors are worse than politicians. Politicians just lie and cheat, but pastors lie and cheat *in the name of the Lord*. Michelle was a real bad girl. She also related how she, while shagging the pastor, was involved with her older sister's husband for six months. The relationship was cut short when her sister caught her husband in bed with another man and divorced him, and he moved to the United Kingdom. These stories were very interesting, more so because they were cementing my opinion that some men get married in order to try and hide their homosexual tendencies from society.

By then only a handful of us were left in the bar and our conversation had evolved to sexual fantasies. The Mosi had attacked my nervous system in a big way and in next to no time I found myself describing to

44

two strangers my deepest fantasy, which before then I had not confided to anyone: 'In this lifetime I have to have a threesome with two nuns.'

I explained to the girls that I was not a bad guy or a pervert. It was more out of curiosity that I wanted to get into bed with two nuns. I had always been intrigued to know whether nuns would genuinely be virgins or whether it was just a myth, I said.

'Have you ever had a threesome with two students?' Michelle asked with a straight face.

'No, never. My focus, at least for now, is on nuns ...'

'No, no, I have never, and I would not mind,' interjected a tall white guy with blue eyes and light brown hair who had obviously been listening to us.

I knew then that it was time to go to bed, so I zigzagged my way to the dormitory. Lizzy and Dave, my dorm mates, were already in dreamland.

The alarm clock woke me up against my wishes. I had a pounding headache and was feeling sick. Nevertheless, I had to get up as it was time to go microlighting over the Victoria Falls.

Peter, a Zambian national, picked me up from the backpackers to drive me to the airstrip. By sunrise I was already going through the formalities (payment, signing an indemnity, etc.). As it was still early in the morning and a bit cold, I was given a fleece to wear. Another Peter, this one from Sweden, was the pilot and the one who was going to take me for a flip.

A microlight is not called a flying lawnmower for nothing. The engine looks too small to have enough power to lift off with two adults on board. The seating is arranged in such a way that the passenger sits at an elevated position right behind the pilot. Although there is nothing wrong with this seating arrangement, the seats are so close to each other that, as a passenger, you have to open your legs in order for the pilot to be able to sit up straight. I could not help but think that if I were a microlight pilot carrying a woman passenger I would crash the damn thing because I would keep looking back.

As soon as I was comfortable in my seat Peter started the engine. By then I had on earphones so that I'd be able to communicate with him.

This was the second time that I had worn earphones in an aircraft. The first was at East Rand Airport in Johannesburg while aerobatic flying on a Pitts Special as part of my 28th birthday celebration. I had almost forgotten how much time a pilot spends talking to air traffic controllers and the importance of this in ensuring a safe flight. As a passenger on a commercial airline you are totally unaware of all this exchange.

The very first thing I asked Peter was, 'So how long have you been flying?'

'Well, my man, that is the most frequently asked question by first-timers,' he said over the earphones as we were taxiing to the main runway.

He never really answered my question.

It was my maiden flight on a microlight. The first few seconds were uncomfortable and everything felt very unstable Within a minute or so, however, the wind on my face made me forget my splitting headache completely. Even a bit of turbulence and having no side panels or roof did not deter me from enjoying the experience and I decided that flying in a microlight, with just two seats, handles and a motor in the back is what floating free in life is all about.

We soon levelled at 1 500 feet Above Ground Level (AGL) and, Peter told me, were doing 42 m.p.h. (about 70 kilometres per hour). From above, the view of Victoria Falls was amazing, incredible, awesome. On the Zambian side I could see Livingstone and the Zambezi Sun and the Royal Livingstone Hotel, as well as the bungee-jumping steel bridge at the falls, which separates/connects Zambia and Zimbabwe. On the Zimbabwean side I spotted the town of Victoria Falls and the Kingdom Hotel.

Nothing, however, could beat the view of the falls themselves, rising like a column of smoke. Were it not for the sound of the microlight's engine, which drowned out all other sounds, the sight would have been accompanied by the thunder of the water as it plunges through the gorge. Studying the twisting course of the river from above, I could half-understand why I had thought we were heading for the falls while we were cruising upstream the previous day. Even in retrospect I was happy to see that it was impossible to have plunged over the edge.

A slight increase in wind suddenly made flying over the falls bumpy and also very scary. I was still enjoying the view, however, and the wind on my face, when I realised that on that very day I was 11 000 days old. I felt that, although unplanned, this was a glorious way to celebrate my 11 000th day on this small blue planet, Earth. In fact, quite honestly, we should not celebrate our date of birth but instead our day of conception because that is when we become part of life.

I had figured out a long time ago that the way we calculate age is not correct: since we determine months according to the Gregorian calendar the number of days in a month fluctuates between 28 and 31. The better way of measuring how long you have lived is to calculate your age in days, hours and minutes. Mind you, the way we measure days and hours is itself arbitrary. Why should it be 60 and not 100 seconds that make a minute, and why do 100 minutes not make an hour? And why 24 hours in a day?

In no time Peter started the descent to the airstrip. The 15 breath-taking minutes of microlighting over the falls had flown by. They felt much shorter than that.

Back in Livingstone, I attended a church service. I knew that during this trip I would need divine intervention now and then and, as if bar-gaining with God, I had decided to go to church although I felt more like going to bed. The service was held in an old, white-walled school hall, right next to the Livingstone Museum.

Since it was a Pentecostal church, there was a lot of singing and clapping. The congregation was led in song by a band and three vo-calists; everyone prayed with arms raised as if they could see Jesus and God, reciting, mantra-like, 'On your left, possess your land. On your right, possess your dream.' The leading devotee would chant 'On your left' and the entire congregation would reply 'Possess the land', upon which the leading devotee would follow with 'On your right' and the congregation with 'Possess your dream.' It was a very appropriate song.

Pentecostal churches emphasise the importance of offering your best. As a congregation, we were encouraged to give our best to the Lord. Everyone who was visiting the church for the first time was then asked to stand. All of us newcomers received a round of applause, hugs and handshakes.

I had spent an hour in the church but, to the displeasure of one of the ushers, I had to leave before 'hearing the Word'. Otherwise, I would have missed the free transfer from the backpackers to the Zimbabwean border. I rushed back to my hotel, picked up my bag and got into the pre-arranged minibus taxi. There wasn't even time to say goodbye to Michelle and her friend. I felt bad that I had to leave Zambia so soon. I loved the spirit, friendliness, cheerfulness and bubblyness, and the enthusiasm of Zambians. I didn't know then that I would be back soon.

Although going to Zimbabwe from Livingstone meant that I would be turning south instead of continuing north, I had decided to do so for two reasons. Firstly, I wanted to witness for myself the effect of Murambatsvina (which translates as 'drive out the trash'), Robert Mugabe's recent urban clean-up campaign, which had destroyed the homes of 700 000 people in the middle of winter. It appeared that the people who lost their houses were suspected of having voted for the opposition Movement for Democratic Change.

Secondly, I wanted to visit Matobo (the colonists corrupted the name to Matopos) National Park just south of Bulawayo. My mission there was to see the grave of Cecil John Rhodes on Malindidzimu Hill, or what the locals call Hill of the Spirits. Legend has it that Rhodes, while standing on this hill, proclaimed that you have a view of the whole world. The hill, hence, is also referred to as World's View.

Rhodes was not only a die-hard imperialist but firmly believed that the British were the superior race, especially when compared with indigenous African people. It is reported that, among other things, he had said, 'I contend that we [British] are the finest race in the world and that the more of the world we inhabit, the better it is for the human race.' Also: 'Remember that you are an Englishman and consequently have won first prize in the lottery of life.'

It has always fascinated and amazed me how a teenage boy who had dropped out of Oxford University could come to South Africa and, through his BSAC, make so much money that when he died in 1902, aged only 49, he was one of the wealthiest people in the world. Luckily, those university graduates among us with an equal measure of intellect, character and physical ability (if Rhodes's instructions are to be followed) have inherited the greater part of his vast fortune, amounting to millions of pounds sterling, in the form of Rhodes scholarships to his alma mater. Bill Clinton is probably the best known recent recipient.

I discovered later that our very own father figure, Nelson Mandela, had agreed to have his name linked to that of Rhodes, whose scholarships are now administered by the Rhodes-Mandela Trust. Rhodes's former mansion, called Groote Schuur (Dutch for 'big barn') until it was renamed Genadendal ('valley of grace') by President Nelson Mandela, has also seen some changes. Bequeathed to the government of South Africa to serve as the official residence of the prime minister of the Cape, it was the venue where Mandela and the then President FW de Klerk signed the Groote Schuur Minute, the commitment to stability and peaceful negotiations that led to our first democratic elections. It is now the Cape home of President Thabo Mbeki. Enough to make an imperialist turn in his grave.

Having started my trip in Cape Town, where Rhodes's statue in the old Company Gardens outside Parliament points north and proclaims 'Your hinterland is there', it felt almost as if I were following Rhodes's directions. There was another reason, however, why I wanted to go to Matobo National Park – I wanted to visit the grave of Mzilikazi Khumalo at Entumbane, which, I had been told, was not far from the Matobo. According to African tradition, Mzilikazi must have been my great, great, great grandfather. Between the two of them, he and Rhodes left a lasting legacy in southern Africa and I thought it was important that I see their graves, even if it meant a detour to the south.

Mzilikazi, the founder of the Ndebele (Matabele) kingdom, was a military genius, second only to King Shaka. He rebelled in 1823, while still one of Shaka's lieutenants, and left Zululand with a large following, moving from one place to the next, warring wherever he went. He settled in Matabeleland in the south of present-day Zimbabwe, 12 years after Shaka's death in 1828. During that time Mzilikazi expanded his army into a formidable machine. Ironically, it was his son, Lobengula Khumalo, who signed the Rudd Concession in 1888, which granted the mineral rights of Matabeleland to Rhodes's BSAC. Lobengula, they say, was manipulated by Rhodes's business associate, Charles Rudd, as well as the doctor who treated him for gout. That medic was none other than Rhodes's friend Sir Leander Starr Jameson of Jameson Raid fame. Like his friend Rhodes, Jameson is buried on Malindidzimu Hill.

Getting stamped out of Zambia and into Zimbabwe went very smoothly. My Achilles tendon, however, was starting to be painful and I decided to take a cab from the border to Victoria Falls station to purchase an overnight train ticket to Bulawayo, Zimbabwe's second largest city (which should actually be kwa-Bulawayo, in Ndebele style).

My cab driver, Sipho Ndlovu, hated Robert Mugabe with a passion.

'He, together with his Shona people, look down on us because we are Matabele,' he told me in Ndebele, which closely resembles Zulu. 'All senior government positions are occupied by Shona people. He is a stupid man who was put in power by the whites. Our leader Joshua Nkomo predicted we Zimbabweans will regret his appointment. Look at the mess he has caused. After how many years of democracy he starts talking about land! Nkomo said a long time ago that we cannot say we are in power if we don't have land. Nobody listened to him.'

'This Shona has messed things up,' he added as we stopped in front of the station building, which, in appearance, could not have changed much since the time of Rhodes and Jameson.

That conversation was an eye-opener for me because, before then, I did not know that ethnicity was so deeply entrenched in Zimbabwe and that the Shona, more than 75 per cent of the population, lived in the north and east of the country while the Ndebele, about 18 per cent, occupied the south and west. Since I was in the southwest of the country, it made sense that I would bump mostly into Ndebeles.

The station was closed, and I had four hours to kill before the ticket office reopened. Sipho took me to the outskirts of town to exchange 65 000 Zambian kwachas for Zimbabwean dollars. According to unofficial blackmarket rates, offered under a big tree, I should have received 433 000 Zim dollars, but our dealer gave me only 430 000 in

10 000-dollar notes. Sipho explained to me that 3 000 was worth so little I should not bother to try to recover this money. The whole thing was very confusing. In reality, I was not sure how much money I had.

I decided to buy a cheese burger and a soft drink at a local Wimpy. The total cost came to 225 000 Zim dollars. Although flabbergasted at how much money I had paid for an admittedly juicy hamburger, the transaction kind of put the value of the local currency in perspective for me.

In the four hours that I had to pass before returning to Victoria Falls station I walked to the Victoria Falls National Park to see the falls once again. Although this was my third visit, it felt like the first. The sheer volume of water plummeting through the gorge, despite its being the dry season, was breathtaking. At a width of 1 700 metres, the Victoria Falls are the greatest curtain of falling water in the world.

Sitting back and enjoying the view, I made a promise to myself (Resolution No. 3) that one day I would make love to my fiancée/wife in the rainforest in the park. Considering the noise made by the water crashing through the gorge, we would not have to worry about our moans being heard by people passing by.

After a quiet and serene two and a half hours, I walked back to the station to buy the ticket to kwa-Bulawayo. When I got to the ticket office there were already about 15 people in the queue. With 90 minutes to spare before the train's departure, I was quite relaxed about having to stand in such a long line of obviously local travellers. The last time I had been at Vic Falls station, about seven years earlier, there were a lot of backpackers milling around. Now I was the only one. I was amazed how things had changed in a few years, thanks to Mugabe.

I must have moved up by just a metre or so during the first hour. Only five of the people who had been standing in line when I joined had been issued tickets. By now, 40, maybe 50, prospective travellers had fallen in behind me in the queue, which for some reason that I could not understand was simply not moving. The ticket officer looked busy enough, although one couldn't tell just what it was he was doing. The odd person joined the queue at the front, but even that was not enough to cause such a long delay. It was Sunday and most of the people in the queue were clearly waiting to take the train back to work in kwa-Bulawayo after the weekend.

Forty-five minutes later, with about six people still in front of me, the train suddenly pulled into the station. All hell broke loose. Everybody simultaneously rushed to the front of the queue, catching me unawares. Most of the people behind me ended up in front of me. All was chaos. Everyone was shouting and trying to speak through the small window, demanding a ticket. On the other side of the glass the ticket-issuing officer looked very relaxed.

I soon realised that I had spent one and a half hours in the queue for nothing: there was no way I was going to get a ticket. I was so angry that I did not have a hard time choosing between the two options that I knew would be open to me after I had found accommodation for the night: either to take a bus to kwa-Bulawayo to try and get a travel company there to take me where I wanted to go – or stuff Cecil John Rhodes, Mzilikazi and Matobo National Park and leave Zimbabwe at first light, head back to Zambia and continue north.

Of course I chose the latter.

I took a cab to a budget hotel just outside town. The hotel was good value for money, except that there was no toilet paper in the toilets, as I discovered a little too late. That night, just to de-stress, I went to the entertainment centre at the Kingdom Hotel, which I had spotted from the air earlier while microlighting. I was the only person besides the depressed-looking barman at the Wild Thing pub there.

After consuming two beers and walking around what looked as if it had once been a thriving city centre, I took a cab back to my hotel. I arranged with the driver, Thulani, to pick me up early the following morning to take me back to the border post. Thulani asked that I pay him in advance so that he could fill his car's petrol tank that night. He needed 3 000 000 dollars, he told me. I had only just met him, but he looked like a trustworthy guy. So I paid him for the following day's services in advance and went to bed with some anxious thoughts about what was going to happen.

The following morning, while I was taking a shower, there was a knock at the door. There stood Thulani, 15 minutes early. It was a good start to the day. He dropped me off on the Zimbabwean side of the border and I exited Zimbabwe without any hassles. I had to walk about two kilometres to the Zambian immigration office and, in the process, crossed over the steel bridge between the two countries, the famous 111-metre bungee-jumping site. The bridge, Rhodes's brain-child, took 14 months to build when they linked Bulawayo to the Copperbelt towns of Kitwe and Ndola.

Midway over the bridge, knowing full well I had a Lusaka-bound bus to catch, I decided to stop and take off my backpack, lean over the handrail and enjoy the view. With the sound of the falls behind me, looking down at the Zambezi River as it meandered through the gorge, with the refreshing early-morning breeze tugging at my T-shirt, memories of my debut bungee jump from the bridge in 1999 (part of my 24th birthday celebration) came flooding back. It was as if I had jumped only the day before.

Your first bungee jump is both nerve-wracking and disorientating. And exhilarating. Once you jump off from the platform, heart pumping ferociously, and start heading down headfirst, there is nothing that goes through your mind except waiting for the bungee cord to pull you back. Although the actual falling takes only a few seconds, it feels much, much longer when your life is totally dependent on a bungee cord. Adrenalin sport, like drugs, is totally addictive. Two months after bungee jumping at Vic Falls, I jumped off at the world's highest commercial bungee site: the 216-metre Bloukrans bridge on the Garden Route, between Plettenberg Bay and Port Elizabeth.

After ten minutes of enriching my soul and having the entire bridge to myself, I continued towards the Zambian immigration office and re-entered Zambia without difficulty. In fact, while I filled out the customs register the two officials were relaxing outside in the sun.

I took a typical Zambian blue cab back to Livingstone and kept asking myself why I had left Zambia in the first place.

On the recommendation of the cab driver – cab drivers are really treasures on travels like mine – I used a cheaper but more comfortable bus company (named Zoom) to take me from Livingstone to

Lusaka than the one on which I had travelled to Livingstone three days earlier. The bus left from the market centre, which was buzzing with activity. I sat back. The cab driver was correct: it was a comfortable bus.

The man next to me must have been in his early sixties. When I told him that I was from South Africa, he became my tour guide. He told me the names of all the towns and townships we passed: Kalomo, Choma, Batoka, Chisekesi, Mazabuka, and pointed out one or two small rivers that we crossed. He also explained to me that the number of tourists visiting Zambia had increased 'ever since Mugabe started doing his thing in Zimbabwe'.

Roughly halfway between Livingstone and Lusaka we had a 30-minute leg stretch. I struck up a conversation with a sister who, to my surprise, could speak a bit of Zulu. I felt ashamed. I did not even know what Zambia's indigenous language or languages were, never mind putting together a string of words in one of them.

Six and a half hours after leaving Livingstone we got to Lusaka, which, I soon discovered, was celebrating its centenary: it was founded in 1905 when Rhodes's railway reached this small, sleepy village, named after Lusaaka, a headman and a skilled elephant hunter. I was certainly going in the same direction as Rhodes's dream railway line – the main street was called Cairo Road.

Because of its central position, Lusaka replaced Livingstone as the capital of what was then Northern Rhodesia in 1935 and, in 1964, became the capital of newly independent Zambia. As a young boy growing up in South Africa I, along with other young stars, used to sing about Lusaka in freedom songs while toyi-toying.

Quite honestly, I toyi-toyied more because it was a way of life in the township than because I understood its significance in the context of the struggle against apartheid. Truth be told, I was a really naïve young boy; I used to think that the political and economic power white people were enjoying was God-given. That is what the system did to us, both black and white: it made us accept things as they were without questioning anything I didn't question white privilege, and how many young white boys questioned the reason for conscription? But along the way my eyes opened and now I question almost everything.

Anyway, it felt good to be in Lusaka, the very city we used to sing about in our freedom songs. There was a lot of activity along Cairo Road. I planned to spend one night in Lusaka and then to continue on my way east.

Although it is possible to travel from Lusaka directly to Tanzania – by making a 36-hour train journey from Kapiri Moshi, less than 200 kilometres north of Lusaka, to Dar es Salaam – I thought I would travel via Malawi in order to see Africa's third largest lake. This would be my second attempt at visiting Lake Malawi.

The first was in the year 2000. I had wanted to visit the lake, but I had not done my homework very well. My plan was to travel through Harare to Blantyre, before proceeding north to Cape Maclear on the southern shores of the lake. What I did not know was that the road between Harare and Blantyre went through Mozambique's Tete Corridor and, as a South African citizen, I needed a transit visa.

At the Mozambican border, at Nyamapanda, I was unceremoniously taken off the bus and had to return to Harare – more than 200 kilometres away – to obtain one. In Harare, still thoroughly pissed off, I decided to head back home instead and run the Indian Ocean marathon from Ballito to Durban North, the final qualifier for the Comrades. Six weeks later, and three days short of my 25th birthday, I ran (and walked) my first Comrades marathon in 11 hours 40 minutes – with only 20 minutes to spare. Those were the days when I was riding the upper crest of my free-spirited, got-to-do-it-all, bachelorhood wave.

Back now in Lusaka, I found that all the backpackers and guest hotels in town were fully booked. A receptionist eventually explained to me why. It was a holiday – Farmers' Day, always on the first Monday of August. As a result, all the bureaus de change along Cairo Road were closed and I had to exchange money at an international hotel, in the foyer of which were 12 to 15 of some of the most outstanding, beautiful, gorgeous women I had ever seen. When I enquired at reception I was told that they were the finalists in the upcoming Miss Zambia competition. Although my budget did not allow for it, I made up my mind to spend the night in that push hotel. However, I decided it would be better to stick to my budget when the receptionist told me that the finalists were there for a photo shoot only.

I left the city centre in a cab and ended up spending the night in one of the guesthouses in the western (read 'poor') suburbs of the city. The place was basically a shebeen moonlighting as a guesthouse. The music coming from the bar, where the locals were playing pool while enjoying their beer, was very loud. Deafening, in fact. My bedroom was not much of a consolation. Although the mattress was big, it was limp and uncomfortable and the bedding old with a terrible smell of mould. The food was not great either: greasy chicken and chips. I ate only the lettuce and carrot.

That night on the television news it was reported that Sudan's deputy president, John Garang, had died in an air crash the previous day, on his way back from Uganda. It was further reported that the news had sparked widespread violence, especially in Sudan's capital city of Khartoum. This was really bad news for me because when doing the Cape to Cairo you simply have to go through Africa's largest country, Sudan. It meant I would have to monitor the situation in Sudan very carefully the following few weeks.

Just before I fell asleep I began to imagine what my life would have been like if my parents had gone to Lusaka (read 'gone into exile'). I would, in all likelihood, have been the son of a cabinet minister and not, as I am, of retired schoolteachers who never lived together. If I were indeed the son of a minister in the government, I would not have been stuck in the corporate world for ten years. I would be the owner of an Investment Holding Company with stakes in the oil, resources, financial, manufacturing, retail, communications, health and tourism sectors. Owning my own company, I would, like a lot of successful black businessmen, have a white Personal Assistant (PA) whom I would spank constantly just for the fun of it. But alas, my parents had never gone to Lusaka ...

In the early hours, at about 2 a.m., there was a knock at my door. From the giggling I could tell it was ladies – they must have spotted me when I went to the restaurant for dinner. I did not open the door.

I went back to sleep and did not wake up until Phiri, the cab driver who had agreed to pick me up and take me to the bus station, turned up the next morning.

I had a ten-past-five appointment with Phiri, which he had confirmed in his parting words the previous day: 'OK, I will see you at zero-five-ten.' (In Zambia time is described differently.) Like his Vic Falls counterpart, Phiri was a few minutes early.

It was still dark when we arrived at the bus station, but the place was already abuzz with activity: hawkers selling fruit, people buying tickets, passengers struggling with luggage, bus drivers hooting and revving engines. Phiri explained to me that, for safety reasons, buses are not allowed to travel at night in Zambia. He helped me to buy a ticket to the eastern town of Chipata, the capital of Zambia's Eastern Province. I found it quite tricky to use Zambian currency because some notes were so old that I could not read the figures. I had to rely on Phiri. Just by looking at the faint colours of the various notes, he could determine the correct amount.

We left the bus rank just after sunrise. Outside Lusaka the driver pulled off the road and, while the engine of the bus was idling, his assistant addressed the passengers. He started by thanking everybody on board for choosing CR Carriers bus company and explained our route, including the stops along the way and the expected time of arrival in Chipata. I was really impressed.

Before he concluded, the driver's assistant asked for a volunteer to lead us in prayer. A man seated somewhere at the back spoke up. The way that man prayed reminded me of my mother: it was a long, highly charged and emotional prayer. I was deeply moved. When eventually the man said 'Amen' the driver's assistant proclaimed, 'Now God is in charge!' Most passengers agreed with a loud 'Amen'.

The bus on the Great East Road to Chipata, once known as Fort Jameson, was even more comfortable than the one on which I had ridden to Lusaka from Livingstone the previous day. It was also very fast. Given the condition of the roads and the speed of the driving, it was little wonder the Zambian government did not allow buses to travel at night. I tried to draw comfort from the assistant driver's concluding words.

We passengers were treated to a film, a Nigerian comedy called *Mr Ibu*, which would have put *Mr Bean* to shame. Mr Ibu reminded me of the American comedian Martin Lawrence: both are always in trouble, either with their loved ones or the law, and both have their own way of solving their problems, which mostly leads to undesired consequences.

I noticed that some passengers were looking at me askance, seemingly finding it very strange that I should laugh so loudly at Mr Ibu's antics. Zambians, especially the women, laugh softly, as if they are shy or unwilling, perhaps because they are such laid-back and easygoing people. This has nothing to do with their sense of humour – they seem to laugh at almost anything. If they cannot understand something, they laugh. If they see something unusual, they laugh, too.

Speaking of an African sense of humour, if there is such a thing, of all the people I met on this trip the Egyptians must be blessed with the driest sense of humour. So dry in fact that it doesn't exist. Give me a Zambian any time of the year.

About an hour and a half after leaving Lusaka, the bus suddenly stopped in the middle of nowhere. Some passengers, both men and women, got out and started relieving the pressure on their bladders on the long grass at the side of the road. Everything worked in a very well-rehearsed and synchronised manner: men on one side, women on the other, all going about their business as if no one were watching. Within a few minutes, with everybody back on board, we continued on our way to Chipata, stopping at Nyimba, a small dusty town dominated by a relatively big market. Despite its size, Nyimba is one of only eight 'district towns' in Zambia's Eastern Province.

As on the previous day's journey from Livingstone to Lusaka, I observed that for most Zambians the preferred mode of transport was a bicycle. In Livingstone and Lusaka poverty was less apparent than in the small towns on the road to Chipata. Notwithstanding its copper mines, which were privatised in 2002, Zambia is rated one of the world's poorest nations, where more than 70 per cent of the population live on less than us$1 a day. Watching from the window of the bus, I could not help but feel that, although we had our own problems in South Africa, our African brothers and sisters seemed to have it even tougher. What was most discouraging was that young kids, instead of being at school, were selling fruit at the market.

After Katete, the condition of the road deteriorated significantly, but the big potholes did not deter the driver from maintaining his high speed. In the record time of seven and a half hours, including brief stops, we covered 515 kilometres and reached the small and seedy town of Chipata. I could have used the opportunity to visit South Luangwa National Park, which is said to offer one of the best animal-viewing experiences in southern Africa. Not, however, for shoe-string-ers like myself. Visitors, apparently, had to spend a minimum of us$80 per day – four times my daily budget.

As I got off the bus I was surrounded by bus touts and INformal CUrrency TRaders – incutras for short, my name for an African pro-fession that should be included in every dictionary on the planet. Somehow, without my saying a word, the locals knew that I was not from their area, regardless of how hard I tried to fit in. I noticed that people in Chipata were much darker than those in Livingstone and Lusaka. One guy, while I was waiting for my backpack to be offloaded from the bus, kept saying to me, 'Come on, big man. Taxi for you. Good price for you. You have Zambia's kwacha, rands or dollars? We give you good price.' Since Chipata is the last town before Malawi, he knew that I would soon be needing Malawian money.

Eventually, I succumbed to the pressure and got 1 200 Malawian kwachas for my 15 000 Zambian kwachas. Malawia's currency was clearly far stronger than Zambia's.

Along with a couple of passengers from the bus, I waited while the sedan (taxi) that was going to take us to the border filled up. A de-fence-force truck drove down the main street. A soldier, seated with two other soldiers in the back, fired his rifle into the air, seemingly for the fun of it. Everybody continued with what they were doing as if nothing had happened. Gunfire, I concluded, was not unusual for the residents of Chipata, but it was the first such incident on my trip and it made me feel very uneasy.

Another surprise was the number of passengers that were loaded into the unroadworthy sedans that took people to the border: four on the back seat, two in front, excluding the driver. As we left Chipata I read the sign on a big billboard: *Aids is a highway to the grave.* Earlier I had read that life expectancy in Zambia had fallen to below 40 years; AIDS was reported to have killed almost 100 000 Zambians in 2004 alone.

The 20-something kilometres between Chipata and the border flew by; the youngster in the driver's seat drove like a maniac despite the large number of bicycles transporting people and luggage across the border, as well as the foot traffic on the road.

It was easy to get stamped out of Zambia, but getting stamped into Malawi was not so simple – the Malawian immigration offices were nowhere to be seen.

I have learned that fantasies must sometimes remain just that. Therefore, I have no intention of fulfilling that threesome fantasy with two nuns in this lifetime. Maybe in the next.

Banda's Malawi

Father of the Nation

Once known as Nyasaland, the independent Commonwealth of Malawi came into existence on 6 July 1964, bringing to an end the Central African Federation comprised of Northern Rhodesia (now Zambia), Southern Rhodesia (now Zimbabwe) and the protectorate of Nyasaland which had been established by Britain in 1907. When Nyasaland was granted self-governing status in 1963, Dr Hastings Kamuzu Banda became the first prime minister.

Kamuzu Banda was born in British Central Africa in 1896 (or, officially, in 1906). He was given the name Hastings when he was baptised into the Church of Scotland, established in the country by missionaries such as David Livingstone, the first European to set eyes on Lake Malawi (in 1859). At the age of 19, Hastings Banda left home on foot for Southern Rhodesia and, two years later, for the gold mines of Johannesburg. Sponsored by the African Methodist Church, he qualified as a medical doctor in New York and, in 1937, enrolled for a second medical degree at the University of Edinburgh in Scotland to enable him to practise in any country in the British Empire. He subsequently spent seven years in West Africa, working as a doctor.

When he returned home, after 42 years abroad, Dr Banda could no longer speak his home language, Chichewa. After five years in office, he declared himself president-for-life (a position he held for 27 years), with the official title His Excellency, Life President of the Republic of Malawi. Also, Ngwazi, which means 'great lion' in Chichewa. During his reign almost all Malawi's landmarks were renamed after him: Kuzi Highway, Kumuzi Bridge, Kumuzi Dam …

Banda's life presidency finally succumbed to uprisings in 1994. After the reintroduction of a multiparty political system, he was succeeded by Bakili Muluzi of the United Democratic Front who, after ten years as president, was succeeded, in 2004, by President Bingu wa Mutharika.

I had heard that in some African countries you travel in what is referred to as 'no man's land' when you are stamped out of one country but have to cover a certain distance before being legally allowed into the neighbouring one. That is exactly what happens between Chipata in Zambia and Mchinji in Malawi. After I had left Zambian territory, I had to catch a taxi to cover the ten kilometres or so to the Malawian immigration office.

The taxis that ran between the border and the Malawian immigration office at Mchinji had to be loaded in strict order, according to how they were lined up. No jumping of the queue was allowed. The taxi I caught looked truly amazing. It was painted in five distinct colours: the boot was the same blue as the front doors; the bonnet was red, the roof white, one back door green, the other silver. It was an old-model Toyota, with holes in the dashboard – in fact, the dashboard was just a shell – no inside panels on any of the doors, no upholstery on the ceiling, and the windows could not open because there were no winding handles.

Obviously the jalopy had to be jumpstarted. The true fun began when the engine eventually started running. There was a heavy rattling sound as if metal was turning on metal. It felt as if there were no shock absorbers at all and, although we were on a tar road, my back was absorbing all the bumps and potholes in the road surface. As the driver increased speed the rattling became even louder. The noise got so bad that it would hardly have been surprising if the whole contraption had fallen apart under us. The only positive thing was that the smoke our taxi was spewing was not black but ultra white. A good sign, I thought. Another comforting thing was that, despite the racket it made, the taxi was moving very slowly. I doubt the driver had any option.

With that rattling sound in my ears I wondered yet again why the border posts were so far apart. But we made it. At the Malawian immigration office I was asked to produce my yellow-fever certificate, which I did. After stamping my passport the immigration officer looked straight into my eyes and said, 'Welcome to the warm heart of Africa.'

It was back to the shaking and rattling for another two kilometres before, a bit worse for wear, I slid out of our multicoloured taxi at the

Mchinji taxi rank opposite Joe's Motel. From there I caught a minibus taxi to Lilongwe, the capital of Malawi and its second largest city.

In general, the roads in Malawi and the houses along the road were of better quality than in neighbouring Zambia. En route to Lilongwe we passed through two roadblocks and at neither did the traffic police raise any objections to the overloading of our taxi, which was carrying 21 passengers and a chicken in addition to the driver and his assistant. Even more amazing was that we were stopped at an army roadblock just outside Lilongwe and our driver, in broad daylight and in front of everyone, handed one of the soldiers some money. I am sure this had something to do with our load. I couldn't see how much it had taken to convince the soldier that we were observing safety regulations, but almost immediately we were given the green light to proceed. It looked as if the Malawian army was doing the work of the traffic police, while the latter were not quite sure what their function was.

Eleven hours after leaving Lusaka we reached Lilongwe, just before sunset. People were walking home in their hundreds. Wongani, my crisply dressed, bushy-haired, English-speaking neighbour in the backseat of the taxi, had promised to show me to a taxi that would take me to a budget hotel in the city. After finding our way through the loads of people at the taxi rank we finally got to the taxi. Wongani asked me for my postal address and gave me his.

The first two budget hotels were fully booked. As in Lusaka, I ended up in a guesthouse. If I had thought the guesthouse in Lusaka was bad, I was totally mistaken: the one in Lilongwe looked more like a ghost house and reminded me of my boarding-school days with its long, uncarpeted corridors with doors on both sides and the bathroom right at the end. The linen was so bad that I had to use my sleeping bag. Even the mosquito net, which smelled horrible, had a big hole in it. Whenever I moved or turned during the night the springs of the mattress screeched.

Since there was no possibility of sleeping, I spent the night wondering what would happen if a Zambian paid a short visit to a friend in Malawi who happened to live in the area between the two immigration offices. He would be stamped out of Zambia and go to meet his friend in Malawi, but would have to go to the immigration office to get a stamp before returning to the friend's house … the same thing when, a few days later, he wanted to return home.

In the same way, a Malawian who lived in this'no man's land'would have to go to his own immigration office to get stamped out and then turn back, past his own house, and proceed to the Zambian border post … the same rigmarole in reverse when he returned from Zambia.

What compounded the problem, to my mind at least, was what would happen if this Malawian wanted to go to Mchinji and Lilongwe, which are both further east in his country: he would have to go'through' his immigration offices but could not be stamped into the country because he was neither leaving nor entering. It would be easier just to climb back and forth through a hole in a fence out of sight of the immigration officer, I thought.

It is my nature at times to be obsessed with how things work in practice. Being of a practical mindset, I have learned, can cause you not to enjoy life; people who live without worrying about how things really work have fewer cares. I am sure that to the Malawians and Zambians in their no man's land this matter would be a non-issue, but to me it was one of those mysteries of life.

The following day, while changing money and sending emails to friends and family, the taxi driver who had picked me up from the ghost house and driven me to the internet café in the city centre disappeared – with my backpack. For a moment I didn't realise what had happened because I was so thrilled by my fiancée's having ended her email with the words *I love you lots, my sweets* – something she would never say to my face. Coming back to my senses, I could not believe how much I had trusted a man I had only just met. To make things worse, I had paid him all his money, including the money for the trip we were yet to make. Then I remembered that we had agreed that he would pick me up in two hours' time. I decided to wait and see and to remain as calm as best I could.

I did not plan to stay long in Lilongwe – my mission in Malawi was to visit the lake. I would have loved to go to Cape Maclear, located on the southern shores of Lake Malawi, but I was not prepared to go that far south. I had heard that the sunsets alone make a visit to Cape Maclear worthwhile, not to speak of Lake Malawi National Park, proclaimed a World Heritage Site in 1980, of which Cape Maclear is part. Instead, I had decided to go to Senga Bay, which meant first taking a taxi and heading in an easterly direction to Salima.

Because of my anxiety my time in the internet café in City Centre in Lilongwe was not a peaceful or a happy one. Lilongwe itself is a two-in-one town, composed of Old Town and a much newer city centre. The banks, embassies and business offices are in City Centre (also referred to as Capital City); the bus rank, dusty, uneven pavements, cheap hotels, the market and the crowds are to be found in Old Town. Old Town started as a small village along the Lilongwe River that grew into a town. Because of its central geographical position Lilongwe replaced the colonial capital of Zomba, in 1975. Lilongwe has kept its capital-city status, but the economic centre of Malawi is Blantyre, which is in the southern part of the country.

After a tense two hours I was greatly relieved to see the taxi driver returning, as agreed, to pick me up from the internet café. Still suspicious, I asked him to open the boot; I wanted to check if my backpack was intact. As we headed off for the taxi rank it became very clear to me that – probably because of where I come from – I had grown not to trust anyone. It dawned on me that I was forever looking over my shoulder and thinking that people, just because they are poor, are criminals. In fact, the more I travelled in Africa, not only in Malawi, the more I discovered that although (or was it because?) people were poor, they were honest and trustworthy.

At Lilongwe's very disorganised taxi rank, where one narrow lane was used as both entrance and exit, 32 of us were crammed into a 22-seater minibus under a mountain of huge red-blue-white striped plastic carrier bags and enormous black suitcases. As I tried to make myself comfortable I wondered why we Africans never travel light.

It took our driver about 20 minutes just to manoeuvre out of the taxi rank into the main road. Taxis entering the rank did not want to reverse to allow others to exit, and vice versa. So, everyone ended up hooting and no one moved. It was the first real chaos I had encountered on my trip. But, at last, I was on my way to the lake.

Along the 140 kilometres to Salima we encountered two road-blocks. Again, the driver paid his way through. From Salima I took a matola (an old bakkie) to Senga Bay. It took half an hour to travel the relatively short distance. Jammed upright in the back of the matola between crates of beer and soft drinks, bulging boxes held together with string, more red-blue-white carrier bags, mattresses and travel-ling bags, I struck up a conversation with Wilson. His uncle, he told me, had a speedboat and if I wanted a trip on the lake he could organise it for me at a good price.

Wilson also showed me where to jump off the matola. As I jumped, six guys who had been sitting under a tree came up to me and said they would like to help me with my luggage and show me the way to my hotel. As the matola began to move away Wilson shouted, 'Trust them. They are good guys, my man.'

I decided I needed just one guy to help me. As I walked with the one guy, who was carrying my jacket, we were followed by the other five, as well as by three more scruffy-looking young men who had been sitting under another tree. So, I had nine guys walking either next to or be-hind me towards some trees. At that moment those trees looked more like a forest into which a stranger could disappear without a trace.

Before long my pseudo bodyguard told me that they were actu-ally businessmen (read 'tour organisers'). They proposed a two-in-one tour for me to 'lizard island' and a hippo tour, including lunch, which they called a barbecue. It sounded like a good idea. As we walked on I started to relax, realising, once again, that these were honest people who were only looking to do some business with me.

We walked through the gateway of my budget hotel and I caught my first glimpse of the lake. As with Swakopmund, it was love at first sight. I could not believe my eyes. The lake had waves! While I was checking into the hotel the receptionist told me that Lake Malawi is referred to as the 'calendar lake' because it is 365 miles long and at its maximum width is 52 miles. This, of course, cannot work in a metric system.

My tour guides were still waiting for me outside the reception area. We soon agreed on the price and time for the tour and they (now my associates) asked me to pay a 60 per cent deposit. Since I did not have change, and neither did they, I ended up paying them 100 per cent. One of the guys reassured me with the words, 'Trust us, we are business-people, my friend.'

We agreed on the time that they would pick me up the following day, and that I could spend as long as I wanted on the island before being 'transported' to see the hippos. All the transporting from the beach to the hippos via the island was going to be done by speedboat. I must admit I was worried, but they managed to convince me that everything would be fine.

As soon as we had agreed on the tour, one of the guys opened his bag and showed me key rings he had made from wood. He wanted to do other business too. I, reluctantly, agreed to buy ten key rings. A split second later, another guy opened his bag and showed me paintings that were done by his sister.

At that moment I understood why so many people had followed me from the matola stop. Each one was hoping to sell me something.

That night I had beef curry while listening to the waves breaking on the shore and, later, whisky on the verandah. From the verandah I could see boats going out to fish overnight on the lake. The breeze from the lake was refreshing and the whisky good company. It was one of those 'life's good' moments.

While having yet another drink I was joined by two couples from Durban – obviously, white – who were on a five-week 4x4 adventure tour through southern Africa. It made me think that while people from Gauteng are busy making money, Durbanites are on holiday and Capetonians are staring at the mountain and wondering what all the fuss is about, and people in the Free State are probably still waiting for Jesus to be born in Bethlehem (in their province). I wondered how, with the Supreme Court of Appeal located in the Free State, efficient administration of justice could be expected from a place still stuck in BC.

With this thought in mind I decided to go to bed, being just compos mentis enough to realise that the whisky had attacked my nervous system again. Instead of a single room or a bed in a dormitory at the hotel, I had opted to sleep in a caravan, which was slightly cheaper than the other options. I tossed and turned all night wondering whether my associates, to whom I had already paid the full fee, would pitch up the next morning.

When I stepped onto the beach just after sunrise, eight guys were waiting for me. One thing about so many associates, I never knew exactly who my tour organiser was. Everyone talked equally, and after we had covered about 100 metres I found I had about 12 guys accompanying me.

As we were walking towards the motorboat, Rasta, who was part of the crew from the previous day, tried to sell me some ganja. 'Malawian ganja is the best. South Africa's is very weak. Don't you want to try the real stuff once you get back from the island?' he asked.

I turned him down politely, but he was not going to give up easily. 'Maybe you can be my merchant back in South Africa. Introduce brothers in South Africa to the real ganja and we will both be very rich.'

I turned down that proposition too. By then we had reached what I was told was a speedboat.

I closed my eyes and looked a second time. A dhow with a motor! It was not a comforting sight. I had to wait a couple of minutes while the other guys were trying to organise the pots that were to be used on the island for my barbecue. Meanwhile, I was introduced to the captain of the speedboat, as well as my two guides, David and Spearman. It was the first time I had seen these three guys.

The pots eventually arrived and we were ready to roll. After pushing the boat from the beach to the edge of the water my companions and I jumped in, just before the motor started – and that was when the trouble began. Although the water was not rough, the motorboat could not cut through the waves, so we went up and down with every dip. This was not only making me seasick but was also scaring me to death, especially because as a result of apartheid (read 'no access to a swimming pool and swimming lessons') I cannot swim. The prospect of capsizing was worse even than the anxiety of being in a small aircraft going through turbulence.

David must have picked up that I was uncomfortable. He tried to comfort me: 'Don't worry, my friend. You are not going to die. We will die first, before you do.' I'm sure he meant well but, for me, the idea was not reassuring. In fact, it made me even more anxious.

'Imagine if you die here. What will we say to your family and Thabo Mbeki?' he continued. By then I was close to shitting in my pants.

The trip to the island took about ten minutes but it felt like an hour. When we got to 'lizard island' I realised that the island was actually just a few gigantic rocks which, from erosion over a long period of time, had been segmented into smaller rocks. We docked on the rocks and I was free to start exploring the island. I soon discovered what lay behind the name 'lizard island': in my entire life I had never seen so many lizards in one place at one time. Some lizards were too big for my liking. I also did not know that lizards came in such a variety of colours – black, electric blue, green, brown, some almost transparent.

One of my guides, Spearman, told me that to have the best view of Senga Bay and the lake I had to climb to the highest point on the island. With Spearman leading the way, we began to ascend the rocks on 'rocky island'.

Although I have not yet climbed Mount Everest, I thought to myself that climbing Mount Everest could not be as bad as climbing 'rocky island'. After squeezing ourselves through a very narrow gorge, we finally reached the summit. By then I was sweating profusely and welcomed the cool and refreshing breeze at the top. Pity I was not carrying the SA flag.

Spearman was right. The views of the fishing village, shoreline and the lake were breathtaking. Owing to an abundance of ants, however, our stay was not long. Within 30 minutes we were back at base camp and that is where the waiting for the barbecue began. David had just started the fire when Spearman took one of the pots to collect water from the lake.

'Don't worry, my friend. This is a freshwater lake,' he assured me. While the water for the rice was boiling David started cutting up the tomatoes, which I had already spotted three lizards nibbling on. In the meantime, the captain was bathing in the lake.

'Don't you want to take a bath? Water from this lake chases away all the evil spirits,' he informed me.

Does it look like I am engulfed by evil spirits, bru, I felt like asking.

Since there was no shade at base camp, I was sitting in the open on the rocks, sweating. While David prepared the barbecue, I had a very interesting conversation with Spearman, who, it turned out, was a conspiracy theorist. For instance, he told me that the real Kamuzu Banda had died overseas while studying medicine. The man who came back to rule Malawi was actually Richard Armstrong from Ghana. Spearman told me that Richard had studied with Banda. He knew that Banda had left Malawi at an early age and figured out that, after years of absence, Malawians would not be able to detect the difference. That is why, when 'Banda' came back, he could not speak his mother tongue.

I dared not ask him if it was true that Banda, known for his resistance to decadent Western fashions and influences, had banned the Simon and Garfunkel song 'Cecilia/I'm down on my knees/I'm begging you to please come home' because his relationship with his mistress, named Cecilia, was going through a bad patch at the time.

Spearman was a real vested guy. He knew things about South Africa I did not even suspect. For instance, that reggae star Lucky Dube was South Africa's ambassador to Jamaica. Naturally we also talked about women. Among other things, Spearman commented that 'food in South Africa must be very delicious. That is why South African women have big bums.'

I had to correct him. 'We don't call it a big bum. To be polite, we call it an African bum.'

'OK, so they have big African bums,' he agreed.

I decided to leave it at that.

After two hours of waiting, just when I thought we were about to have a meal, the captain got into the speedboat and left. When I enquired what was happening, Spearman responded in a very calm voice, 'He is going to get a fish and will be back now.'

About 20 minutes later the captain returned with two fishes.

Spearman cut them up and washed them at the very same spot where the captain had had a bath earlier on. Altogether, the barbecue preparations took three hours. Then, rice and spinach, sprinkled with boiled tomatoes and fish, were served by David.

What does not make you sick makes you fat, I thought as I munched away. To my surprise the dish was not just tasty, it was delicious. I finished off the fish and vegetables; the rice was too much. By then I had told my various tour guides that I was cancelling the hippo tour.

Cruising back to the mainland was much quicker than the outward trip. Rasta was waiting for me and he just would not give up on his insistence that I would be 'a very good business partner'. I ignored him completely. Being stuck in a corporate environment was not the best thing, but exchanging it for a career in smuggling could not be an improvement.

I parted company with the guys at the village. We promised to see each other soon.

That night I had dinner with Elizabeth, an American blonde. She was on a month's Malawi-Tanzania-Kenya vacation and was very easy to talk to.

One thing about being brought up in apartheid South Africa is that I never really interacted with people from other races until I went to a tertiary institution. Even then, interaction was very limited: 'wit okes' hung out together and so did darkies. The democratic dispensation had not changed things much. The only white people I interacted with were my former colleagues and we met, by and large, only during working hours. After hours and during weekends we all hung out with our own. So, to find an attractive white woman who had no hangups/frills and who judged me by what I am and not by my race was a breath of fresh air.

Thanks to apartheid I, like the majority of black South African men, grew up thinking it was a privilege, blessing and honour to sleep with a white woman. If my memory serves me correctly, it was almost every black man's fantasy. Those very few black men who got lucky would often relate the story, even five years after the actual event, and the unlucky ones would listen attentively while turning green with envy. Even if the white woman was ugly and unattractive, who cared? As long as the black brother had done it with *ungamla* (tsotsi taal for a white person), he was The Man and he was given all the respect he deserved.

Elizabeth was attractive and very nice to me, but I did not try my luck. Later that night she came to my caravan to pour her heart out. She told me that the real reason she was doing the African trip was to discover herself after she had found her fiancé in bed with her best friend. Again, being such an introvert, I was not sure what to say to console her. I changed the subject. It did not work. She appeared very hurt. I told her what I thought would make her feel better: 'Your fiancé is a dog and your best friend is a whore.'

I am not sure if that consoled her, but soon thereafter she left.

The next morning I took a matola to Salima, stacked under people this time, not between luggage. In fact, we were so many in the back of that bakkie that I had to put my backpack on the roof of the cabin, hanging onto it with one hand.

I had thought of taking the Ilala boat on its weekly trip to the northern part of Malawi but realised, after checking the schedule, that I would have to disembark at Nkatha Bay at one o'clock in the morning. That was definitely not my cup of coffee. I decided instead to go back to Lilongwe and begin the, reportedly, uncomfortable 26-hour bus ride to Dar es Salaam, Tanzania.

Returning to Lilongwe, I spotted three funeral processions although it was a weekday – another reminder that people were dying in numbers. Although it was reported by UNAIDS, the joint United Nations programme on HIV/AIDS, that 90 000 Malawians died from HIV/AIDS-related illnesses in 2003, I felt that, given the poor living conditions and lack of infrastructure I saw along the road between Salima and Lilongwe, the figure might have been even higher.

In 2002, Malawi had experienced the worst famine in four decades and hundreds of people died as a result. Malawi's agricultural sector is the country's biggest employer, as well as the biggest exporter, especially of tea, tobacco and sugar. As much as I was enjoying the trip, the suffering of my fellow African brothers and sisters was a constant reminder of the seemingly insurmountable problems facing our continent.

When we arrived in Lilongwe I was told that there were two direct buses to Dar es Salaam in the next three days, but both were fully booked. That meant I either had to stay in Lilongwe for four days or do the trip in stages. Although I hated the prospect, I felt I had no option but to catch a minibus the next day to Mzuzu, Malawi's third largest city after Blantyre and Lilongwe, with a view to reaching the border town of Karonga a few hours later. I spent the night in a basic hotel in the centre of Old Town.

It was another early morning. I was woken up around five by the muezzin's call to prayer. I was amazed by the number of mosques in Malawi, more so even than in Zambia. Before the trip I had thought the number of Muslims in sub-Saharan Africa was negligible. The abundance of mosques convinced me otherwise.

I had read that Islam came to northern Africa via Egypt in the 7th century and spread westwards to today's Libya, Algeria and Morocco. So, the majority of people in North Africa would naturally be Muslim. Much later, in the 18th and 19th centuries, Islam was introduced to East Africa by Arab and Persian sailors and traders, and from there westwards along the slave routes to countries in central Africa.

Christianity also came to North Africa via Egypt, but much earlier – apparently, Mark the Evangelist had already built the first church in Alexandria in the 1st century. However, Christianity didn't stick so well around Mediterranean Africa and it is a minority religion there today, unlike further south, where Christianity is still the biggest religion.

It is the missionaries who must be credited for successfully spreading Christianity in sub-Saharan Africa. The likes of Robert Moffat and Dr Livingstone – whose motto could have been Christianity, Commerce and Civilisation – were among the first to come to convert 'dark' Africa, but soon many from different missionary societies and countries (especially from those who 'scrambled' for Africa) followed their example.

The muezzin's call to prayer, and the fact that some African brothers and sisters are so big on Christianity that they see those, like me, who still believe in the ancestors, as both uncivilised and barbaric and possessed by the devil, got me wondering why we Africans never exported our own religion, our ancestor belief, to other parts of the world. Why is it only we who are dropping what our forefathers believed in while others spread and are still busy exporting their religion to the four corners of the globe? Why are we only consuming and not producing where religion, too, is concerned?

An hour later, I was at the taxi rank. In terms of chaos, nothing beats Lilongwe's taxi rank for me. It is a mad house at its worst. While hawkers were still unpacking fresh fish from the lake, everyone was shouting, screaming and trying to get the attention of potential customers, making it almost impossible for me, carrying a backpack, to get to where another 22-seater was waiting, bound for Mzuzu.

After 90 minutes the minibus was finally full and ready to hit the road. There was a minor problem, though – it would not start. It took a lot of effort from a few other taxi drivers to create enough space amid the chaos to allow the minibus to roll down a slight incline to get it jump-started. Thirty minutes later we were finally on our way. As soon as we hit the main road, I realised that reaching Karonga the same day was a pipe dream. The minibus was moving at a tortoise's pace and it was clear that I would have to sleep over in Mzuzu.

A note here on a few words used in Malawi that may cause confusion: what we black South Africans – after all, we are just about the only ones that take them – call a taxi (*itekisi* in Zulu), Malawians call a minibus; what we call a cab (i.e., a metered taxi) they call a taxi. But their taxis (what we call a cab) are not metered, as is normally the case with taxis in the outside world. You agree on a price at the start of the journey, never mind how long the journey, and that's it. Malawians are right, though, to call what we call a taxi a minibus because it is, in fact, a minibus. Or is it a minibus taxi? In which case, both of us are 50 per cent correct.

The Malawians also seem to call every shop a shopping centre. Thus, in a tiny rural town you may have three shopping centres. Outside one, an innovative sign caught my eye, this time over a mortuary: *Energy Coffins*.

In the few days that I was in Malawi, I had discovered that Malawians are a very creative and poetic people. Among other things, I spotted some quite unusual names of businesses:

Joy Online (for a telephone bureau)
Natural Mistake (for a telephone bureau)
Someone-Say-Something-So-What (for a bottle store)
Let Them Talk (for a general dealer)

Malawians also have a different way of breastfeeding. Mind you, it is not only in Malawi but also in Zambia that when women suckle their babies they do not hold their breasts; they just let it all hang out and nobody seems to notice and/or care – except me, of course.

An hour or so after leaving Lilongwe it started to drizzle. The minibus had only one wiper working, but the real problem was that it was the one on the passenger's not the driver's side. This meant that the driver had to stop a few times to get out of the bus and wipe the windscreen by hand.

Six hours, 320 kilometres and four roadblocks later, we were welcomed to Mzuzu by a billboard with a simple but powerful message: *Speed thrills but also kills*. By now, I was convinced that Malawians are natural poets. Between Lilongwe and Mzuzu I had not seen a single speeding car; what I did notice was that most vehicles looked unroadworthy.

I found a room in a guesthouse in Kitutu, within walking distance of Mzuzu. My hostess was Mama Maggie, a woman in her early fifties. Slightly overweight, definitely not tall and with thick glasses, she welcomed me warmly and showed me to a room with only a narrow bed, where I dropped my bags before walking back to town. There, I strolled into the market, no longer stressing about being in unfamiliar surroundings. I was feeling very comfortable among my black brothers and sisters. Later, I noticed that quite a few tourists walked from the residential area of Kitutu to Mzuzu, or back, even late at night.

With time on my hands in Mzuzu, I decided to have my hair done.

...ed to be washed before being plaited again. I went to the big, crowded, dusty market right next to the taxi and bus station and, after window shopping for a few minutes, went through the small gate that separated the market from the bus station. There I found a salon occupied by five sisters, all hairdressers I presumed, and one client who was having her hair relaxed. I told one of the sisters that I wanted my plaits to be undone and my hair washed and re-plaited. She looked at me for few seconds without saying a word. Then she asked, her eyes round with amazement, 'So you want me to do your hair?'

Well, you're a hairstylist. So that is what you do – you style people's hair. No, I could not say that. Instead I said, 'Yes, please, I want you to do my hair.'

'Where you from?' she asked, looking at me as if I came from another planet.

'South Africa.'

She shook her head, turned around and spoke to the other sisters in a language I could not understand. Even the woman who was having her hair relaxed turned around and stared at me. Then they all started laughing. Somehow I figured out what the problem was: in some African countries, and especially in small towns such as Mzuzu, only women have their hair plaited. Although it did not feel right that they should laugh at a potential client, I understood why they were giggling. To them I was not man enough. After all, I'm sure they were asking themselves, what type of a man has his hair plaited?

The sister, nevertheless, undid all the plaiting done in Swakopmund and then asked me to bow my head over the sink. This was a strange request because in a hair salon you usually sit with your back to the sink, face upwards, so that the hairdresser can wash your hair from your forehead backwards without the shampoo running into your eyes. In Mzuzu it is exactly the opposite.

I bent over while facing the sink. Only when the sister took a jar full of water from the table did I realise that the taps on the sink were not connected to the water supply. The sister applied a nice-smelling shampoo to my hair before leaving the salon with an empty 10-litre bucket. I was still standing bent over the sink when, a couple of seconds later, she returned with a full bucket. She used the jar to scoop water from the bucket and poured it over my head until all the shampoo was rinsed out. I did not mind the long process, except that the water, which was fetched from a public tap not far from the salon, was very cold.

The cold water, however, was just what the doctor ordered: I felt much more awake after that. My hair was blow-dried with an electric hair dryer, and then the plaiting started.

Oh my sister, you are such a rough rider, I thought to myself as she pulled my hair so tightly that I could feel my eyes widen; it was as if she were warning me that I, a man, should not ever plait my hair again. I figured that I could not complain because that would cement the women's view that I was a sissy.

At that moment I noticed that two brothers, who looked like taxi drivers, had come into the salon. I am not sure why they were there but they stood on one side of me, with the sister on the other, and chatted over my head in an incomprehensible local language, all the while looking at my hair and having a good laugh.

Sporting a new hairdo, I walked back to my guesthouse and had a cold beer. The hair was so tight that I had to have a second beer to numb the pain while watching a two-hour programme on prime-time television called 'President's Diary'. I discovered some interesting similarities between Malawi's former president, Bakili Muluzi, and his counterpart in Zambia, Frank Chiluba. Chiluba spearheaded the reintroduction of democracy in Zambia but subsequently tried to amend the constitution in order to enjoy a third term in office; Muluzi spearheaded the reintroduction of democracy in Malawi and so ended Banda's reign of terror, but he, too, attempted to have the constitution amended to allow him a third presidential term. Like Chiluba, Muluzi did not succeed in extending his presidency beyond ten years.

For two hours, while sipping cold Kuche beer, I saw in great detail what Malawi's first citizen had been up to during the previous week. He obviously loved arriving in a howling motorcade of expensive German cars while women ululated and children waved small Malawian flags. All this fuss because he was opening a clinic in some remote town. Talk about good Saturday evening viewing! Some things never change.

Banda had forced women not to wear trousers and men not to have long hair; Malawi's third president, Bingu wa Mutharika, was committing an equal offence by forcing Malawians to swallow him during prime time.

I resumed my trip to the border early the next morning, on the very first minibus to leave Mzuzu for Karonga. I was sitting next to a man in an old T-shirt, grey trousers and slops (flip-flops) named Zeblon Nkosi who told me he was born in Zambia but his father had moved to Malawi while still a young man. His forefathers, he said, were originally from Swaziland, which explained his very familiar surname. As we left the town, the jacarandas in full bloom along the main road, I was briefly reminded of Pretoria, i.e., Tshwane, the new name for the city that Afrikaners can pronounce but appear to hate.

As we drove past certain villages, Zeblon would tell me their names and history. Between villages he complained about how corrupt the government was. 'They all want to be voted in so that they can enrich themselves once in the office. All of them are rich and have big stomachs while the people are suffering,' he complained.

About halfway between Mzuzu and Karonga we passed Phwezi High School, a world-renowned boarding school, according to Zeblon. Kids from as far away as Mozambique, Namibia and even South Africa applied to study there, he told me. To say I was astonished to hear this is an understatement. According to Zeblon, most people who had made it big in Malawi and Mozambique had gone to Phwezi. To me, as we were driving past, it looked like any school in a South African township. It did not have that **wow** factor you associate with Kearsney College or Michael House, two of the highly regarded private schools in my part of the world. But life has proved over and over again that it is not correct to judge a book by its cover and I was prepared to give Zeblon the benefit of the doubt. Phwezi may indeed have been an exceptional place of learning and it was possible that I would one day apply for my daughter Nala to go there.

In total, there were six roadblocks on the winding road between Mzuzu and Karonga, the last two just two drums on either side of the road with a wooden beam across. The army performed its job of questioning the driver and looking inside the minibus with enthusiasm and a smile. The road led through Ngara, a small town with rolling hills on the left, and Lake Malawi on the right, where I would certainly have stopped had I been travelling in my own car. It looked like a soul-enriching place.

Just before we entered Karonga Zeblon turned to me and said, 'My friend, I have a friend in Karonga whose name is Joshua. He has a taxi and can take you to the Tanzanian border for a good price.'

It was a scorching hot day. I soon noticed that some of the people at the taxi rank were speaking Swahili. These Swahili-speaking people, Zeblon explained, were in fact Tanzanians who had come down to Karonga to sell their wares. Malawians bought from them and then sold the goods, mostly garments, further south in Mzuzu, Lilongwe and Blantyre.

In no time Zeblon located Joshua in the dusty Karonga taxi rank. It turned out that what Joshua had was not a taxi but a cab. We agreed on the price, Zeblon accompanying us to the border town of Songwe. I did not have enough Malawian kwachas on me to pay the fare, but I knew that, as at any other African border post, there would be incutras waiting for people like me. Indeed, after a few enquiries on the Malawian side we were referred to a hut about a hundred metres from the border gate. The guys in the hut took the term 'black market' literally: it was pitch dark inside the thatch-roofed mud hut. Zeblon did all the talking in Chechewa. Our money dealer then left us, literally in the dark, for more than ten minutes. I couldn't work out where he had gone and why it was taking him so long to come back.

'You see, my friend, sometimes in this black market a few individuals have to be approached, especially if loads of money is involved,' Zeblon explained. In my case we wanted to change us$10 and us$100 for Malawian kwachas and Tanzanian shillings, respectively.

When he finally returned, the incutra was accompanied by a youngster who must have been in his late teens. I enquired about the going exchange rate and received a very long answer. 'The rate is not fixed. The more money you change the better the rate. Seeing that you are changing quite a bit of cash, you will get a reasonable rate' was what that youngster, who spoke fluent English, told me.

This rate thing was really confusing me: first, as per their calculations, they converted US dollars to Malawian kwachas and only then kwachas to shillings. When I questioned this, the youngster explained, 'This is the standard procedure and it is the only way that they, as the merchants, know that they are not short-changing themselves.'

I left the hut convinced that in one way or another I had been compromised. Almost all shilling notes are multiples of thousands, which made it even more confusing. After paying Joshua and giving Zeblon my postal address and taking a photo (they insisted) of them, it was time to leave Malawi. It was a sad farewell; Zeblon had really helped me on my way. I shook his hand and he promised to write.

There was nobody at the counter in the brick-walled, tin-roofed Malawian immigration office. After a couple of minutes an officer pitched up and gave me an exit form to fill in. Everything went smoothly. I stepped out of the office and found that the black-market youngster was waiting for me. As we walked towards the Songwe bridge, which separates Malawi from Tanzania, he asked me a few basic questions and suddenly turned around and said, 'I really like you. Will you be my friend?'

I was stunned. The last time a person asked me whether we could be friends was during my lower-primary schooldays. (I am discounting those dumb women, later in my life, who would turn me down when I proposed love to them, saying, 'Let's just be friends.')

I responded convincingly, 'Of course. For sure. Hey! Why not?'

'My name is Tandai Gondwe,' he said. 'Will you please give me your postal and website address?' I gave him my email address as we walked together towards the Tanzanian border post.

The only regret I have about Malawi is that I did not comfort the American girl Elizabeth in a more personal and humane way.

Nyerere's Tanzania

Father of the Nation

For more than 2 000 years Arab traders visited the east coast of Africa before they started to settle there in the 8th century. The Portuguese arrived in 1505 to secure ports of call on the trade route to the East. Until 1698, when the Arabs finally broke their hold, the two groups were in constant conflict.

Almost 300 years later, Julius Kambarage Nyerere became president of Tanganyika, a country on the east coast of Africa administrated by Germany as a protectorate from 1885 to 1922, and then by Great Britain under a mandate from the League of Nations. Britain changed the name from Deutsch-Ostafrika to Tanganyika Territory in 1922.

Nyerere was born in Tanganyika in the same year, the son of a local chief. He studied at Makerere University in Uganda and at the University of Edinburgh – the first Tanganyikan to study at a British university. On his return he was employed as a teacher, but was forced to resign after he became president of the Tanganyika African National Union. As such, he helped to ensure that Tanganyika achieved independence without war or bloodshed, on 9 December 1961.

Nicknamed Mwalimu ('teacher' in Swahili), Nyerere was president of the Republic of Tanganyika for three years and, after Zanzibar was incorporated in 1964, of a unified Tanzania for a further 21 years. He eventually stepped down in 1985, amidst the dismal failure of his ujama policy, a combination of socialism and African communal living. In his farewell speech he said quite openly, 'I failed. Let's admit it.' Nyerere died of leukemia in London at the age of 70.

Nyerere was succeeded by Ali Hassam Mwinji, who was president for ten years, and then by Benjamin Mkapa who was also in office for a decade. Mkapa was succeeded by President Jakaya Mrisho Kikwete in 2005.

Like KK in Zambia, Nyerere was instrumental in the liberation of South Africa. For that I am grateful.

As we crossed the Songwe River, incutras from Tanzania began to harass me to change some currency, but my new Malawian friend Tandai told them, in Swahili, that I was already sorted. A short distance from the Tanzanian customs office he asked if I could take a snap of him, which I did, and he promised to write within a few days. And off he went.

There were three officials sitting outside the Tanzanian customs office, which somewhat resembled a shack. 'Do you have anything to declare, my friend?' the youngest asked.

'No, I don't,' I replied.

'Do you have a camera?' asked another officer.

'Yes, I do,' I said hesitantly.

'How much?'

For a second I was confused and then I replied, politely, 'But, Sir, that one is mine.'

'Come on, my friend, I will give you a good price,' he insisted.

'I only have one, Sir,' I said firmly.

The third officer, who had not said a word until then, intervened and pointed me towards the immigration offices where I had to go next.

For the first time on the trip I was asked for a visa, which I did not have. I did not know that South Africans needed a visa to enter Tanzania. Fortunately, I could get one on the spot at the border post for us$50.

After stamping my passport the official said, 'Karibu.'

I just stood there and he repeated, louder this time, 'Karibu.'

I was even more confused.

He smiled and said, 'Welcome.'

Only then did it click that 'karibu' is 'welcome' in Swahili. Although I had learned a few key phrases in Swahili before leaving South Africa, it is one thing to learn phrases while sitting on a comfortable sofa with a beer in one hand and something totally different to remember those phrases when interacting with locals.

From the moment I walked out of that immigration office I was subjected to the worst harassment ever from young boys, mainly incutras. They were grabbing and tugging at my backpack, trying to get my attention. I realised that I could not allow my temper to rise, but if I were back home in Mzansi I would have slapped at least one of them.

The fact that I could not speak Swahili made things worse. Even after I told them, in English of course, that I had already changed money, they continued to walk next to me, just staring at me and not saying a word. That made me very uncomfortable. And I felt really stupid that I could not construct even a single simple sentence in Swahili, the most-spoken language in East Africa.

Tandai had advised me to take a minibus to Kiyela and another from there to Mbeya, where I was heading. From Kiyela, he told me, more people were going to Mbeya than from the border.

People on the Kiyela-bound minibus were really shocked that there was a black African person on board who could not speak Swahili. Growing up in apartheid South Africa, I was made to believe that as long as I could speak my home language (Zulu) and the 'universal' language (English) the world would be my oyster. My first few minutes in Tanzania disproved this myth completely. I discovered that quite the opposite was true when the guy sitting next to me asked, 'My friend, besides English, what other language can you speak?'

'Zulu,' I said, confidently.

'What?' he asked in amazement.

I was beginning to feel that my Tanzanian brothers were somehow rougher in their responses than their Malawian neighbours.

I got to Kiyela just in time to take a 35-seater to Mbeya. As I entered the minibus it suddenly hit me: I had to piss. Without thinking twice I turned around, took two steps and – right on Kiyela's main road – I let fly. It felt so good, with so many people looking on. When nature calls every living species shall answer, I thought to myself. Not that I cared, and nobody else raised an eyebrow either.

It was refreshing not to be in an overcrowded minibus. There were only about 25 of us, plus five chickens, heading towards Mbeya. I wondered why so many people in this part of the world carried chickens with them. But, unlike in Malawi, where luggage consisted mainly of big bags, in Tanzania it was mostly empty 20-litre plastic drums, the purpose of which was never revealed to me.

From the outset I was struck by differences between the two countries. The grass and shrubs were far greener in Tanzania than in Malawi. I was impressed, too, by the bright and colourful garments worn by women in Tanzania, where the Muslim way of dressing, head covered, was much more noticeable than in Malawi.

I soon realised that it was an illusion that minibuses in Tanzania did not overload. Kiyela was only the first stop; thereafter the minibus stopped frequently, at different villages along the way, to pick up passengers. It was Sunday and everyone seemed to be heading back to Mbeya; at one stage we were, as far as I could count, 45 passengers in the minibus. The other passengers would talk to me in Swahili and I would reply very softly, 'What? Me do not understand', while using a bit of sign language. I felt really bad. In Malawi I had promised myself that when I returned to South Africa I would go for swimming lessons – Resolution No. 4 of my trip. My first few hours in Tanzania made me come up with another goal for when I got back to South Africa: Learn Swahili – Resolution No. 5.

I might not have understood Swahili, but to my surprise I suddenly heard a lady on the bus saying 'Soweto'. My excitement was wasted: it turned out to be the name of a bus stop. Ironically, there was a Mandela grocery store at that stop. I had always suspected that Madiba invested far and wide. After deliberating on the matter for a while, however, I came to the conclusion that maybe it was Ebrahim Patel's shop – just using Mandela's name (again).

Although the roads were far better than in Malawi, we came upon two minibus-taxi accidents. Both vehicles had overturned, but there seemed to be no casualties.

A few kilometres beyond the Soweto bus stop we entered a small town where everyone seemed to be disembarking. I asked the lady next to me if the town was Mbeya. She looked at me for a while and then nodded her head.

Just to make sure I was jumping off at the right place, I asked the assistant driver, who was busy offloading bags at the back of the minibus, whether we had indeed reached Mbeya. He answered me in Swahili and, because I could not understand what he said, I just stood there, my backpack next to me, looking at the antiquated cars driving by. The assistant driver suddenly grabbed me by my hand and shoved me back into the minibus while uttering more Swahili. He sounded peeved. I sat back in my seat and sighed – Tanzania was really proving to be a bit too rough for my liking.

Almost ten hours after leaving Mzuzu in Malawi, I finally arrived at the spread-out town of Mbeya. At the right spot, the driver's assistant told me, by hand signal, to get off.

Mbeya, to my surprise, was a big town with some modern buildings. Most of them, however, looked old and in need of attention. As all budget accommodation was fully booked, I had no alternative but to try a mid-luxury hotel. The bearded receptionist there told me that they too were fully booked and explained that it would be impossible to get accommodation in Mbeya because 'there is a big festival to celebrate the farmers' day tomorrow'.

Without thinking I said at the top of my voice: 'Again? Another Farmers' Day?'

The man looked confused and told me that they only have one Farmers' Day – on 8 August – every year. By then I had realised that the other Farmers' Day celebrations (on the first Monday of August) had been in Zambia the previous week.

With no place to sleep, I enquired whether there were any overnight buses to Dar es Salaam. I was told the buses for Dar, as it is popularly referred to by the locals, left only in the mornings. The receptionist, sensing that I was really stuck, gave me directions to a budget hotel that he promised was never fully booked. This turned out to be a two-storey building with a roof bar, just down the road from the mid-luxury hotel, in the reception area of which about 20 local guys were watching an English Premiership game on a big-screen television. To my relief there were indeed rooms available.

To get to my room I had to step through the local guys, who immediately lost interest in the game and stared at me as if I were a creature from another planet – among other reasons probably because of my hairdo. As in Lilongwe, the hotel had a long corridor. The difference was that this corridor smelled strongly of stale urine. My room was not as bad as the corridor, I was pleased to discover. It was pretty basic and clean and contained twin beds with mosquito nets.

Finding accommodation was not the end; I still had to get the bus ticket to Dar, and to do that I had to take a cab to the bus station outside the town. The cab driver did not speak a word of English and, only after quite a few hand signals, succeeded finally in understanding where I wanted to go. On our way to the bus station the huge speed humps gave me a business idea: Business Idea One. I would simply have to come back to Mbeya and open an exhaust and shock absorber outlet. With speed humps of these dimensions there would always be a queue of customers.

At the bus station all the bus touts wanted me to buy a ticket from the bus company they represented. A white shirt and black tie made one of the young guys look much more respectable than the rest and I decided that he probably represented a better bus company. As there were no buses to speak of at that moment in that huge station, it was difficult to know whether or not I was buying a bus ticket from a reputable company.

When the ticket was issued I noticed that the time of departure from the station was 11:00, even though the ticket officer had told me it was 05:00. The explanation was quite simple: 'The time on your ticket is Swahili time.'

I had no clue how Swahili time worked and it took a lot of explaining from a man at the bus rank for me to grasp it. Tanzanians, it appeared, start counting their day at 6 a.m. English time. So when it's 7 a.m. English time, it is 01:00 Swahili time; 8 a.m. English time is 02:00 Swahili time, and so on. Hence 5 a.m. English time and 11:00 Swahili time are one and the same.

I took the same cab back to my hotel. Still using hand signals, I tried to explain to the cab driver that he must pick me up the following morning. I was so desperate to ensure that he got the message that I even showed him my bus ticket. After he dropped me off I was hopeful, but not convinced, that he would turn up the next morning.

Later that evening, as I was having a warm beer and reflecting on the harassment I had experienced at the border post at Songwe, there was a knock at the door. The receptionist had a message for me: 'You have a visitor. His name is Paul.'

I had not met any Paul in Mbeya and was curious to see this person who wanted to speak to me so late at night. At reception I recognised Paul, but I was not sure where from. He was quick to remind me that he was the one who had explained the difference between English and Swahili time to me at the bus rank.

Paul was eager to continue the explanation: 'English and Swahili time was very confusing to me as well when I first got here seven years ago. You see, my friend, I was born in Malawi, but I came to Tanzania because of better job opportunities here than in my native land.' He further explained that he had been to four hotels looking for me.

'So the bus for tomorrow has been cancelled?' I said, jumping the gun to encourage him to get to the point.

'No. You see, since the bus gets to Dar at about sunset, it is important that your accommodation should be booked before you get there.' Without allowing me to say anything, he continued, 'You see, my younger brother works for a good but very reasonable hotel in Dar. I can organise a room at a discount for you.'

The name of the hotel he mentioned was one of the three hotels in Dar I had considered while preparing myself for the Cape to Cairo. I had no problem with Paul helping me, as long as there was no exchange of money involved, at least not with him. In addition to getting me a room, he promised he would organise a pick-up car from the bus station to the hotel. He was helping his brother, he explained, to get a commission from the hotel. It sounded like a good deal.

Just when I thought he was about to leave, Paul had another deal for me: 'You see, I can organise the boat for you if you want to cross to Zanzibar, as well as a bus ticket from Dar to Lilongwe.'

'I've been to Zanzibar before,' I responded quickly. 'I do not intend going there this time, and from Dar I'm flying back to Johannesburg.'

From the look in his eyes I figured he knew that I was lying, but there was nothing he could do about it.

As Paul was leaving, I was told my dinner – chicken and rice – was ready. Considering the state of the hotel, the food was not bad at all and, when I finished my meal, a peeled orange was put on the table. Dessert, Tanzanian style.

Since Tanzania was the first country on the trip that was on GMT+3, the next morning was my earliest morning yet. I was dressed and ready to go before 4 a.m. SA time. After standing around in the dark courtyard for five minutes, anxiously awaiting my cab driver of the previous evening, I saw a car with one working headlight stopping outside the hotel. It turned out to be my man.

On our way to the bus rank we did not converse because of the language barrier, but as I got out of the taxi I turned and said, 'Asante.' The cab driver was so surprised that I could thank him in Swahili that he responded, 'Oh! Goodbye, Mister.'

I was about to close the door when he gave me a piece of paper. Yes, it was his postal address. That was another major motivation for me to implement Resolution No. 5 (to learn Swahili).

Although it was still very dark, the bus station was a hive of activity. Loads of people with loads of luggage – mainly agricultural products – milling around. It soon became obvious to me that the bus company I was travelling with was one of the worst at the bus rank; the other buses there looked far more comfortable. There was no way, however, that I was going to forfeit 55 000 shillings and buy another bus ticket. I realised that I should never have judged the bus company by the appearance of its tout.

I boarded the bus and, to my surprise, saw Paul entering the same bus at that early hour of the morning. He stood in the aisle next to my seat in the first row from the back and said, 'I am also going to Dar and my seat is in front.'

It sounded strange, but I did not take much notice. A few minutes later he finally came out with it: 'Look, my man, I have to buy rice for my wife in Dar. She will give me the money when we get there. Can you please borrow me 200 000 shillings?'

I gently refused and he soon walked back to the front of the bus.

Meanwhile, other passengers were boarding the bus amid the (for me, at least) deafening sound of the morning-prayer call from the mosque. It made me think that if you are born in a country where you are exposed to this noise every morning of your life, you are drawn into Islam from birth.

When the bus left Mbeya it was still dark. I soon realised how wrong I had been in my pre-judgement: that old piece of machinery was moving at great speed and it was not all that uncomfortable either. Like the bus from Lusaka to Chipata, it stopped in the middle of nowhere about three hours into the journey. There we did it again: passengers jumped out, men and women going in different directions into the long grass on the side of the road. It was then that I discovered that Paul was not on the bus and began to suspect that the hotel and a pick-up car in Dar were empty promises.

In no time everybody was back in the bus and we continued on our way to the coast. Moments later the driver's assistant came to the back and said a few words in Swahili to the people in the last three rows. From the guy who sat next to me I gathered the gist of what was happening. In the few words of English that he managed to string together he told me that most of the land around Mbeya was used for growing crops and that people from Mbeya and surrounding areas traded their agricultural produce with people from the coastal region. The government was against buses being overloaded with agricultural products, hence it encouraged traders to use trucks for transportation to the coast. To make sure that their fruit and vegetables were not transported from Mbeya to Dar by passenger bus, buses were weighed.

It was for this reason that the driver's assistant came to ask us to stand in the aisle at the very front of the bus at the next weigh bridge, in order to 'balance' the load – apparently most agricultural produce was loaded at the back of the bus. The trick must have worked because our bus had no sooner been put on the scale than it was given a print-out as proof that it was within the weight limit and was given the green light.

Between Mbeya and Dar, we went through three weigh bridges in total, and each time the passengers in the last three rows had to go through the same procedure. I wondered if the authorities genuinely did not know about this trick. Also, try as I might, I could not figure out, technically and practically speaking, what the 'balancing' of the load meant. But the driver's assistant believed in it and so did the passengers, who moved to the front whenever the bus went through a weigh bridge.

Soon after the first weigh-in we stopped at Iringa Hotel, the only hotel in Iringa, to give passengers the opportunity to buy something to eat. Although it was still early morning, people bought full meals: rice and chicken and portions of chips and chicken, all of which were served in really large portions. Half an hour later we were on our way again. From time to time, police in white uniforms stopped us to check the weighbridge print-outs. With big speed humps between Mbeya and Dar, my Business Idea One, i.e., going into the shocks-and-exhausts business, was reignited.

Ten hours, 829 kilometres and nine roadblocks after setting off from Mbeya, we disembarked in hot, humid and badly maintained Dar es Salaam, a typical African city with a sprinkling of skyscrapers and lots of dilapidated old buildings.

Once known as Mzizima, Dar is one of the oldest cities on the east coast of Africa. The Arabs gave it the name Dar es Salaam, meaning 'abode of peace' or 'haven of peace' in Arabic. Although it is not the capital of the country, it is the trade and economic hub of Tanzania, as is Blantyre in Malawi. That explains why the once medium-sized port has grown into a sprawling and overcrowded city.

Dar is both hot and very humid, more intensely so than my home town of Durban. The feeling of discomfort is made worse by continuous traffic jams and the vast numbers of people who seem to walk, non-stop, up and down the severely potholed streets. Legend has it that people had to become street smart to survive in the city during the Nyerere era, hence Dar's nickname Bongo ('brains' in Swahili) and Bongoland, for Tanzania.

As I suspected, Paul had just been blowing hot air. There was no pickup car for me at Dar's bus station; I had to take a cab. Something I found really strange was the distance of the bus station from the city centre

– 11 kilometres – almost as far out as the international airport. This, I was told, was to alleviate noise and traffic congestion in the city centre.

When I arrived at the hotel, where Paul was supposed to have re-served a room for me through his brother, I was told that it was fully booked. It didn't take long for me to realise that all the promises he had made were nothing but an investment in winning my trust so that I would give him the 200 000 Tanzanian shillings he had asked for on the bus. Since even the budget hotels nearby were fully booked, I ended up in a mid-luxury hotel in a scruffy neighbourhood.

It was the first time on the trip that I had a room with a fully en-closed bathroom, TV, air-conditioner and a mini fridge. It was already evening when I booked in and I decided to have dinner at the in-house restaurant. After enjoying scrumptious fish and chips I asked for the bill and was given a beer. I am not a complaining type, so I enjoyed the beer. When I asked for the bill for the second time, I received another beer. Although I drank the second beer, I used a hand signal to ensure that on the third request I got the bill and not a beer. Of course I paid for the beers with a broad smile on my face. After all, I was a bit tipsy.

Just before I went to bed I checked for email on the free internet ser-vice for hotel guests. I was relieved to know that my fiancée's concern that the thug who had broken into my car might return was unfounded. However, she informed me that my friend Vukani Hlatshwayo, known as Merv, had died in a car accident.

The last time I had seen Merv was at my bon voyage party two days prior to my departure. As he said goodbye he wished me well and asked me if I had taken all the necessary vaccinations. He warned me about malaria as well as the importance of using a condom in case I got lucky. Before I left Merv had been involved in two accidents, the second within 24 hours of collecting his car from the panel beaters. After the second accident the car was written off and he bought a new car – the one that killed him.

Merv's death made me realise, again, that life is both fragile and short and that we must get on with it and do the things we want to do without procrastinating. It was a sobering note on which to retire.

Lala ngoxolo qhawe. Rest in peace, our hero.

Financially speaking, my grand plan was to separate my Cape to Cairo trip into stages. Logistically and practically speaking, it meant that I did not travel as the crow flies but sometimes followed the meandering line of my own interest, with Cairo my ultimate but not direct goal. My first stage was scheduled to end in Zanzibar.

As the US dollars I was carrying on me had run out, I needed a swiping machine to draw enough foreign currency to take me from Dar es Salaam via the 'spice island' to Nairobi. At the black market at the Songwe border post I had changed my last couple of US dollars to Tanzanian shillings, all of which I had already spent.

I could not find a swiping machine. Only foreign exchange bureaus in Dar, I soon learned, provided forex, and they only changed one currency (either in cash or travellers' cheques) to another. I ended up going from one bank to another, trying without success to buy just enough Tanzanian shillings with my credit card to get me to Nairobi.

In the process I procured the services of an interpreter, who referred to me as Bafana because of our national soccer team, Bafana Bafana. He took me to different banks and foreign exchange agencies. Everywhere I received the same response: I could not buy the local or any currency using my credit card. The only place with such a facility, someone in a bank suggested, was at the domestic terminal at the airport. I took a bus to Julius Nyerere International Airport and was promptly sent back to town.

I was so desperate I even considered flying back to Johannesburg to attend Merv's funeral and get all the cash I needed before flying back to Dar. Eventually, after about three hours of solidly looking for a swiping facility, I found an official foreign exchange bureau where I could buy foreign currency by swiping a credit card. It was right next to the bank that I had tried earlier that day! The commission was high and it had a relatively small daily maximum allowance, but the relief was great.

Since Dar was so hot and humid and the traffic so congested, I decided that I would cross directly to Zanzibar by ferry. It was high season and the one reasonably-priced ferry on which I could book a seat was leaving only later in the evening. Since the difference in price between taking a ferry and flying was only US$15, I decided, instead, to book a flight to Zanzibar and return to Dar by ferry. I had about three hours to kill before my flight, so I left my backpack at the booking office and went to the National Museum of Tanzania.

The museum offered an insight into the history of Tanganyika/ Tanzania, along with a graphic commemorative display by a Japanese NGO of the dropping of atomic bombs on Hiroshima and Nagasaki in August 1945. After two hours of looking around the museum I went to wait for the cab at the main entrance, having agreed with the driver that he would pick me up at a fixed time. I waited and waited but the cab driver did not turn up.

Accepting that I had been let down was a horrible moment for me. My backpack was at the booking office and, although I had paid for my plane ticket, the ticket had not been issued yet. I was supposed to collect it together with my bag. My other problem was that I really had no clue where this office was located. Even worse: what if the cab driver had gone back to the office, picked up my bag and disappeared with it?

The only thing I could remember about the office was that it was not far from a church.

Given the language problem, the two cab drivers I approached had absolutely no clue as to what I was talking about. It was I who was now *ikwerekwere* (the derogatory term used back home to describe our African brothers and sisters who come looking for a better life in South Africa). It was at that moment that I made Resolution No. 6: not ever to call another person ikwerekwere.

By then I was in a state of panic. The third cab driver I spoke to looked as if he had a faint idea of what I was so urgently gesticulating about. I got into his car and after a few minutes discovered, little though I knew Dar, that we were going in the wrong direction. We had to turn around.

I tried making the hand signal for praying and the sign of the cross to describe the church to the cab driver. I even tried to hand signal a ferry sailing through water. That confused the poor man all the more. I was still trying to figure out what hand signals to use when, from the corner of my eye, I saw the church I was looking for. Not far from the church, I spotted the office. I shouted 'Stop!' and hammered on the dashboard, leapt out and rushed over to the booking office to find my backpack quietly waiting for me inside.

From an old, grey-haired man at the office I learned that someone would be waiting for me at the airport, so I didn't need to be issued with an air ticket. At my insistence (I was not taking any chances at this stage) he phoned to confirm that this was so. It sounded confusing but, relieved more than anything else that I still had my bag and without time to ask any further questions, I jumped into the cab waiting for me, as agreed, in front of the office. When I got to the airport, there, indeed, was a young man awaiting me at the domestic terminal drop-off zone. He hastily ushered me through security, as well as through the only passenger gate, all the way to the waiting area without anyone ever asking for any documentation/ticket/boarding pass.

We waited for about 15 minutes before boarding time was announced. As we were approaching the boarding gates my companion suddenly remembered that I had to pay us$10 domestic departure tax. Since I did not a have us$10, I gave him a us$20 note to change. That was the last I saw of him.

I continued walking and went through the exit/boarding gate and still nobody asked me for anything. I could not believe that there I was, carrying my heavy backpack, walking towards a small airplane without a ticket or boarding pass. Quite a few passengers were in front of me. From what I could see when I boarded the Cessna Caravan the other passengers also didn't have boarding passes.

I chose a seat right behind the pilot. There was only one seat left unoccupied when a white couple, obviously tourists, came on board. Without being asked, a gentleman, a black Tanzanian wearing a black suit and carrying a briefcase, volunteered to leave the plane to make space for the two tourists. As the plane lined up on the runway the pilot turned around and asked, 'Is everyone here going to Pemba island?'

Before he could finish, I was already screaming at the top of my voice: 'No, no, I am going to Zanzibar!'

'We are going to Pemba via Zanzibar,' he replied, with one hand on the joystick and the other on the headphone so that he could hear what I was saying. It turned out, meanwhile, that the person I thought was the co-pilot was, in fact, another passenger.

The aerial view of Dar from the Cessna as we flew off was just endless square kilometres of corrugated iron, clear water and picturesque shoreline. Although it was a cloudless day the turbulence in the small plane was strong. But I was already shaken enough not to worry about such a small matter. Besides, it was a very short flight. In no time we were descending to Unguja, as Zanzibar is called by the locals, and I caught my first glimpse of the palms for which Zanzibar is world renowned.

I learned later that 'Unguja' is Swahili for 'So you came?' or 'Oh! You came?'– the first question asked of a person coming to the island from the mainland. Visiting Arabs only later called the island Zangibar –'land of blacks'. The rest, as they say, is history.

Zanzibar, Honolulu, Fiji, Timbuktu – these must be some of the most exotic place names in the world. Zanzibar is certainly one of Africa's top tourist destinations.

Three events have put the island on the world map. One, it boasts the shortest war in recorded history – the Anglo-Zanzibar War of 27 August 1896, which lasted a mere 45 minutes. Two, it was one of the most active slave-trading centres on the East African coast. Three, a boy by the name of Farrokh Bulsara, better known as Freddie Mercury, was born there on 5 September 1946.

From the airport I took a 1960s Peugeot cab to Stone Town. I really felt like a tourist in Zanzibar, which looked completely different from any place I had visited before. Stone Town is a conglomeration of innumerable small alleys, and the drivers of all manner of vehicles were hooting all the time. I learned the following day that one of the biggest offences on Zanzibar's roads is to have a car/bike without a hooter. In fact, it is required by law to hoot so that other road users will know you are around.

After checking into my hotel I thought it fitting that I should have a drink at Mercury's. While sipping a Kilimanjaro beer in this restaurant I was treated to one of the most beautiful sunsets I have seen in my life.

I had begun to see that the trip was making me appreciate the simple things in life: sunsets, waterfalls, a good conversation with a stranger. Perhaps it was the beer attacking my central nervous system, but I was greatly moved by the thought.

Lazing away the hours, I watched the international tourists, who all seemed to be madly in love, holding hands and gazing into each other's eyes instead of looking at the scenery, and the youngsters playing soccer on the beach and the heavily covered local women, dressed in black. I was blissfully content until I discovered that I had completely forgotten the name of my hotel. I had gone completely blank. To jolt my memory I walked around the night flea market, where I spotted a few tall Masai men in red kikois selling art and beads. I was still blank but then, all of a sudden, it hit me: the name of the hotel was Gavu.

Being an arrogant male, I did not want to ask for directions to the hotel, even after getting lost in the tiny alleys of Stone Town. Various people had told me that all first-timers get lost in Stone Town and, wanting to disprove them, I kept on trying to find my way about. Eventually, after an hour, I had to swallow my pride and ask for directions. It turned out that the place I was looking for was, in fact, not the Gavu but the Vuga Hotel.

I blamed it all on the Kilimanjaro.

Naturally, on my first morning in Zanzibar I had to join a tour group for a one-day tour to the spice plantations, which are on the northern part of the island. Prior to joining the tour, I dropped off my laundry at the hotel's reception desk. I had been on the road for almost a month and my clothes were really dirty.

There were about 15 of us on the tour. On our way to the plantations, which are all government-owned, we drove past David Livingstone House. While the tireless explorer was outfitting his last expedition to the mainland of Africa in 1866, Sultan Seyyid Majid placed this big, square, triple-storey house at his disposal for a few weeks.

Our first stop was at the Kizimbani plantation. Like other spice plantations and farms, it looked more like a garden where spice shrubs and grasses grew together in the shade of mango, jackfruit and other fruit trees. Our guide, Abdullah, showed us foods such as rose apple and guava carambola and tamarind, as well as spices in their natural form: cloves, cinnamon, nutmeg, cardamom, vanilla, black pepper and many others.

Like many Zanzibaris, Abdullah was of mixed Indian and African descent. He was very informative and took his job seriously. He told us that the East Indies and southern China were originally the source of almost all the spices that were traded, and that the cloves for which Zanzibar is famous, and other spices, were introduced by the Arabs in the early 18th century to break the spice monopoly of the East.

The highlight of the trip for me was not spices and fruits, however. It was the rain. Actually, it did not rain; it poured. And since we were in the middle of nowhere, we had nowhere to go. Except to hide under the metre-and-a-half-high shrubs that grew along the side of the plantation. For me, there was something about those moments, crouching under a shrub in a rainstorm, that was bringing me back to nature. For the second time in two consecutive days I felt the trip was changing my appreciation of life's pleasures.

After touring the plantations we had a delicious and very filling lunch of some local fish and rice in one of the villages and proceeded to the chambers where slaves were secretly kept after the British had tried to stop trafficking in slaves in 1873. For another 33 years or so, right up to 1906, the Arabs continued trading in humans, hiding their African captives in these secret chambers. Slaves, captured or bought on the African mainland, were marched in chains to Bagamoyo (near present-day Dar es Salaam), which in Swahili means 'lost hope'. Once you got to Bagamoyo it was clear your chances of escape were very small.

'It was during this period of secret trading that a slave ship was arrested by the British off the Durban coast and all the slaves were dumped in Durban,' Abdullah told me when he discovered I was from South Africa. It suddenly dawned on me why there is a small, close-knit Zanzibari community in Durban, whom we Zulus call amaZinzimbane.

The secret chambers – dark, damp caverns where many captives died of suffocation and starvation – were located in the forest, entirely underground; only the roof stuck out above ground. In the old days entry was by way of a small hut and a big hole.

The tour was a sobering experience for me, but one frivolous thought kept popping into my head – were it not for the Arabs, Africa would have won the FIFA Soccer World Cup a few times already. Imagine Pele playing for Malawi, Ronaldo for Tanzania and Ronaldinho for Zambia! Before visiting the secret slave chambers I had never thought that the Arabs had contributed so massively to today's global demographics.

On our way back to Stone Town I asked Abdullah what he considered to be his nationality since Zanzibar, although it is part of Tanzania, has its own president. His answer was: 'I am a Zanzibari of Tanzanian nationality.'

If you understand that, shake your booty.

Although I was not looking forward to visiting the old slave market, it was one of the reasons I had chosen to go to Zanzibar. I could have joined a half-day tour of the place but decided to go there on my own. I felt that I needed time to absorb everything at my own pace. I was right. I saw groups of tourists being shunted around by tour guides and knew that if I had joined the tour group I would have done myself a disservice.

Visiting the old market was a very moving and emotional experience. Standing in front of the statue of four chained slaves, I could not understand how people could be so evil, inhuman and barbaric for the sole reason of accumulating wealth. Bitter as the site made me feel, it is one of those places that I wish everyone would visit.

Later, I stood outside the Catholic Church that was built on the actual site of the slave market and reflected on the pain and agony slaves must have felt when they were whipped to establish the price they could fetch. The value of a slave was determined, it seems, by four factors: gender, age, physique and, for a male, how much pain he could take at the whipping post. If a slave showed low resistance to pain by crying out at the very first whipping, the seller would normally not go through with the sale because the slave was likely to go for a low price. For the slave that meant going back to the slave chambers until the next auction day. But the most disturbing thought was that the auction, however awful, was just the beginning of a dismal life in bondage – first, an appalling sea journey, which few survived, and then, working like an animal in the service of another human being. Mainly, it seemed, on plantations: sugar plantations in Brazil, the West Indies and the French colonies of Madagascar, Réunion and Mauritius; cotton plantations in the American Deep South.

Depressing as the old slave market was, I was glad I went there. Among other things, it changed the way I look at Arabs. The history books that we studied during the Bantu Education era never mentioned the role and magnitude of Arab influence in Africa. They concentrated on European colonialism. The slave tour in Zanzibar opened my eyes to the reality of a thriving trade in African slaves on the African continent long before European powers even started colonising Africa. In fact, it is ironic that it was mainly Britain, the arch imperial power, that finally put an end to slavery, with the active involvement of the very missionaries, guys like Livingstone, about whom I have such ambiguous feelings.

Nowadays, Arabs are mostly portrayed as fighting a just cause against American imperialism. To me, however, it seems that their forefathers screwed Africans in a big way. They took away our dignity and pride and converted our forefathers, including women and children, into goods with a monetary value. Not that the African kings and chiefs were innocent. It is well documented that local traditional leaders used to barter their own subjects or captive members of other clans with Arab slave-traders.

Like Robben Island, Zanzibar is one of those places that for ever changes your perception of certain groups of people because of their treatment of others.

While waiting for the sunset and watching the dhows ferrying tourists along the bay, I decided to go for a barefoot walk on the beach. It was time for reflection.

Later that evening I spotted a once-in-a-lifetime photo opportunity: two Masai men surfing the net in a public internet café. Excuse my ignorance, but I had always thought of Masai as warriors who kill lions on the plains of the Serengeti, as portrayed by the media. The Masai in the internet café reminded me of another contradiction: the name of the rock group Guns and Roses.

It was at that moment that a brilliant idea leapt into my mind – Business Idea Two. What if I were to produce a world-class music album by fusing the music of a few Masai musicians and a number of Zulu mbaqanga musicians with Australian Aboriginal tunes? The name of this confusing group would be Organ Donors in Waiting and the album would be called *Open Secret* and it would contain tracks with names like:

> 'Dentist with a toothache'
> 'An honest politician'
> 'Divorced marriage counsellor'
> 'Dermatologist with acne'
> 'A trustworthy pastor'

And – the smash hit at number one –'Pregnant nun'. One thing about doing the Cape to Cairo, you really start thinking outside the box.

The following morning a scheduled half-day trip to the beaches along the east coast of the island was cancelled because of bad weather. I spent the morning still getting lost in the small alleys of Stone Town. In the afternoon I went to the harbour to catch a ferry back to Dar es Salaam. As I was walking towards the boat, I was stopped by a policeman who told me that I had to go through immigration.

'But I am only going to Dar es Salaam,' I said, rather peeved.

'I know, but you still have to be stamped out.'

I found that really confusing. How can you be stamped out while you're still in the country?

At the immigration place I was the last one in the long queue of tourists. It appeared that there was even a form to be completed. When I eventually got to the counter and handed in my passport, the officer did not give me the form to fill in. Instead he simply asked,'Bafana Bafana?'

I replied,'Yes, sure. Bafana.'

I wasn't sure what he wanted to know – whether I was part of the Bafana team or, highly likely, to confirm that our national soccer team was indeed Bafana Bafana. Whatever it was, my response worked. He stamped my ferry ticket, not my passport. Only then was I free to board the ferry back to Dar.

At the dock there was much chaos and many people with big bags pushing and trying to get on the ferry first. When I at last got on board I found that there weren't all that many seats, which explained why everyone had tried to get there first. I ended up on the sundeck with some other tourists. The ferry left on time.

As I watched Zanzibar recede, I vowed to visit that magical and exotic place again – Resolution No. 7. The perfect sunsets alone would be worth the trip. I also loved the laid-back culture, the cosmopolitan nature of the residents, some of them, especially on the government plantations, living in dire poverty. One thing though, I had to learn Swahili first (Resolution No. 5).

After about half an hour on the ferry the sea started to get rough, owing to bad weather. As time progressed it got much rougher and the ferry, although relatively large, lurched up and down over the big swells. I was really taking strain. I was starting to feel seasick. A few moments later I witnessed something that I'm sure I will never see again in this lifetime: a large number of people all throwing up at the same time. Because of poor judgement most of them stood facing the wind and almost everything blew right back into their faces.

Among this crowd was a sister who must have been in her late thirties. She was afraid to stand up and hold onto the railings before bending over to throw up into the sea. As soon as she got close to the railings, she would start reversing. Eventually, she just sat on the edge of the deck and messed up her legs and feet.

Just when I thought I had seen it all a young girl came running towards the edge of the deck, but she could not hold it in any longer. She boiled over just before she reached the edge. Coincidentally, this girl was upwind from the woman who had sat down near the edge of the deck. So everything, and I mean everything, blew into the older sister's head and the back of her neck.

Regardless of how seasick I myself was, it was such a hilarious moment that it had to be enjoyed. Like others on the ferry, I laughed out loud. That young girl must have eaten a lot of brown rice in Zanzibar because all I could see on the sister's head and neck was brown rice. Only then did the ferry's ticket examiner start handing out plastic bags.

While all this was happening I had spotted a very attractive sister who was also carrying a backpack. She must have spent a lot of time in the sun because she looked chocolate white. She was really attractive, with fine, shapely legs and juicy lips and boobs. She was so stunning that I thought to myself that I would really not be a man if I did not pounce on this sexy thing.

In just over two hours we got to Dar and, while people were disembarking from the ferry, I decided it was time to put my charms to the test. 'Which backpackers are you off to?' I asked for starters.

Before I could finish my ice-breaker, she said, 'I cannot remember the name but there is a pre-arranged cab waiting for me. If you want, you can join me.'

I could not believe my luck. We started chatting about her travels and other general stuff while I surreptitiously examined her cleavage. Just what the doctor ordered, I thought. We waited until all the other passengers had disembarked and, as we descended the steep narrow stairways, I allowed her to walk in front in order to get a view from the rear. Her backside, as to be expected of a European woman, was small and not really my type, but generally speaking I was very happy. She was going to be in Dar for one night and then fly back to Amsterdam, via Nairobi.

When I stepped off the ferry, the cab driver who had failed to collect me from the museum four days ago suddenly showed up. He started to explain that he had had a flat tyre, but he discovered within seconds that he was the last man on the planet I wanted to see. I did not care whether or not he called his gang to sort me out. That man had almost ruined my trip, and now he wanted to separate me from Leonie.

I learned that the cab that was supposed to pick her up had not pitched. And that is when the trouble started. More than ten cab drivers began to shove their keys into our faces, trying to get our attention so that they could take us to our hotel. As the man, I had to take responsibility. Since Leonie's driver had not shown up, it was my duty to organise an alternative cab quickly. I did all the negotiations while she held onto my left arm. Eventually we agreed on a price with the driver who shouted the loudest and were on our way to the backpackers where she had a reservation.

We discovered when we got to the backpackers that it was fully booked. But since Leonie had pre-booked she had a bed – I was the one without a place to sleep. I had to think fast. 'What if we book a room in another hotel and share the cost?' I asked with a disarming smile.

She kept quiet for a while and then said, 'No.'

Before she could continue, I had another proposal. 'I will pay for the room. You just have to bring yourself.'

She kept quiet, looking at me with a silly smile. By then my heart was pumping hard and blood was running from one head to the other.

'Let's give it a rest. In about 48 hours I will be with my man. Maybe if we had met earlier … I am sorry,' she said, really looking sorry.

I took a deep breath, knowing that I had given it my best shot. We shook hands. She wanted to give me a hug but I resisted, trying to make her feel guilty and, hopefully, change her mind.

This also did not work. I had to go and find accommodation for myself somewhere else.

As we were driving to another hotel the cab driver, Stanley, started laughing at me. 'The secret, my brother, is to keep eye contact all the time. Women feel under pressure when you look right through their eyes,' he advised me. The man could not only speak a bit of Zulu, but was curious about something that is well known about Zulus among other black South Africans. 'Why,' he asked me, 'don't Zulus want to learn other languages?'

'That is a long story, a very long story,' I told him, thinking about what could have been but was not.

Stanley didn't seem to notice that my mind was elsewhere. He explained to me why the drivers were shoving car keys into our faces as we left the ferry. It seemed that touts who did not drive cabs also tried to get passengers from the ferry in order to show them to a cab. On whatever the cab driver charged, they would then claim a commission. You could distinguish between the two groups: cab drivers had keys, touts didn't.

Having decided to take it easy in Dar for a day, I went for a walk on the main street, Samora Machel Street. I could not help noticing how beautiful Dar's women were. Pure beauty, natural African beauty.

That was another motivating factor for me to learn Swahili.

Later that afternoon I went to an international hotel to use the internet. The difference between the relaxed people at backpackers and the stuck-up and serious people at international hotels immediately struck me. It was with that in mind that I decided to do something I have always wanted to do: watch porn in public on the internet.

All those serious, uppity people who were walking past could not believe what they were seeing. I was even tilting my head from one side to the other in order to have a better view of what was displayed on the screen. I noticed that, much as they pretended to be disgusted with what I was doing, the men passing by spent more time looking at the screen than at me. What a bunch of hypocrites!

After a full day of relaxation in Dar, contemplating its beautiful women and old buildings, I was ready for the 11-hour trip to Mombasa, Kenya, on, as it turned out, a bus that was really luxurious. It even had seatbelts throughout the cabin and the driver's assistant would check at intervals that everyone was still buckled up. We were well looked after on the bus: biscuits, 350-ml soft drinks and 600-ml bottles of water were served throughout the journey. But, as on other bus trips, we stopped in the middle of nowhere and things proceeded in now familiar synchronised fashion, women on one side and men on the other.

We came across the first weigh bridge on the outskirts of Dar. There must have been something wrong because, after 20 minutes of heated argument between our driver and the weigh-bridge operators, we were required to make a U-turn to be weighed again. Only after the bus was weighed for the second time were we given the go-ahead.

Otherwise, the journey was uneventful. We took a well-deserved break in the small rural town of Tanga, consisting mainly of old houses with corrugated-iron roofs. From there, for the first time on this trip, the road surface was not tar but gravel – all the way to the border at Horohoro, which we reached about two hours later. The borders on previous occasions had all been rivers – Orange, Zambezi, Songwe. This border, however, ran right through the middle of a featureless landscape.

To Leonie, the Dutch woman I met on the Zanzibar to Dar es Salaam ferry: thanks for nothing.

Kenyatta's Kenya

Father of the Nation

Arab settlement in what is now Kenya began in the 8th century, along with trade in ivory and slaves. The Portuguese seafarer Vasco da Gama arrived at Mombasa in 1498 and, seven years later, Portuguese ships followed to establish a permanent presence there. By 1730 the Arabs had managed to expel the Portuguese and, by 1839, all the major ports along the East African coast were governed from the island of Zanzibar. Britain took over in 1890, when Germany gave up the protectorate it had established in 1885, and British East Africa (Kenya, Uganda and Tanganyika) came into being.

Kenya became independent on 12 December 1963, under a government led by Jomo Kenyatta, alias Kamau waNgengi, alias John Peter, alias Johnstone Kamau. By the time of his death in 1978, he was commonly known as Mzee ('old man' in Swahili). Born in British East Africa (some say in 1889, others 1893), Kenyatta spent several years in London and a year in Moscow as a student. After his return to Kenya, in 1946, he founded the Pan-African Federation with Kwame Nkrumah, and became president of the Kenya African Union. In 1953 he was sentenced to seven years hard labour for organising the Mau Mau rebellion and, on his release, was sent into exile in a remote part of Kenya.

Kenyatta was re-elected president in 1966 and the next year changed the constitution to gain extended powers. He was re-elected in 1974 in one-party elections in which he was the sole presidential candidate. He was Kenya's prime minister for a year and president for 14 years. He died in office (Kenya's largest landowner at the time), and was succeeded by Daniel Toroitich Arap Moi, who was president for 24 years until he was defeated in 2002 by Mwai Kibaki.

Mzee is credited with the Kenyan policy of harambee – 'pulling together' in Swahili – which encourages communities to work together as part of building a new nation.

Exiting Tanzania at the Horohoro border post was a really slow process. All our luggage had to removed from the bus and each person had to claim his or her bags and take them to the customs office. Thank goodness, the offloading of bags was halted when it started to rain. Those passengers whose bags had not yet been checked were presumed innocent, myself among them.

It was a short drive to Lunga Lunga, the Kenyan border post. After checking my passport, the Kenyan immigration officer there said, 'Oh, Bafana Bafana.'

I politely replied, 'Yes.'

Again it worked, and he stamped me in. I understood then that our national soccer team was a big brand name in the rest of Africa.

Besides a few incutras, there was hardly anyone at the border and, as a result, no new passengers joined us. We got back on the bus relieved, although a little damp, and continued on our journey to Mombasa. The man who had been sitting next to me on the bus all the way from Dar must have eaten Malawian beans during the break for it was not long before he started to fart. And he did not stop. There was no smell, thank goodness, but the loud, very loud, noises were unmistakable. The inflated man didn't seem to care though.

I have always heard that yawning is contagious. What I didn't know was just how contagious farting is. Before I knew it I had a sudden but very urgent need to expel some wind myself. I am sure all of us have found ourselves in a situation where the more you try to suppress wind, the more pressure it creates in the bowel. My bowel could take only so much pressure, but as a gentleman I could not fart out loud. So, after slightly shifting and lifting my left cheek while faking an endless cough, I let out one of those quiet but very long and great reliever-farts. I felt like saying 'Aaaaahh ...'

A few seconds later, smelling strongly skunk, I realised that it had not been a good idea to cough so much. But it was too late.

The fart seemed to have been an ice-breaker. Soon thereafter my neighbour and I started chatting about women, food and politics. He remarked that so many Tanzanians were forced to move to Dar es Salaam and other big cities because of the failure of the socialist-inspired agricultural system where ordinary farmers had no choice but to comply with government directives.

The vegetation on the Kenyan side of the border was exactly the same as in Tanzania: palm trees, banana trees, long green grass and evergreen bush. I was surprised to see such lush greenery because I'd read that only about 20 per cent of land in Kenya is considered suitable for agriculture; most of the land, especially in the northern part of the country, is semi-arid. Only the coastal belt, through which we were travelling, received sufficient rainfall – 1 000 millimetres more per year than the rest of the country – for agricultural purposes.

It took us just short of two hours to cover the 100 kilometres or less from Lunga Lunga to Mombasa, Kenya's second largest city. Although it is near the coast, Lunga Lunga is a very isolated place in the middle of nowhere. Nevertheless, we went through four roadblocks en route to Mombasa. When travelling in this wonderful continent called Africa there is one thing you can be assured of – roadblocks. On our journey, soldiers would stop the bus and talk to the driver for a few seconds before allowing us to go through. I wondered, in Kenya and in other countries too, what the point of the roadblocks was. I never discovered what they were looking for. Whereas roadblocks in northern Malawi consisted of two drums and a wooden beam, in Kenya a spike chain was stretched across the road. Because it was after sunset, a lamp was added.

I had not known that the city of Mombasa is built on a 15 square-kilometre island (Mombasa Island), which is separated from the mainland by two 'creeks' – narrow channels of water. From the south, the direction from which we arrived, people and cars cross over to the island on the Likoni ferry. It was already dark when our bus, together with a few cars and some pedestrians, was ferried across to the city. I booked into a cheap motel recommended by the cab driver in a suburb called Kibokoni.

Whatever I had expected of Mombasa, it was a surprise to see how deserted the streets were, considering that it was not even three hours after sunset. At the bus station a few cab drivers were waiting for business, otherwise all was quiet. Even on our way to the motel we encountered only a few cars on the road. The streets were lined with mostly old and not very tall buildings, some modern office blocks providing variety. Mombasa reminded me of Mgungundlovu (Pietermaritzburg) back home, an historical and now important administrative city with little nightlife.

As he dropped me off the cab driver remarked, 'If you want to have a great time, that small white building down the road has beautiful girls who can de-stress you.'

'Thanks for the tip,' I said as I took my backpack. I held back from asking him, Do I look stressed to you?

The non-descript hotel had five floors and long zigzagging grey corridors. Inside, suddenly there was life. While checking in at reception, I could see through an open door that people had hung their washing on a line in the adjacent courtyard. Considering the number of people hanging around in the reception area and the kids under the age of three running freely up and down in the corridors making a noise, it felt and looked more like a block of flats than a regular hotel.

My room on the fourth floor, which I reached by a flight of stairs, offered a single bed, a small table with a red plastic chair and a shower with cold water. For the time being, it was enough.

The next morning I made my way to one of Mombasa's landmarks – the strange star-shaped fortification known as Fort Jesus, built in the 16th century by those stalwarts of Christianity, the Portuguese, to secure their dominance over the trade route to the East. After years of fighting, it was captured by the Arabs in 1698, hence the local name for Mombasa, Kisiwa Cha Mvita, which means 'island of war' in Swahili.

The main reason for the battles between the Arabs and the Portuguese and, later on, between the British and the Arabs was economic. Mombasa, with its natural harbour, was and still is ideally situated for purposes of trade along the East African coast. Although Malindi offers port facilities further north, Mombasa remains the major trade centre in the eastern and central African region. Fort Jesus sits at the mouth of the harbour and, therefore, whoever controlled

the fort controlled the port and Mombasa Island. And whoever controlled the port controlled the economy.

Fort Jesus has seen it all: starvation, murder, battles, siege ... The
fort was built with such thick and high walls that it was impossible to
get either in or out by climbing over them. From the entrance there
are steep stairs that lead into the courtyard where cannons are still
mounted, ready for action. While Kenya was under British rule, Fort
Jesus was used for over 60 years as a prison, where criminals were in-
carcerated for a variety of offences. Today, along with the museum located inside it, it is the main tourist attraction in Mombasa.

What I didn't know, excuse my ignorance, is that Swahili, too, developed for economic reasons. Naturally, the Arabs and their African
trading partners could not communicate at first, so over time a lin-
gua franca evolved through absorption of many Arab words into the
original Bantu language (meaning a language that indicates 'person'
with -ntu) of the coast. The word Swahili comes from the Arabic *sahel*
–'boundary' or 'coast'. With the addition of *ki-* ('language'), it becomes
'coastal language' – Kiswahili.

Kiswahili is still the most commonly spoken language, not just in
Tanzania, Kenya and Uganda (where it is an official language) but also in
Rwanda, Burundi, Congo, Somalia, Comoros Islands and Mozambique
(where it has become the second language of millions of people).
I simply have to learn to speak it. As the most widely spoken language
of sub-Saharan Africa, it is now the only African language used as an
official working language by the African Union.

In Mombasa it struck me, for the second time, that the history I was
taught at school did not reflect the role that the Arabs had played on
the African continent. I had been brought up to believe that the British
and other Europeans colonised Africa, but what I learned in Zanzibar
and Mombasa was that Africa had lost its virginity to the Arabs centuries before Europeans even began lusting after our continent. By the
time Europeans got to East Africa, Arabs had fully established trade
routes and were transporting not only Africa's natural resources but
human cargo as well. In the Fort Jesus Museum these facts are graphi-
cally illustrated with artifacts and short descriptions.

Having immersed myself in the history of the place, I went next to Mombasa's Old Town. It is not as old and big as Zanzibar's but has the same kind of carved wooden doors and small alleys. Unlike Zanzibar's Old Town, Mombasa's does not have a lot of traffic.

While I was walking around, I was twice approached by men who shook my hand and, after a small chat, said, 'Karibu'. I had thought they would try to sell me something but, to my surprise, they just greeted me and went on their way. The third one even said, 'Feel at home, my brother.' I am still not sure how they knew that I was not a Kenyan.

That, amongst other things, is what makes us Africans African: the desire to make a stranger feel at home. It's a great pity Europeans and Arabs took advantage of our natural hospitality and exploited it with such dire consequences.

I must have wandered around the Old Town for about an hour, getting lost twice. Some things just never change. I consoled myself with the thought that not having a sense of direction was a weakness I had to live with. How else could you explain that I had left my job to do this trip? I'm fortunate that my fiancée, although she does not always understand my directionlessness, never tries to put me on the straight and narrow. In fact, she sometimes even joins me in my incomprehensible pursuits. For example, when I started parachuting she did not want to know about it, but in January 2005 I bought her a tandem-sky-diving ticket as a birthday present. It was at 10 000 feet above Umdloti (north of Durban), just before leaping out of the plane – while attached to the tandem master – that I proposed to her. Obviously, she said yes. Who would not like to get married to an adventurous and handsome guy like me?

In the afternoon, I discarded the idea of going to Mombasa's northern beaches and, instead, went for a walk in the city centre, mainly along Moi and Nkrumah roads.

Although the relaxed Swahili culture of Mombasa was much to my taste, I had to take a bus to Kenya's capital city, Nairobi, the following morning. Like Dar, Mombasa was proving to be hot and humid and, sitting at the bus stop, I was sweating as if I were in a sauna.

Everyone else also seemed to be sweating and at that moment I had another brilliant commercial idea, Business Idea Three: sell handkerchiefs in Mombasa. Later I noticed that my idea had been stolen – there were quite a few hawkers selling handkerchiefs. I had to conclude it was a non-starter.

The Scandinavian Express bus to Nairobi had ultra comfortable seats and seatbelts throughout, so I sat back and relaxed. Soon the air-conditioning had cooled the whole cabin and they were handing out biscuits, 350-ml cans of soft drinks and 500-ml bottles of water. Although the road was initially very rough, owing to roadworks, it improved within an hour and before I knew it we were cruising on a highway.

The further we travelled from the coast the more the vegetation changed, from tall palms to short trees and shrubs. The traffic stayed the same – mostly big trucks carrying cargo, which underlined the strategic importance of Mombasa and its shipping facilities for the rest of the country.

Our itinerary included dropping off passengers at Jomo Kenyatta International Airport, the busiest airport in central and eastern Africa, about 20 kilometres from Nairobi. Approaching the airport I remembered that a few days earlier Leonie (remember her, that good-for-nothing, useless Dutch gal with messed-up morals I met in Dar?) must have boarded the plane back to her man in Amsterdam at that very place. I put the thought out of my mind.

As we dropped off the passengers near the domestic terminal I could see – in the distance among the airplanes parked in the international area – a plane that belonged to SAA. The sight of the tail painted in the colours of the South African flag instantly made me homesick. The thought of jumping off the bus and flying back to Johannesburg crossed my mind but I suppressed such a stupid idea. It was like when you are out running and you suddenly see people having a braai. The thought of stopping and joining them shoots into your head and you start asking yourself, especially when you are tired, questions such as: Why do I have to do a difficult thing when there are easy things to do? That was exactly what I was thinking as the bus drove out of Jomo Kenyatta International Airport.

Apart from the airport distraction, the seven-hour trip from Mombasa was uneventful and, suddenly, we were in the urban environment of Nairobi. Although I am not a city person at heart, it felt good to be in the big city again, among skyscrapers, traffic, crowds of people. As we got to the city centre it was becoming dark and the traffic was bumper to bumper. It looked as if urbanisation was happening at a faster pace in Nairobi than the authorities had anticipated.

Nairobi – from the Masai *ewaso nairobi* or 'stream of cold water' – started off in 1899 as a railway camp, called Mile 327, on the 1 400-kilometre line built by the British (not Rhodes), using Indian labour, between Mombasa and Kampala in Uganda. The compound soon grew into a town. By 1907 it had become so well established that it was made the capital of British East Africa, the newly-formed federation of Kenya, Tanganyika and Uganda. A hundred years later, Nairobi is one of Africa's major cities.

Being in 'Nairobbery', as it is sometimes referred to because of the prevalence of crime, aroused mixed feelings in me. I was happy that I had reached the unofficial halfway point of my Cape to Cairo trip unscathed. At the same time, I was filled with vague feelings of anxiety. I knew that the second half would be more difficult and probably also more dangerous.

From the bus station I took a cab to a Nairobi backpackers on the outskirts of the city, the address of which I had found in a guidebook. It felt wonderful to be in a good dormitory in a properly run establishment. What I like about backpackers is that they are informal, the surroundings casual, the patrons unpretentious, without issues and always willing to give advice and supply recommendations. As usual, most of the patrons were from the US and UK, each and every one of them besotted with Africa and either heading to or from Lamu, an archipelago of low-lying desert islands that seems to epitomise Swahili culture. I looked at the map and saw that Lamu was quite near the Somalian border and too far from the track I was beating for me to contemplate a visit.

The next morning I set off for the Ethiopian embassy, which was only a 15-minute walk from my backpackers. By the time I arrived there were five people waiting in the queue. Getting an Ethiopian visa looked like a straightforward process: fill in a simple form, attach your photo and hand it to the attractive lady at the counter, together with the required amount of money.

All five people in front of me did exactly that. When I got to the counter, the officer looked at my form and, instead of asking for payment as she had done with other applicants, picked up the phone. After a conversation in a language I couldn't understand she put the phone down and said, 'Take a seat.'

I tried to pretend that I was not stressing but, deep down, I really was. Five minutes later another lady came to reception to call me. I followed her as she led me to the last office at the end of the passage. The sign on the door said *Head of Consulate*. That sign almost made me wet my pants.

In my visa application I had lied about two things. Firstly, I felt I could not say that I was unemployed. So I had put down the name of my fiancée's employer. Secondly, and not as serious, I had lied about the hotel where I was going to stay in Addis Ababa. On the form I had given the name of a five-star hotel. I thought the embassy might have phoned either my 'employer' to confirm my employment or, possibly, the hotel to confirm my booking.

As I knocked on the door of the Head of Consulate I knew that I had been caught out, one way or another, for supplying false information. So I made up my mind: if they declined to issue me an Ethiopian visa I would go to Uganda instead and bungee jump at Jinja before heading back to South Africa by public transport.

There were two well-dressed gentlemen in the huge office, one sitting behind an L-shaped desk and the other on a three-seater couch. I decided to sit down on the three-seater. As I sat down I realised that I had not been invited to sit. I stood up. A split second later I thought, what the heck, I have already sat down. So I sat down again. All of this – sitting down, getting up and sitting down again – happened in quick succession before either of the two gentlemen had said anything to me.

Then the Head of Consulate – I assumed it was he because he was seated behind the desk – said to me, 'Hi, Khumalo. So are you Zulu?'

With my plaited hair I never expected anyone to mistake me for a Zulu, but I had to admit that I was indeed *umZulu* (a Zulu).

'So are you Nkatha?'

I learned a long time ago that answering 'yes' or 'no' is not necessarily a good thing. 'Mmm,' I said, trying to keep calm. 'As much as most of Inkatha members are Zulu, I think not all Zulus are Inkatha members.'

'You have not answered my question,' the Head of Consulate replied quickly.

At that moment the gentleman seated opposite me on the couch asked, 'Do you smoke?'

I told him that I did not but I had puffed on a cigarette once or twice in my more youthful days.

The Head of Consulate, who was now paging through my passport, asked me another question: 'Why did you go to Bangkok?', referring to my trip to Thailand a few years back.

There was no specific reason why I had visited Bangkok except that it was the cheapest international destination I could find to visit as part of my 23rd birthday celebrations. Obviously, I could not state the truth. Instead I replied, 'I wanted to experience the Thai culture, Sir.'

The other gentleman then asked me, 'And why do you want to visit Ethiopia?'

The honest answer would have been: 'Because from Kenya to Egypt the only safe route goes through Ethiopia and Sudan.' But I could not say that, of course, so I mumbled something like: 'A colleague of mine visited Ethiopia a few months ago and he liked it so much he convinced me that it is one of the countries I should visit before I die.'

At this the Head of Consulate looked at me and said, 'OK. We will give you 30 days.'

I felt like standing up and hugging him. I had already given up on getting an Ethiopian visa and within an hour I was leaving the embassy with a visa that I had thought would, if I got it, take about two days to process. The bad news was I had 30 days effective from the issuing date to travel through northern Kenya as well as Ethiopia. Given the rumoured irregular modes of transport further north and the reportedly slow Ethiopian public-transport system, as well as the well-documented long waiting period for a Sudanese visa in Addis Ababa, I knew I had to cut short my stay in Nairobi.

From the Ethiopian embassy I walked to the city centre, past Uhuru Park, the one that was saved by Wangari Muta Maathai when then President Arab Moi wanted to build a 60-storey building there. Wangari, both environmental and political activist, was the first African woman to win the Nobel Peace Prize, in 2004, for her efforts in sustainable development, mainly involving women planting trees. The park is indeed a green haven in the middle of a concrete jungle.

By the time I got to the bank I was saying to myself, Wow, if I thought the women in Dar were beautiful, I have to think again. The ladies in Nairobi looked even more stunning. They had a more sophisticated and cosmopolitan, yet natural, African look about them, like former Miss South Africa turned businesswoman, Bastsane Khumalo (née Makgalemele).

While I was gazing at the slim-limbed, elegant creatures I suddenly remembered that I had another small problem: the cash I had in hand was not enough to get me to Cairo. Changing money in Nairobi was not as bad as in Dar, however. Within two hours a bank had sorted me out and I had my US dollars.

After once again appreciating the gorgeous ladies of Nairobi, I decided to go to the museum. There is something special about museums: they give you insight into a country that you cannot normally get from a book. The National Museum in Nairobi has been operating for more than 70 years and its collections cover a wide range, from handicraft and cultural exhibits to Kenyan wildlife to history, starting from prehistoric times up to the Kenyan struggle for *uhuru* – freedom. It was the first time that I truly understood the loss of life exacted by the Mau Mau rebellion. By the time the revolt was suppressed in 1956, more than 13 500 black Kenyans and just over 100 Europeans had died. Out of that struggle, the man to emerge most strongly was Jomo Kenyatta.

Right next to the museum is the snake park. I don't think anyone can be more terrified of snakes than I am; I'm one of those people who can't even watch a snake on television. So, for obvious reasons,

I steered clear of the place. I sat on a bench under a tree in the city gardens, enjoying the sight of people lounging on the green lawns.

Nairobi, I discovered, is not nicknamed the safari capital of the world for nothing. Almost everything in Nairobi is touristy: safari this, safari that, safari this, that and the other. Although I would have loved to visit the Masai Mara National Reserve, the most famous and most visited park in Kenya, it seemed as if prices were aimed at super-rich tourists. Considering that it was the time of the annual migration of wildebeest and zebra from the Serengeti plains to the lush grasslands, I am sure prices had been increased further to cash in on the two-month natural extravaganza. As with the South Luangwa National Park in Zambia, which I had missed out on because of the high admission price, I decided to give Kenya's best animal reserve a miss. Thus I couldn't see for myself the dozen different species – buffalo, eland, elephant, gazelle, giraffe, hyena, kongoni, lion, ostrich, topi, wildebeest and zebra – that they say can be seen all at the same time.

Before leaving Nairobi I decided to get a letter of introduction from the South African High Commission to use in Addis Ababa when applying for a visa to Sudan. One thing about this kind of trip: you learn, very quickly, to think ahead and be on your toes all the time.

The High Commission was about half an hour on foot from my backpackers. I hoped that, as at the Ethiopian embassy, I would be invited to the Head of Consulate's office. But it was not to be. Instead, while my letter was being prepared, a forty-something lady came to talk to me through the window that shielded those behind the reception desk from those in front. She asked in Zulu where was I heading and why.

It was nice to be able to communicate in Zulu again. It was just basic chatting and it was good to see my people representing us in foreign lands. As she was about to leave she said, 'Ndiyavuya ukukwazi. Uhambe kakuhle' – I am happy to meet you. Travel safely.

'Ngiyajabula ukukwazi nami,' I replied. 'Ngiyabonga kakhulu, sisi' – I am happy to meet you too. Thanks a lot, sister.

Being the eternal optimist, I was hoping that maybe, just maybe,

I would bump into a sexy young South African working at the High Commission. Or, even better, a home girl visiting Nairobi for pleasure, or perhaps business. Well, again, it was not to be.

As I left the building I knew that one day I would simply have to be my country's High Commissioner in some exotic place like the Bahamas, Maldives or Fiji. It wasn't a resolution, it was a dream. And dreams can come true: within two days of arriving in Nairobi, I already had my Ethiopian visa and a letter of introduction to be used in Addis when applying for my Sudanese visa. I knew then that I was on my way to fulfilling my childhood dream of travelling from Cape to Cairo. I found myself happily humming the words of Bob Marley's song, 'Don't worry about a thing, 'cause every little thing will be alright'.

Returning to the city centre later that day I noticed a modern build-ing named Integrity Centre. On closer inspection I discovered that it housed the offices of the Anti-Corruption Commission. The small parking area next to building had a sign that read *This is a corrupt-free zone* I'm sure they meant well, but for some people, including myself, it created a very bad impression.

Since it was my last night in Nairobi I decided to have dinner at an upmarket restaurant to celebrate reaching the halfway mark of my trip. As I walked into the posh restaurant in the Hilton Hotel I spotted a fine-looking young woman sitting all alone. She was also looking at me with her big eyes while sucking a cocktail through a straw. Being such a faithful man to my fiancée, I totally ignored her while I placed an order.

Have you ever had the feeling that someone is constantly and con-tinuously staring at you? That is what I felt. With reason. That woman had her eyes all over me when I went to dish from the salad valet, making me feel uncomfortable in a very pleasant way.

After downing my first beer I started to feel bad about ignoring such a beautiful sister. When I looked up to order another beer, our eyes locked. That was it. I went straight to her table. We had just started chatting when I felt a tap on my shoulder. I turned around and there was this Mike Tyson look-alike standing right behind me. The only difference was that he was pitch black. He asked me something in Swahili, pointing to the sister who also looked freaked out.

I just sat there looking straight into his eyes, pretending to be fine, whereas I was feeling shit-scared. Without another word the boxer type grabbed me by the scruff of my neck and pulled me out of my chair. Thank goodness, two waiters came over and pushed him away.

I headed straight for the door – not running, just walking fast and checking over my shoulder to see if Iron Mike was following me. As I was about to exit I looked back one last time and saw that he was arguing with the woman. I got into a taxi in order to get to my backpackers as soon as possible.

Nairobi, especially in the recent past, has experienced phenomenal population growth. As a result, there is heavy traffic congestion even at night. From the passenger seat in the front of the cab I kept looking at the side rearview mirror just to double-check that Iron Mike was not pursuing me as we were stuck in traffic literally a few metres from the front door of the restaurant. It was at that moment that I knew, for sure, I had to leave Nairobi.

Back at the backpackers, even the dog that assisted the guard with security duties at night wanted to bite me. I was more than ever convinced that I had to leave Nairobi the next day.

That night I tried having a local beer just to calm my nerves, but it tasted awful. I paid and left – I was still not used to the idea of having a beer and writing my name in the black book so they could charge it to my account, to be paid when I settled the rest of my bill. The problem was that no one monitored the process. You could, therefore, have quite a few beers without writing your name in the black book and no one would have noticed. You drank beer on trust at this particular backpackers.

I woke up the next day feeling lethargic. It had nothing to do with the previous evening's Mike Tyson episode. It suddenly hit me: the last time I had had a bath was in Mombasa, three days ago. I was definitely not doing things I didn't want to do, like I often did back home.

After a cold shower I felt like a brand-new person. I went for a last-minute stroll in the city centre, past the City Hall and into City Square, where Jomo Kenyatta's statue sits facing a courtyard and the flickering flames that guard this monument. I continued past Parliament. Needless to say, I had to wear a cap just in case I ran into Iron Mike. I didn't bump into him, but I did bump into two beautiful ladies who made it very clear they were not interested in me.

In the afternoon, I headed for Eastleigh on the outskirts of Nairobi to catch a bus north. Eastleigh is a scruffy and neglected part of the city, inhabited mostly by Ethiopians, Somalis and Eritreans. I was much relieved when I was told that there was a bus going straight to the border town of Moyale. Ticket in hand, I made my way towards the bus. When it was pointed out to me I could not believe what I was seeing – a converted truck pulling the shell of a bus, with everything expertly welded together. Being a converted truck, the passengers could not see the bus driver.

We left Nairobi at sunset.

I was aware that we were following a dangerous route. A month before I arrived in Nairobi there had been a massacre at Marsabit in which schoolchildren were attacked and killed. Marsabit lay on the bus route to Moyale. The bus, however, was not likely to be attacked, the cab driver who had taken me to Eastleigh reassured me, because it was owned by the bandits who were causing all the trouble in the northern part of Kenya.

For a converted truck, the bus was really speeding, probably because it would be dark soon. As we were fast approaching the equator, twilight – the time just before sunrise and just after sunset – was very short, lasting only about five minutes. To me the change from light to dark looked abnormal and unnatural. And crossing the equator by air is very different from crossing it by road. Unless you are the pilot, you are never sure of the exact moment of crossing the 'big red line' when you are flying, whereas if you are travelling by road you can stop right on top of nought degrees latitude. Bam!

Inside the truck-bus the passenger cab was soon very dark, but instead of worrying about that I found myself thinking that if only there were an open-minded woman sitting next to me my fingers could do the walking/talking. Unfortunately, I was seated next to an old Muslim woman with a five-year-old boy on her lap, her head covered with a black scarf.

Our first stop was at the small town of Nanyuki, located right next to the equator. Actually, the airport sits on one side of the equator while the town, which is dominated by a huge market, lies right on top of the equatorial line. Tourists who come to Kenya to view wildlife end up coming up to this old settler town just have their photos taken next to the yellow board at Nanyuki – *This sign is on the Equator* – which confirms that they are now standing exactly halfway between north and south. Although I know that the equator is an imaginary line, I found myself subconsciously looking for that straight line that cuts the globe into two equal hemispheres.

Other tourists come to Nanyuki as a transit point on their way to trekking on Africa's second highest mountain, Mount Kenya, which lies between 40 and 50 kilometres to the southeast as the crow flies.

We continued north and stopped again, just before midnight, in a very seedy-looking town named Isiolo, situated, apparently, on the border between the fertile highlands and the desert – it was too dark to see. From Nairobi to Isiolo we had travelled on a very good tarmac road, a puzzle because I had been told, back in Nairobi, that the road to Moyale was bad. Just after Isiolo, however, the real African journey began.

I had expected that somewhere along the line we were going to drive on gravel, but I did not think it would be like this. The whole body of the bus started shaking and vibrating heavily as we hit the road. I found it impossible to sleep although it was after midnight. The bus was still speeding and it felt as if I were sitting on a jack hammer. In addition, the windows were rattling non-stop. Under those conditions sleeping, for me at least, was totally impossible. Other passengers, however, were in dreamland, judging by the deep breathing and the occasional snore.

In the middle of nowhere, the bus stopped to pick up an elderly Masai man. Within minutes this Masai, who was seated next to the aisle a couple of rows in front of me, decided to start singing at the top of his voice. Obviously I did not know the song, but I could tell that he was repeating the same line over and over again. I could hear, as well, that he was miles off the right tune. He had a hoarse voice – he sounded like Eric Clapton trying to sing opera.

It was Friday night/early Saturday morning and it dawned on me that, had I not made the decision to leave my job and backpack to Cairo, I would be sleeping comfortably at home, as is normal in the middle of the night. Instead, my whole body was vibrating in a truck converted into a bus while I was forced to listen to a Masai singing loudly out of tune. For the first time on the trip I regretted having left the comfort zone. The shaking was so bad that, although the luggage on top of the bus had been tightly fastened, the driver's three assistants had to take turns to check that nothing had fallen off the roof rack.

We arrived in the dusty town of Marsabit in northern Kenya, 550 kilometres from Nairobi, just after sunrise. We spent two hours waiting in this town, supposedly a fascinating hill oasis in the desert, parked outside an old, run-down building the most striking feature of which was its peeling red paint. I thought we were waiting to join a convoy as I had read that vehicles going from Marsabit to Moyale travel, for security reasons, in convoy. To my surprise, there was neither armed guard nor convoy when we left two hours later.

As if that were not enough, the bus broke down about an hour outside Marsabit. Something had gone terribly wrong with its wheel alignment. We were ordered to disembark and that is when I got the shock of my life. The reason why the bus was shaking and vibrating so badly was because we were more or less driving on rocks. That also explained why a converted truck was used instead of a bus. No bus could survive continuous driving on such a rocky surface.

Within half an hour, after one of the assistant drivers had used a rope to tighten something on the inside of the right-front wheel, the journey to Moyale was resumed.

The next stop was in a small town called Torbi, which is actually not a town but two shops. I was standing around looking at the desert when Saddam, a local guy in an off-white robe, approached me and asked in no uncertain terms, 'What do you want, my friend, a gun or drugs?'

After turning him down politely, I knew it was time to get back into the hot bus and wait there for the other passengers to finish having lunch and quenching their thirst in the only restaurant in town. (All the shaking and vibrating had made me lose my appetite.) It was a very hot and dry day. I sat back and reflected on the distinct difference between the south and the north in Kenya: the easygoing Swahili (read 'black African') culture of the south and the austere atmosphere of the hot and arid north, where people follow a nomadic lifestyle and move around with their camels, cattle and other domestic animals. They also speak a language in the north that sounds totally different from the languages spoken in Nairobi and Mombasa. It was as if I were in another country.

Resuming our journey, we encountered three roadblocks between Marsabit and Moyale. Just after the second one, soldiers in a 4x4 overtook and stopped us. Without a word they arrested one of the driver's assistants who was at the time seated on top of the bus checking the luggage. He was taken to the 4x4 and the soldiers left with him. The passengers were talking under their breath to each other. Certainly none of them dared to challenge the soldiers. Neither did the driver.

Soldiers at the third and last roadblock wanted us to produce identity documents or passports. Quite a few passengers had neither. Naturally, the passengers without documents had to make a plan with the soldiers. In front of everyone they paid the soldiers money, how much I do not know. What interested me more was how fully accepted bribery was. Not that you could blame the people who paid the bribes. At the mercy of soldiers in the middle of nowhere, you do not insist on your rights.

We were allowed to continue the journey, but one of the soldiers got on the bus and stayed with us until we reached Moyale. Why, I never knew and, without a common language, there was no one I could ask. The old lady and child had left the bus at Marsabit, and the Masai man got off even earlier.

Twenty-one hours after leaving Nairobi we reached Moyale, where the unbelievable happened. Instead of going to the bus rank, the bus with all its passengers was directed to the police station. From what I could gather from my extremely limited understanding of what was being said, it had to do with the assistant driver having been allowed to ride on top of the bus.

While the driver and his two remaining assistants went to negotiate with the police, the passengers were instructed to stay put. Two policemen ensured that no one moved. We baked in that bus for about an hour before the driver and his assistant returned and the bus was at last allowed to move to the bus rank, which was within walking distance of the Ethiopian border.

I waited for my backpack to be offloaded, amid youngsters with wheelbarrows who were eagerly offering their services, no doubt to carry my luggage. While these young boys were trying to get my attention, a young man, more or less my age, came to introduce himself, to my great relief in English. 'My name is Fucking but my friends call me FK,' he told me with a straight face.

'OK, I will call you FK,' I said, blushing.

'I'll help you through customs.'

I thanked him, pleased that there was someone who could speak English and because, being older, he looked more trustworthy. I carried my backpack as we walked to the Ethiopian border while FK carried my jacket. As at the Tanzanian border, there were about six youngsters walking next to me, none of them saying a word, just staring at me.

Before the immigration official stamped me out of Kenya, he looked at me and asked, 'How is Thabo Mbeki?'

That was another first for me. 'I am sure he is fine,' I replied.

After I was stamped out, I had to go to a customs official who searched my bag thoroughly.

On the Ethiopian side things were somewhat more complex, but at least FK was around and he was clearly clued up on process and procedure.

To the two waiters in Nairobi who saved me from the Mike Tyson look-alike: Asante sana, thank you very much.

Haile Selassie's Ethiopia

Father of the Nation

Ethiopia, officially the Federal Democratic Republic of Ethiopia, is one of the oldest nations in the world. It claims to be 'the only African country that has never been colonised'. (Ethiopians discount the bumbling five-year military occupation of their country by Italy from 1936 to 1941.) The only contestant, Liberia, although always independent, was founded by African-American slaves.

Ethiopia's last emperor, Lij (literally 'child', a term usually bestowed upon nobility) Tafari Makonnen, known to the world as Haile Selassie I, came from a royal line that is traced 3 000 years back to the Queen of Sheba and King Solomon. He inherited his imperial blood through his paternal grand-mother, Princess Tenagnework Sahle Selassie, who was an aunt of Emperor Menelik II, said to be a direct descendant of the Queen of Sheba. Emperor of Ethiopia for over 40 years (1930–1974), Haile Selassie spent the five years of Italian occupation in exile in England. When ousted by the Derg, a com-mittee of military officers, he was 82 years old.

Under the leadership of Mengistu Haile Mariam, the Derg ruled Ethiopia for 17 years. Mengistu was tried in absentia in 2006 and sentenced to life imprisonment for his involvement in a campaign in 1977–1978 in which more than a million people were killed. After rebel forces toppled the Derg, Ethiopia's current president, Meles Zenawi, became interim president and, in 1995, prime minister.

Ethiopia, historically also known as Abyssinia, is the second most popu-lous country in Africa – with only 70 people per square kilometre. It is the second oldest Christian country in the world, having converted officially to Christianity in 4 AD. Although his name is commonly associated with the Rastafarian movement, among whose followers he is known as God Incarnate, Haile Selassie himself was a devout Christian.

After checking my visa, the two gentlemen standing outside the Ethiopian customs office instructed me to leave my backpack behind and go to the immigration office, which was about 100 metres from the customs office. FK assured me that my bag would be safe. On the way to the immigration office we encountered three incutras, who wanted to change money. I knew I had to buy some Ethiopian birr, but I totally ignored them because at that moment all my energies were focused on dealing with the bureaucracy.

The immigration official was not fluent in English and FK had to act as interpreter. He asked me basic questions like: why was I visiting Ethiopia, for how long was I going to stay, etc. Once I was stamped into the country I had to go back to the customs office, where I was ordered to go to another office across the road. There I had to fill in the entrance register. Once that was done, I was officially in Ethiopia.

The first surprise was that cars in Ethiopia drive on the wrong side of the road. Excuse my ignorance, but I had thought that all of Africa drove on the left, British style. I wondered whether Ethiopians had driven on the left or the right before the Italians arrived in 1936.

The two towns on either side of the border are both called Moyale and the inhabitants of both looked equally rough and ready for war. Freshly arrived in their territory, I received that 'what-do-you-want-here' type of look from some guys on the Ethiopian side. FK excepted, the way the Ethiopians stared at me did not make me feel welcome in their country. For the first time on the trip I felt strongly conscious of being different: although an African in Africa, I was sticking out like a sore thumb.

FK told me he could show me a comfortable place to spend the night. 'That lodge is mostly used by businesspeople,' he assured me as we walked towards it, followed by about seven guys, all incutras. Having tried unsuccessfully to obtain Ethiopian birr in Nairobi, I decided to use the most decent-looking of the seven, who were all insisting that I change money with them. As I had an idea of the official exchange rate, the transaction on the side of the road went relatively smoothly.

Checking in at the lodge – which looked more like a humble rural school than a place for businessmen – I realised that the businesspeople

FK was talking about were hawkers who bought clothes in Nairobi and sold them in Addis Ababa. The lodge, which was crawling with guests, had a number of tiny rooms joined to each other in an L-shape. In the courtyard were three showers for common use. Considering the number of hawkers and the size of the lodge, I was convinced that there must have been five or more hawkers to a room.

After a cold, trickling shower in the courtyard I tried to have my first meal of the day in a shop next to the lodge, which, according to FK, sold 'very tasty Ethiopian food called injera'. This looked like pizza but with a very soft and flexible pancake as the base. The topping seemed to be a mixture of minced meat and vegetables.

Since my last meal had been in Nairobi, about 26 hours earlier, my first bite of injera was huge. I am not sure what I expected, but I could not force myself to swallow even that first bite. It tasted like raw flour mixed with a concoction of vegetables that had been boiled in over-used oil. I am not a fussy person, but injera proved to be too much for me. FK ended up eating first his portion and then polishing off mine, delighted that I had passed it on to him, almost untouched. Then FK and I parted ways.

On my way back to the lodge I met Bajir, the incutra from whom I got my birr earlier. As he could speak a smattering of English we agreed that he would accompany me to the bus station the following day – I had been warned earlier by a gentleman at the lodge's reception desk against walking in the dark in Moyale. Since buses left very early in the morning, Bajir, unknown to him, was going to be my bodyguard.

Unable to eat injera, I returned to my room with an empty stomach. I sat on the bed, an ancient thing and the only piece of furniture in the room, with a splitting headache. I knew that I was really stressing and that the headache had as much to do with my last hour in Kenya baking in the bus as with my having had nothing to eat for more than a day, and the fact that I could not speak a word of Amharic, Ethiopia's national language. That night, while sitting on the bed in that bleak room, I realised that the trip was beginning to take its toll on me. I was beginning to feel lonely. I missed my fiancée and daughter; it was three days since I last exchanged emails with home. I was hungry, the place was depressing and I did not know when I would be able to converse again with someone beyond the basics. I was also beginning to question seriously whether it had been a good decision in the first place to resign my job in order to undertake what had become a truly challenging journey. For the first time, sitting on that sagging bed, I wondered whether my ex-colleagues and friends had not been right when they accused me of having a screw loose in undertaking this journey with all it implied.

I had a terrible night. People knocked continually on my door. I had been warned, again by the gentleman at the reception desk, that I should not open my door to anyone. Mostly, he explained, the people who knocked on doors were touts who wanted to sell you a bus ticket at an inflated price.

Ethiopia is renowned for the early starting times of its long-distance buses. I had set my alarm for 04:00 so as to be ready in time for the next day's 500-kilometre journey from Moyale to Shashamane (or Shashemene, as it is also called) in the north. As in Tanzania, there were two times: English and Amharic. Like Swahili time in Tanzania, 01:00 Amharic time was 07:00 English time. The bus was scheduled to leave at 11:00 Amharic time, which meant 05:00 English time.

I was just about to fall into a peaceful sleep when my alarm clock went off. Time to get ready for Bajir. I switched on the light but nothing happened. I tried again. Again, nothing happened. I tried for the third time and still there was no light.

In a state of total confusion in the pitch-dark room, I searched for and, to my great relief, managed to find the door handle. Contrary to my assumption that when I awoke there would be a lot of people preparing to go to the bus station, I was perplexed to find that the lodge was deadly quiet. Seemingly, everybody was still asleep. For a moment I was tempted to go back to bed myself and take a minibus taxi to the north later on in the day.

I tried to pack my bag in the dark but it proved impossible. Even with the door open, which I knew was risky, it was impossible to see my backpack and the pieces of clothing I had left at the bottom of

the bed. While contemplating my next move I heard voices and footsteps coming towards my room. It was Bajir with about six other guys.
I asked him about the electricity. The power cut was due to the town's
energy-conservation programme, he told me. They switched the power
off at night and it came on again at 6 a.m. English time.

As I continued packing in darkness I could not help but think that
whoever said this was a dark continent was right after all. Bajir and
his mates waited outside the room. When I stepped through the door
everybody wanted to grab my bag, but I insisted that only Bajir could
touch it. Halfway to the bus station I discovered that I had misplaced
my passport. This was my worst nightmare come true. What could possibly be more terrible than losing your passport while you are travelling, especially where I was?

After checking through my pockets once more I decided that I might
have left the passport in my room and that we should go back to the
lodge to check. Fortunately, the man at reception was back at his post
and accompanied us to my room. What was more, he had a torch. After
a few seconds, while I scrambled around looking for my passport, he
started to complain that his batteries were being used up. A couple of
seconds later he left and I had no alternative but to check through my
luggage in the courtyard by the light of half a moon.

I was about to open my backpack when I remembered that I had
put on shorts after taking a shower the previous day. When I checked
my shorts, under the watchful eyes of Bajir and his mates, I found the
passport in the back pocket. I almost shouted with relief.

Then it was the same story all over again: all of Bajir's mates trying to take my bag. Again I insisted that only Bajir could touch it. We
walked back to the bus station guided by moonlight, like the shepherds
looking for the newborn Jesus. All the way to the bus station Bajir and
the other guys argued about who should carry the bag. I could smell
alcohol on some of the other guys.

When we got to the town's main road a full-on fight ensued between Bajir and one of his mates. Bajir pulled one of those Mike Tyson
shots. Within two seconds the other guy's nose was bleeding, with
blood spilling onto my sleeping mat, which was attached to the top

of my backpack. It was all I needed. The combatants were eventually separated by people who were also on their way to the bus station.

At the bus station I gave both Bajir and Rasta a tip. (The other Rasta I met on the trip was at Lake Malawi.) I gave Bajir a tip because, although an incutra, he looked like a guy who was trying to make an honest living. I tipped Rasta, whose nose was still bleeding profusely, because I felt sorry for him. He was in the wrong, but it seemed the right thing to do.

Just when I thought everything was settled, another of Bajir's mates, one who had been quiet all this time, appeared next to me inside the bus and started begging. I totally ignored him, but I was already seated and he had all the time in the world to get my attention. I pretended not to see him. He did not give up. He did not say much, but he kept both his hands a few inches below my chin. Almost all the passengers were looking at me by now. Eventually, to force me to take notice of him, he knelt in the aisle of the bus, still holding both his hands in front of my chin. I could not take it anymore, so I gave him a tip as well.

By then the engine of the bus had started running. I took a deep breath, knowing that we were about to leave. The sun had not even risen yet and I was already stressed, regretting that I had ever embarked on this damn frustrating journey. As the bus pulled out of the rank I was fighting back tears. Not only had two people who, if not friends were at least acquaintances, fought fiercely for my tip, but another young man had chosen to dehumanise himself in front of about 35 passengers by begging on his knees for something – anything. I could not bear to think about it. I could not bear the thought that poverty was reducing people to such depths of dependency and self-abasement.

The bus had hardly left the station when we had to stop at a roadblock on the main street. According to the guy sitting next to me, who could speak some English, the government was trying to prevent hawkers from bringing clothing illegally into the country, mostly from Kenya, to sell in Addis Ababa.

Unlike the roadblocks we encountered later, this one was very thorough. First, all the passengers were ordered to disembark and had to undergo a thorough body search. After that, the customs officials searched all the bags inside the bus. Just when I thought we were about to leave, the officials got on top of the bus to search the luggage stowed there. To complicate matters, some of the passengers had locked their bags with padlocks. That meant they had to throw their keys to the driver's assistant, who had accompanied the officials onto the roof of the bus to help with the opening of bags. Naturally, not all people are good throwers, so some keys landed in the wrong spot. If I had thought the Lilongwe taxi rank was chaotic, clearly I was mistaken. The first roadblock outside Moyale was a real eye-opener.

While all this was happening, two guys who had been part of Bajir's entourage showed up and started speaking to me in Amharic. As translated by one of the passengers, they said I had not paid them for carrying my bag earlier that morning. I told them, through the interpreter, to get lost. With straight faces, they accused me of not having paid for services rendered. Eventually, after almost an hour, the officials finished inspecting the bags on top of the bus and we were all ordered back into the bus. The two guys followed suit, insisting that I pay them. Of course I stood my ground.

When everyone was at last seated, the two guys were still blocking the aisle. I could see that the majority of passengers were irritated that I could be so mean. After some time the bus driver came down the aisle and told me in no uncertain terms, through the interpreter, that I must give the two their fee because I was delaying everybody. It was daylight robbery, but I had no choice but to pay the alcohol-smelling impostors for nothing.

E n route at last to Shashamane, back on a tarred road, thank goodness, we encountered the next roadblock within an hour or so. The same procedure ensued: passengers were searched while disembarking, officials searched the inside of the bus and, last but not least, the top. This was proving to be a nightmare for me, but I could see that other people weren't troubled at all. Around midday, the bus stopped in a small town; it was lunch time.

By then I was starving and the only food available in that two-camel town was injera. I had no choice but to give it another try. From its appearance this version was even worse than the one in Moyale. As on the previous occasion, I could not swallow even the small piece I bit off. I went and stood next to the bus, which was parked on the side of the road. With my back against its smooth side I waited for the others to finish eating, thoroughly disenchanted. After the lunch hour we got going again and, just outside the town, ran into the third roadblock. The same procedure applied. It was proving to be a very trying day.

The fourth and last roadblock was a show-stopper. Instead of searching us as we left the bus, the officials allowed us to disembark unchecked and then started searching the inside and the top of the bus. The passengers were searched only when we returned to the bus and, for some reason, all the people wearing leather jackets (fake and real) were asked to remove them.

In total, eight jackets were taken away from their owners and into the customs office. Then, the negotiations began. It took another half an hour for all the jackets to be released. Since the negotiations were conducted in the shack that served as the customs office, I could not see if any money exchanged hands.

Back on the road I could not believe how green everything was. Sometimes it was difficult to see the thatched huts between banana trees and long grass. I could not understand why a country with such fertile soil was one of the poorest countries in the world. In fact, it was hard to comprehend that in a country that looked so bounteous more than a million people had died from starvation in 1984–1985.

The other thing that amazed me on the Moyale–Shashamane road was how popular table tennis was. As we passed through villages I spotted many young stars playing the game. I read, later, that since 2000 the French, in particular, have been supporting the development of the game in Ethiopia by providing equipment, and that Ethiopia came second in the African Table Tennis Championships in 2004.

It took us 11 hours to reach the sprawling town of Shashamane, which looked like one big junction and nothing more. Roads from the south, north, east, west, and southeast all connected there. I booked into a lodge right next to the bus station and was pleasantly surprised to find that a young Somalian guy who had been with me on the Nairobi–Moyale as well as the Moyale–Shashamane bus had also booked into the same lodge. He was in Ethiopia to apply for a UK visa, he told me in halting English.

'My friend, it is much easier to get the UK visa in Ethiopia than in any other African country within the region,' he assured me. He also boasted to me how his 'friend' had let him through the Ethiopian border without the proper documents. He was convinced that I was either selling something illegal or had travelled all this way to see my wife/ girlfriend in Addis Ababa. He could not believe that someone would travel from Cape Town all the way here just for the fun of it.

'Really that would be very stupid,' he concluded. After my most recent experiences I wasn't sure that he didn't have a point.

Since there was no in-house restaurant in the lodge, I again went to bed without eating. That meant I had not eaten for more than two days. I wasn't feeling particularly cheerful. I am sure there were other types of food to be found in Shashamane besides injera, but I didn't want to walk in the streets after dark on my own (two people in the bus had warned me against wandering around in the town after sunset) and the Somalian traveller had expressed no desire to go and eat somewhere else. As in Moyale, my room at the lodge was very basic: an old bed and nothing else. The showers, which were located outside at the back, were far worse. One look at the filth and grubbiness on the walls and the floor and I was convinced that I would get some kind of infection if I dared to use them. Hungry and unwashed, I went to bed.

Although I had been told that there was a large Rastafarian commune about two kilometres from the centre of town, in the direction of Addis Ababa, I did not see a single Rastafarian during the hours I spent in Shashamane. In 1963, Haile Selassie donated 500 hectares of land to a group of West Indians, mainly Jamaicans, who wanted to come back and settle in Africa. The Rastas have lived there ever since, spreading their religion of love, peace and smoking of the ganja pipe.

Early the next morning I left Shashamane, on the final leg of the journey to Addis Ababa. As in Mbeya, Tanzania, a loud call from the mosque ensured that I did not oversleep. It was still dark when my Somalian friend and I flagged down a minibus on the main road running through Shashamane. It so happened that the minibus was on its way to Addis, as the locals call their capital city.

Without further ado, still on an empty stomach, I embarked on the 250-kilometre journey in a 25-seater, with Amharic music blasting from a powerful sound system. I couldn't help but remember that I had wanted to drive to Durban airport in a similar fashion the day I left. Of course I did not at the time know Amharic music, which sounded quite a bit like the Indian music on Radio Lotus. Not at all like Toto and Salif Keita.

There were mainly men on board the bus. My seat was in the back on the right-hand side, the Somali next to me. It was really taking time for me to get used to the Ethiopian style of driving on the right; it felt wrong and outright dangerous.

Soon we entered the Great Rift Valley, which starts somewhere south of Shashamane, a lush greenness surrounding us. Between Shashamane and Mojo, where we would exit the Rift Valley again, there are no fewer than five large lakes. The first that we encountered was Lake Langano, the rising sun reflecting off its sparkling surface. It gave me that 'it's a brand-new day' feeling. For the first time on the trip, I felt that Cairo was attainable.

That view of utter peace so early in the morning, with no signs of human activity, gave me hope. In no time I was truly glad that I had embarked on the journey. It's amazing how emotionally unstable you become on this kind of trip. Just the previous day I was seriously considering throwing in the towel and here I was, only one day later, convinced that I was going to make it to Cairo. It helped, too, that we were not stopped at any of the three roadblocks on the way because, I guess, we were in a small local minibus. Buses had to go through the same rigorous procedure every time.

Within three hours of leaving Shashamane we were in Addis. It was still early in the morning and people were going to work in their thousands.

Addis looked totally different from every other city I had visited. Skyscrapers and shacks, goats and donkeys, beggars and well-dressed people, filthy-rich and poverty-stricken, all shared the same space.

There was no city centre to talk of. I am reluctant even to call Addis a city – it is more like the world's largest village. It was in this village, back in May 1963, that the Organisation of African Unity (read 'African Dictators Club') was formed.

When the minibus dropped us off in one of the busiest streets in Addis, I quickly realised that my Somalian companion did not know where he was going. 'You know, my friend,' he said in a very soft voice, 'we must hang out together and support each other here in Addis.' He also mumbled something about running out of cash and that he wanted me to loan him some money.

At that moment I knew that I was not going to 'adopt' a twenty-something-year-old son. I flagged down a cab and took off for the budget hotel I had picked from my guidebook, which by then had more or less become my Bible/Koran, leaving my travelling companion standing there on the street. With so many people in Addis, I could no longer see him when I turned around. Within a second or two he had been swallowed by the crowds. Although I pretended it was fine, deep down I felt genuinely sorry for him.

It did not take me long after checking into my hotel to realise that I was coming down with flu. I was sure it was related to stress and to not having eaten for more than two days. Although it was morning and an ideal time to go sightseeing, I decided to take it easy. I took some flu tablets that I had been carrying with me all the way from Durban and went to bed.

In the afternoon, instead of continuing with the medication, I decided to have three double, locally-stoked brandies. The barman promised that I would awake the next morning feeling like a new man.

I had a good night's sleep, but I woke up the following day feeling much sicker, and with a pounding headache. I considered sleeping the whole day but opted in the end to go and apply for a Sudanese visa instead, before returning to bed. I was worried about the visa. After all, I had read a lot of negative stories about how difficult it was to obtain one. I decided that, rather than use the letter of introduction from Nairobi, it would be wise to get a letter from the South African embassy in Addis. I was willing to try anything just to get a, reportedly highly elusive, Sudanese visa.

When I arrived at the embassy I was astounded by the number of Ethiopians applying for a visa to enter South Africa. I seemed to be the only non-Ethiopian there. I told the lady at the counter that I was a South African passport-holder who needed a letter of introduction. 'Why?' was her immediate response.

I did not expect that question, especially from a South African working there. I was dumbstruck. While I was still trying to explain the reason, she started paging through my passport and told me that I would not have a problem obtaining a Sudanese visa and shoved my passport back at me. She really had an attitude problem. Judging from appearances, she must have been feeling menopausal.

I left the South African embassy disappointed and discouraged and went to the Sudanese embassy, already in a dejected state. The sign at the gate stated that they dealt with visa applications only on Mondays, Wednesdays and Fridays. Since it was a Tuesday I had no choice but to return the following day. I regretted that I had wasted so much time by going to both the South African and Sudanese embassies instead of sleeping. It was still mid-morning and time, I decided, to go back to bed and take some proper medication.

In the afternoon, when I told the waiter that I had travelled from Cape Town to Addis by public transport, he exclaimed, 'That is fuckin' beautiful!' I did not know that Ethiopians used the f-word so freely.

Abstaining from alcohol really worked. I woke up the following morning feeling refreshed, energetic and ready to face the Sudanese embassy. When I got there I could not believe my eyes: about 70 people were already in the queue. I showed my passport to the security guard and he ushered me to the front of the line amid filthy looks from some of the people queuing. I glimpsed men who were obviously business-people and young people who could have been students; the rest appeared to be just ordinary folk. My spirits lifted even more at the prospect that, having been shown such privilege, I might walk out with a visa in an hour, as had happened at the Ethiopian embassy in Nairobi.

An officer in the open-plan embassy office gave me an application form to complete. The form, I reckon, had to be filled in from right to left because when entering information I wrote, as usual, in the empty block to the right of the question, which left a row of empty boxes on the left and a row of unanswered questions on the right.

When I handed back the form the officer asked, 'Do you know anyone in Sudan?'

'No,' I replied. Mindful of what I was told at the South African embassy earlier, I did not bother mentioning my letter of introduction from Nairobi.

With my application form in his hand, the officer asked me the same question again. I again said no. He asked me the same question for the third time. By then I felt like changing my answer because I could see that he was not impressed by the fact that I didn't know anybody in Sudan. But I stuck to my original reply.

Looking straight at me for the first time, he handed me a piece of paper and said, 'All visa applications are processed in Khartoum. Sami is my name and this is my number. Phone me on Monday afternoon.'

'But today is Wednesday?' I said, somewhat puzzled.

Sounding irritated, he replied, 'I know. Phone me on Monday,' and turned around to help the mostly Ethiopian applicants in the queue, which by then seemed to have reached a total of a hundred or more persons.

I walked out of that office very disappointed and confused. The more I thought about it, the more complex the whole thing seemed. If I had to phone on Monday afternoon and they dealt with visa applications only on Mondays, Wednesdays and Fridays, then even if my visa was approved I would, at the earliest, get it only on the following Wednesday. That meant I could not leave Addis before the following Thursday. And, I asked myself, what if they turn down my application after I've waited for more than a week? Another puzzling thing was that Sami took only my application form and not my passport.

Addis seemed interesting, but I did not want to spend so much time in one place, and the places I wanted to visit in Ethiopia – Bahir Dar and Gondar – were both in the northern part of the country through which I would travel on my way to Sudan. Visiting these two towns for a couple of days and then coming back to Addis was totally out of the question.

Maybe I should use the time to apply for an Egyptian visa, I thought, so that I would not have to do so in Khartoum. But what if the Egyptian embassy gave me a 30-day visa, with effect from the issue date? It would mean rushing through northern Ethiopia, Sudan and Egypt in order to ensure that the visa did not expire before I was ready to leave Egypt.

One option was to give a far-into-the-future date as my date of entry when applying for the Egyptian visa. The problem with that possibility was that my application for a Sudanese visa might be turned down and my Ethiopian visa might expire before my Egyptian visa was valid. And if I synchronised my Ethiopian expiry date with my Egyptian entry date and was turned down by the Sudanese embassy, I would be stuck in Ethiopia waiting for that far-into-the-future date to arrive!

My good mood had evaporated. Once again, I was finding that being obsessed with how things would, or could, work out in practice made it very difficult for me just to enjoy life and take things as they come.

With all these confusing thoughts buzzing in my mind, I decided to go, as my guidebook suggested, to the newly refurbished Ethnological Museum.

I asked a taxi driver to take me there and the man dropped me off right outside the entrance. After paying the entrance fee I was joined by a free guide who, in relatively good English, started going on and on about vertebrate and invertebrate animals. He also talked about Ethiopia's fauna and flora. Something was wrong somewhere. Only then did I see a big sign: *Zoology Section.*

I went out even more stressed than when I entered.

As I walked down the street my attention was caught by a very large modern building that, to judge by the architecture, could only be a place of worship. On closer inspection it turned out to be the Holy Trinity Cathedral. I felt in need of some solace and gladly paid the small entrance fee required of tourists, which included the services of a guide.

According to my guide, the cornerstone of the cathedral – its proper name is Kiddist Selassie Cathedral – was laid by Emperor Haile Selassie in 1933. The cathedral was inaugurated by him in 1942, as part of the celebrations following the defeat of the Italians, who had occupied

Ethiopia for the preceding five years. It took me two hours to go through and around the cathedral. It was evident that no effort was spared in the creation of that great piece of architecture, in the construction of which the best Ethiopian architects, sculptors, artists and painters were used. The interior is a showcase of religious paintings in both the modern and medieval Ethiopian style.

The Emperor, his wife and five of their six children are all buried in Kiddist Selassie Cathedral, and the locals come in continuously to pray either in the courtyard or the main body of the church. I discovered later that Haile Selassie was, originally, buried next to a toilet and was reburied here only in November 2000 at a ceremony that was attended by, among others, Bob Marley's wife, Rita, and a large group of Rastafarians from all over the globe. I had to have a photo taken of myself next to the late Emperor's huge granite tomb, which is housed next to an identical tomb holding his wife's remains in a chamber at the front of the cathedral.

Ethiopians, it struck me, are deeply religious. When we entered the cathedral, my guide, like everyone else, made the sign of the cross in the manner of Catholics. I followed his lead, smiling nervously, because it was the first time ever that I crossed myself.

I learned quite a few things during that tour, among others that the seats used by the Emperor and his wife had not been occupied since Haile Selassie was smothered to death in 1974. My guide, a junior pastor in the church, told me that between Haile Selassie and his ancestor Menelik I, the son of the Queen of Sheba and Solomon, King of Judea, 254 kings of the same bloodline had ruled Ethiopia. Menelik had been allowed to visit his father, Solomon, in Jerusalem, where he was showered with gifts, including the Ark of the Covenant, which is now kept in one of the Orthodox churches in Axum, in northeastern Ethiopia. The general public is not allowed to see the Ark, he said. In fact, only one holy priest is allowed to enter the chamber where the Ark is stored. On his death, the duty passes on to another priest.

I understood after talking to the junior pastor why there is a lion, the symbol of the King of Judea, on the Ethiopian flag. I decided that when I returned to South Africa, I would study the Bible and other books in detail to check on the claim that King Solomon and Haile Selassie were distantly related and that the Ark of the Covenant had ended up in Ethiopia. That was my Resolution No. 8 and the only one I have thus far executed. When I got back to Durban I did read the Bible carefully – you can do, too: 2 Chronicles chapter 9, verses 1-12, and 1 Kings chapter 10, verses 1-13.

When I emerged from the cathedral, still trying to come up with the best solution to my visa problems, I decided to do some window shopping in Piazza, where a number of shops are found in a relatively small area in downtown Addis Ababa. While looking around I noticed that some of the women in Addis displayed a distinctly African bum. I had grown up with images of malnourished Ethiopians with kwashiorkor. What I saw in Addis was, by and large, a thin but very healthy population.

I had to concede, again, that I had made a very big mistake. After I had a good look around Nairobi, I had to revise my opinion that the women of Dar es Salaam were the most beautiful on the continent. Now I had to admit that I was wrong to think that Nairobi's women were the most beautiful. Ethiopian women were far more striking than their Kenyan sisters. I guess it is their cosmopolitan look – a mixture of African and Indian, spiced with Italian blood – that makes them so stunning.

Lying in bed that night, I kept asking myself why the Sudanese official Sami had asked me three times if I knew anyone in Sudan. I decided that if I didn't get a Sudanese visa I would simply fly from Addis to Cairo. As I dozed off I thought of another alternative: fly to Cairo, apply for a Sudanese visa in Cairo and then do Cairo to Khartoum. The following day would make it exactly 40 days since I left Cape Town. I was happy with my progress. At the same time I felt that I had rushed the trip and maybe a few days in Addis would not be so bad after all.

The next day I decided I might as well check out Merkato – Africa's largest open-air market. Upon entering this vast area of roads, lined with small shops of every description, I was approached by several young boys, intent on taking me to the 'cheapest' stalls. By now, however, I had mastered the art of ignoring hustlers. I hadn't gone there to buy in any case, only to pass the time. There was plenty to look at: curios, cassettes with local music, crosses, traditional clothes and hand-woven cloth, silver and gold jewellery, spices, fresh vegetables, dried beans and pulses.

Three different people in three different places in Merkato said I looked like an Ethiopian. That was really good news for me because it meant I had lost weight and that my bulging tummy was getting smaller. I could not have asked for more. I probably lost a bit more weight that day because I kept getting lost in the maze of stalls and small streets. In fact, I could not find my way back to the taxi rank and eventually had to swallow my pride and ask for directions.

That evening I went to the bar in the Debra Damo Hotel where I was staying. I spent some time studying the magazines that, for some reason, had been left there by NGOs working in Somalia and Eritrea. Unexpectedly, the barman said to me, 'My friend, it is impossible to travel from Cape Town to Addis by public transport.' After I had described my route to him, he replied, 'OK, but if it was really possible it would take more than six months to reach Addis,' and shook his head incredulously.

To a certain extent I could understand why the barman regarded Cape Town as such a far, unreachable place – he was using Ethiopia's slow public transport system as a point of departure. When I told him the trip had taken me slightly more than a month he found it hilarious, very funny. I, in turn, found it hilarious that he was finding this so funny and so we both had a good laugh.

I spent the next day lazing around. I was really becoming a local. Some of the Addis Ababans were even calling me by name – 'Sikle'. In the afternoon I went for another session at the hairdressers. At a good walking distance from the Debra Damo I found the corrugated-iron shack to which the barman had directed me. To my surprise, it had good plumbing and was staffed by two very beautiful girls. I was happy to let the more stunning of the two start immediately on redoing my plaits. As the girls could not speak much English, we had to depend on hand gestures to communicate. I was getting used to girls playing with my hair and savoured every minute of relatively gentle treatment while the girls continued to speak Amharic almost non-stop to each other. The barman nodded his approval later that evening.

The next day I woke up to the news on television that local runner Kenenisa Bekele, the son of a farmer, had broken his own 10-kilometre world record in Finland. The 22-year-old Bekele's accomplishment made me think that there must definitely be something called talent that causes people with few resources and no infrastructure to achieve greatness.

As far as talent is concerned it is clear we are not all born equal. But I'm sure that everyone must have some talent; it is just a pity that most people live their lives without ever discovering what their particular talent is. I fear I'm part of that majority, except that I seem to have the talent to find (crazy) ways to celebrate my birthday each year, and the talent to continuously and consistently – without asking for directions – get lost in big markets and small and ancient towns.

Since Addis is renowned for its club scene, I decided to check it out that evening. I went to what was literally an underground club. I entered via a flight of stairs with mirrors on both sides and another big mirror at the bottom of the stairway. In the club with an unpronounceable name a live band was playing Amharic music.

The Ethiopians at the club showed themselves to be truly cosmopolitan. Their dancing was a mixture of very different movements:

> Indian: moving of the head from side to side
> Masai: jumping high up and down
> Xhosa: *ukuxhensa* – moving and shaking the upper body
> Latino: abdomen wiggling
> Western: moon walking à la Michael Jackson

The DJ took over as soon as the local band had finished playing, but before I could show my skills on the dance floor I had some serious business to attend to: I had to introduce myself to the sexy leading vocalist whom I had been eyeing throughout the band's performance and whose Latino moves had impressed me. Starting a conversation with her was very easy. As a well-known DJ and top producer in South Africa, there was naturally a lot about me that she wanted to know. In fact, I quickly explained that an association with me would open doors wide for her.

Unfortunately, most of this was lost on her as she did not speak much English. She was, nevertheless, getting really excited about the gist of all the prospects in view and called another member of the band to interpret for her. By now even a recording deal was in the pipeline. The interpreter, however, saw right through me and, my cover blown, I had to return to the bar.

I soon noticed that the ratio of women to men in that club was somewhat skew. There were many more women than men. Initially, with so many ladies showing an interest in me, my bruised ego was enjoying being well stroked, but after a while, especially when it became clear that these were bar women looking for a bit of extra income, I lost interest.

For the first time since I arrived in Addis, I became aware of a large number of older white men in one spot. They were having a good time, thoroughly enjoying the attention the ladies were lavishing on them. I had witnessed something very similar in Bangkok when I went there to celebrate my 23rd birthday.

Looking at the way those old men were behaving, I was sure they were widivodorced (a phenomenon that occurs when your ex-spouse, whom you still adore, dies, making you a widivodorcee). I could have been wrong, of course – maybe they were still married. After all, history has proved over and over again that married men are worse in their behaviour than their single brothers: for married men every opportunity counts because they are forever living on borrowed time.

Later on, tipsy from drinking too much beer, I took to the dance floor. As I have already mentioned, Ethiopians have the rhythm – which is to be expected; after all, they are Africans. They were so good that it would have been very difficult to beat them at contemporary dance moves, so, being drunk and flexible in my thinking, I decided to perform a dance I was sure they had never seen before: *isipantsula*. It stopped the show. Shuffling my feet back and forth while shaking my hands as if

I suffered from Parkinson's, all the while slightly bent yet keeping my head straight in military fashion and wearing not the standard frozen look but a broad smile on my face, I moved to the rhythm of whatever music came from the loudspeakers. When I noticed just how impressed the ladies were, I bent my body further and further towards the floor. Just before I broke my back I retired to my stool next to the bar.

Overall I had a really good time. It had been years since I danced in a club until I was dripping with sweat. When I took a cab back to my hotel I saw that the driver had not switched on the headlights. Although the sun had not yet risen, there was already enough light to drive without lights.

After only three hours of sleep I was awoken by my alarm clock. It was time for church.

Waiting for the Sudanese visa was like a ton of bricks on my shoulders and I had decided that I needed to lessen the weight by attending the service in an Ethiopian Orthodox Church just a ten-minute walk from my hotel. Apart from two funeral services in Durban, it was the first time I attended what looked very much like a Roman Catholic service to me.

Like members of any religious group, the members of the Ethiopian Orthodox Church have their own procedures and special ways of doing things. Even in English and Zulu it would have been difficult to follow the ancient rituals; in Amharic I was completely and utterly lost. I spent most of the time trying to keep a straight face. I didn't know where we were in the prayerbook, when to kneel and when to sit, when to say 'Amen' and when not. Twice, I almost choked trying to suppress a nervous laugh. And I might have fallen over and had a good sleep during the sermon were it not for the bearded old man next to me who kept nudging me with his left elbow.

After the service I went straight back to bed, the weight on my shoulders having spread to my legs as well. I needed to be rested for the next day, Monday, the day for telephoning the Sudanese embassy. I knew that if my visa application was turned down my Cape to Cairo dream would be shattered.

Since I was supposed to phone the embassy in the afternoon, I decided to apply for an Egyptian visa on Monday morning. I had to catch a cab to the Egyptian embassy as I had no idea where it was. Security was very tight. The consulate hours, according to the notice board, were 09:00–12:00 and you could pick up your visa the following afternoon. Well, that was the theory. In practice, the other applicants and I had to wait from 09:00–12:00 for the Head of Consulate to accept the application, which was no guarantee that the visa would be issued. All but two of the applications were accepted.

There was still time to visit the National Museum of Ethiopia before making the dreaded phone call to Sami at the Sudanese embassy. The National Museum, a ten-minute uphill walk from Arat Kilo, one of the two major traffic circles in Addis, is one of the best museums in Africa. (Arat Kilo means 'four kilometres' in Amharic, indicating that the circle is four kilometres from the city centre.) The highlight for me was seeing Lucy – or, at least, a very realistic replica of the skull that was discovered in northeastern Ethiopia in 1974.

Lucy, called Dinkquinesh ('thou art wonderful') by Ethiopians, is believed to be 3,5 million years old and is regarded as a 'scientific' link between humans and chimpanzees: she walked upright, had no tail, a very small brain and was only 1,1 metres tall. The discovery caused archaeologists to completely rethink human evolution because Lucy proved that our ancestors were walking upright 2,5 million years earlier than was thought. Looking at Lucy, who you could easily mistake for a stone if you saw her lying on the side of a mountain somewhere, it was difficult to believe that she had caused such a stir.

When I finally called the Sudanese embassy from the reception at my hotel and introduced myself, I was asked: 'Do you work for the African Union?'

I was tempted to say yes, but on second thought decided it was not a good idea. When I stated the truth I was told that they had not heard anything from Khartoum yet and that I should phone the following day.

That was a good excuse for me to get drunk, and I kept the barman at the hotel company for an hour or two. Waiting for the Sudanese visa was really testing my patience to its limits.

I woke up the next morning with a terrible headache, and with an even bigger problem: I had misplaced my passport (again). I turned my backpack inside out looking for the small blue book without which I'd be truly stuck. It was only after two hours of thorough searching that it clicked – I had left my passport at the Egyptian embassy. The relief was great but not complete because I still had to make that phone call to the Sudanese embassy.

When I did, the phone rang for a long time before a lady finally answered. 'Sami, the official you are looking for, is not available,' she said. 'Phone this afternoon.' Phoning later was not a problem, except that I was scheduled to pick up my Egyptian visa that very same afternoon. The bureaucracy was stressing me out big time and I was again beginning to think that, maybe, the whole Cape to Cairo thing was misconceived from the start. I was even missing having my own office and some type of routine. I found myself pondering the thought that dull and deadening comfort was not so bad after all.

At the Egyptian embassy, the security officer asked for any type of identification. When I gave him my driver's licence, he opened a drawer and, without saying a word, handed me my passport. Very reluctantly I opened it – there, neatly stamped, was an Egyptian visa. Within 30 seconds I was out of there with my visa and, to top it all, I had not paid a cent for it. Like all other visas I had been issued, it was valid for 30 days from the date of issue.

I was in high spirits although I still had to rush back to the hotel to phone the Sudanese embassy. The same thing happened: the phone rang for a long time and when someone eventually picked up they could not find Sami. I was told to phone the following day.

Later that afternoon there was a downpour that caused a two-hour power failure in our hotel. The day was really moving from bad to worse. Not even the good lamb stew at a restaurant near the Debra Damo could restore my spirits. And it took a while to get used to waiters who, when serving your food, would add, 'I wish you a good appetite.'

The waiter who was serving me suggested, just before I settled my bill, that in order to relax I should chew khat (also sometimes spelt 'chat'). He gave me a sample in a plastic bag. I tried it out in my room by chewing a fairly large portion; it looked and tasted like grass. It dried my mouth out and, quite honestly, did nothing to improve my mood.

That night, while under the mellow influence of khat, I tossed and turned, thinking about the options available to me if I did not get the Sudanese visa. There were seven:

1 Give up on the dream and fly from Addis straight back to South Africa.
2 Fly to Cairo, apply for the Sudanese visa there and then do the Cairo to Khartoum.
3 Travel east, by land, to the port of Djibouti and from there hitch a lift by cargo vessel to one of the Egyptian cities on the Red Sea.
4 Head back by road to Nairobi and from there to Uganda and then fly back to South Africa.
5 Fly to Cairo, apply for a Moroccan visa and return via the Atlantic route.
6 Return to Nairobi by road and fly to Madagascar before heading back to South Africa.
7 Return to South Africa by road.

At this point I laughed at myself to think how sick in my head I was getting.

I woke feeling very thirsty. It must have been the khat.

My mission that day was the same as on previous days: to phone Sami at the Sudanese embassy. I didn't wait until the afternoon. After countless rings someone picked up and told me that the official I was looking for was unavailable. I begged him to check my application. I had been waiting for the visa for more than a week, I said. He asked me to hold while he checked the application forms.

A few seconds later he returned to the phone and said, 'OK, come at ten.' I was so shocked I didn't know what to say to the man.

When I got to the embassy I was, again, shunted to the front of the queue. I spotted my application at once, on top of a huge pile of application forms that made me genuinely and quietly sympathise with those who had to work through them. I began to understand why the process, which was complicated further by the applications having to go via Khartoum, took so long.

The official behind the desk asked me for the fee of us$61 (roughly R400). By then I was so relieved to be getting such a highly elusive visa that I didn't mind paying. He gave me a receipt and said, 'Friday.'

'No, today is Wednesday,' I replied, thinking he was confusing days.

'Yes, come back on Friday,' he said, placing my passport and application form on top of another big pile of forms. I walked out of the office with very mixed feelings: on the one hand bitterly disappointed that I still did not have a visa, on the other hand happy that within 48 hours I would have one. The mad speed with which I had been travelling was broken and I was slowly getting used to the leisurely pace at which things moved in this part of the world.

It was back to chewing khat and drinking cheap local whisky. At the last moment I decided to go to the club I had visited before, although it was a Wednesday. (Ethiopians party on weekends and all week long.) As before, I was harassed by the ladies and the old white men were still taking advantage of beautiful young Ethiopian girls. And there was, again, a lot of smoking – people in Ethiopia had obviously never heard of a woman by the name of Nkosazana Dlamini Zuma and her passion for banning smoking in the interests of health. They happily continued to smoke in clubs and other public spaces.

I enjoyed dancing to both Amharic and Western music. I returned to the hotel just before sunrise and spent most of the following day sleeping and nursing a hangover. In the afternoon I went to the station to buy a bus ticket to Bahir Dar for Saturday. After all, the following day was Friday, when I was finally going to get my visa and prepare to set off for Sudan.

It was almost too good to be true.

I decided to go to the embassy early so that I could revisit Merkato directly afterwards. As usual, there was a security guard at the gate. I showed him my receipt with pride. Without looking at it, he said, 'Come back at four.'

To say I was surprised is an understatement. I really could not understand what was happening, but I had been broken in like a wild bull and the last thing I was going to do was argue with him. Tail between my legs, I slunk into Merkato again. The place is huge and, being a person without any sense of direction in life, I got lost again. My mind was elsewhere in any case. I kept asking myself what would happen if I went back to the embassy at four and found that the offices closed early on Friday. Just to make sure that I did not spend another weekend in Addis, I decided to go back to the embassy immediately.

As on previous occasions, there was a long line of Ethiopians applying for a Sudanese visa, and this time I had to join the queue at the back like everybody else. However, after about ten minutes, a well-dressed man from the office (not Sami) came straight to me and asked to see my receipt. A minute later he returned, handed me my passport and said, 'Enjoy Sudan.'

I almost knelt before him (to show, in a traditional African way, my respect and appreciation) as I took my passport from him.

I could not believe that, finally, I had in my possession the hard-to-come-by Sudanese visa. The accomplishment called for a celebration. I headed straight for the bar at the Debra Damo Hotel. A little intoxicated and super relaxed, I started chatting to a fifty-something man who had been sitting quietly in the corner with a female companion, who had just gone off somewhere. His name was Mattheus and he was from Germany and on holiday with his wife. They were celebrating their 25th wedding anniversary.

After chatting for a while I discovered that Mattheus and his wife had hired a 4x4 and, like me, were going to Bahir Dar the following day. When Mattheus suggested that we share the vehicle I could not believe my luck. I was going to be in a 4x4 instead of a bus! The day was really getting better by the minute.

After half an hour or so Mattheus was ready to head for bed. We agreed on the next day's departure time and, since I was not going to be travelling by bus the following day and considering it was Friday, I decided to return to the club and paint Addis red.

People in Ethiopia are very trusting. For instance, they allow patrons to run up a tab in a packed nightclub. What makes it more amazing is that the toilets are usually outside the club, making slipping away easy. Sitting there in the club, I decided that I would visit Addis one day with my South African friends and run up a tab, run up a tab, run up a tab and run (typical darkie, to take the money and run – just like not being able to swim). It was not a resolution or a business idea, just a mad fantasy that I blame partly on apartheid: I grew up struggling financially, hence I am forever thinking about freebies.

That night at the club it was mostly Chinese men (or Japanese or Koreans – I find it hard to tell the difference) who were hanging around Addis's beautiful girls. I spent more time at the bar than on the dance floor and went back to the hotel earlier than on the two previous occasions. I would have only four hours of sleep, but I was not worried since I was not going to be using public transport and would be swept along in comfort the next day.

On leaving my room the following morning I noticed that the driver had already arrived with his big 4x4 and was chatting to Mattheus and his wife. When I got closer to the car Mattheus's wife gave me that 'can I help you' look. Sensing something was wrong, Mattheus spoke to her in German. I could see that he had forgotten to tell her that I would be driving with them to Bahir Dar.

For a couple of seconds there was dead silence. By then the bus to Bahir Dar would almost surely have left, and I was determined not to spend another day loitering in Addis. It was really an uncomfortable situation. What I could not work out was whether Mattheus's wife was angry because she had not been consulted about an additional passenger or whether she just did not want to travel with me. To say she looked furious is putting it mildly. Eventually she said something like she hoped I was going to pay.

Have you been married to this woman for 25 years? I felt like asking Mattheus.

Although we had not discussed costs the previous night at the bar, I knew that I was expected to meet them halfway. I sat in front with the driver and Mattheus and his peeved wife occupied the rear seat of a very comfortable and powerful four-wheel-drive. I was happy that I was about to leave Addis at last, although sad to be leaving such friendly and high-spirited people.

What made it even more sad was that the Ethiopians were about to celebrate New Year. Although it was September 2005 according to the Gregorian calendar, on the Orthodox Ethiopian calendar it was still 1997, and there were only seven days left before the start of 1998. Even shops sported New Year stickers and banners. To celebrate the event one of the top hotels in Addis was staging a huge show featuring mega international artist Wycleaf Jean.

When I first heard about the Ethiopian New Year the question I wanted to ask was, Where did they get left behind? Even the explanation that the Ethiopian calendar has 13 months – the first 12 each have 30 days and the last only 5 – was not an adequate explanation, because one still ended up with the same number of days in the year as in our calendar.

Anyway, I missed a big party. It would have been great to go through New Year's Eve three times in 366 days: I celebrated my 2005 New Year's Eve at the Flux Festival in Hidden Valley, just outside Mooi River in the Natal Midlands, which was renowned for its multiracial crowd and great line-up of artists before the sponsors stopped funding it. At the time I didn't know it, but my 2006 New Year's Eve would be spent seriously partying at Tofo Beach in Inhambane, Mozambique. Had I managed to spend a few more days in Addis, I would have added a third New Year's Eve – sandwiched between the other two.

I slept during most of the 565-kilometre journey from Addis to Bahir Dar. I would wake up now and then when we stopped at roadblocks, but since we were in a marked tourist-company vehicle there were no hassles whatsoever. Even though I spent most of the time dozing off, I noticed that we were driving past lots of animals – goats, donkeys and mules – on the winding road. Most of the time the driver was travelling very slowly. We were tourists – we had to enjoy the scenery and have time to take it all in.

Mattheus woke me up when we crossed the spectacular bridge across the beautiful gorge of the Blue Nile. It made perfect sense that, since we were going north, the Blue Nile (which originates in Ethiopia's largest lake, Lake Tana, where we were heading) would be flowing south, before turning in a northwesterly direction to Khartoum to meet the White Nile.

Almost seven hours after leaving Addis Ababa, we came in sight of Bahir Dar. I was surprised that Mattheus's wife (we were never introduced formally and I never caught her name) was turning out to be a nice person. She was the one who insisted that, instead of dropping me off in the middle of town to find my own way, they should take me to the budget hotel where I planned to stay, in a prime location right on the shores of Lake Tana. When I got out I gave Mattheus what I thought was a fair share of the costs and, although he looked a little hesitant, he took the money.

The capital of the Amhara region (one of the eight regions into which Ethiopia is divided), Bahir Dar is an attractive town with wide palm-lined streets. In comparison with Addis it has a very relaxed ambience, the result, perhaps, of the sticky tropical atmosphere. As it was Saturday, market day, and only about two o'clock in the afternoon, I thought I would squeeze in a visit to the local *merkato*, which I had been told was one of the finest in the country.

As I stepped outside the hotel grounds I found I had company. A young boy, probably in his teens, wanted to be my guide. Regardless of how hard I tried to ignore him, he persisted. Naturally I ended up employing Yishwas, and he proved to be a really good guide despite his limited English vocabulary. He kept saying to me, 'Have a look. They don't charge if you just look.'

I was becoming more and more like a woman – a compulsive buyer. Although I had already bought some souvenirs for my family in Addis, I ended up buying more stuff in Bahir Dar: a dress for my fiancée and for Nala a pair of cotton pants and a matching top with *Ethiopia* embroidered on the chest in Rasta colours. Sellers would try to get my attention while I was walking among the stalls and I thought it would be polite to thank them in their own language. 'Thank you' in Amharic is *ameseganallo*. Somehow, whenever I said 'thank you' in Amharic, the sellers looked really puzzled. I, too, felt that whatever I was saying did not sound quite right. It was only when I left the markct that I realised that instead of saying *amesegenallo* I was saying 'abracadabra'.

At the end of my shopping expedition it was, unfortunately, time to say goodbye to Yishwas. After I had given him a tip he shook my hand and said, 'See you next lifetime.'

Much as I liked Bahir Dar, I was worried about the irregular transport between Ethiopia and Sudan that everyone had warned me about, and so decided not to spend another night there. That meant I was not going to see the monasteries.

There are no fewer than 20 monasteries on the islands and peninsulas of Lake Tana. Although most of them were founded before the 15th century, these churches are still used today. In this part of Ethiopia, I was told, Christians outnumber Muslims four to one. From an architectural point of view, the churches of Tigray and Lasta, hewn out of solid rock, are, apparently, the best. Visually, Ura Kidhane Mihret, which I could easily have reached from Bahir Dar, is the most beautiful and is covered from top to bottom with 16th century paintings.

I consoled myself with the thought that within the next five years I was going to do the Cape to Cairo in a sponsored four-wheel-drive – Resolution No. 9. On that trip, I would also visit Ethiopia's holiest town of Axum (Aksum), which is considered to be the cradle of Ethiopian culture and Christianity and the site of Ethiopia's first church. Also Lalibela, 2 630 metres above sea level, where you find 800-year-old churches carved underground into the mountain – Resolution No. 10. The rocky escarpment in and on which Lalibela is set is said to resemble South Africa's highest mountain range, the Drakensberg.

The calmness of the lake in front of my hotel, with its pelicans and abundant birdlife (there were hippos and crocodiles too, but I did not see them), made me feel that I was making the wrong decision by not spending at least two nights in Bahir Dar. With its scenic views and its lush surroundings, the place really gave me that 'I can live here forever' feeling. I would rate it as one of Ethiopia's major attractions.

Just before sunset I took a walk on the paved walkway along the edge of the lake. A soft drizzle was coming down and, although I was walking alone, it felt very romantic. They were a surprising number of couples, especially from Germany, who had booked into the same hotel as I had. Seeing all these couples, as well as the locals, walking hand in hand along the edge of the lake, I could not but feel that, for all its advantages, travelling alone has severe limitations.

In Bahir Dar, as in most African cities and towns that I visited, the loud call to prayer from the mosque made it unnecessary to set an alarm clock. You really have to get used to the noise, which can be very irritating, especially if it is the first thing you hear in the morning.

It was another early start for me because, as in Zambia, Ethiopian buses were not allowed to travel at night and I had to reach my next destination before sunset. When I packed my bag I was still wondering whether it was a good idea not to spend another day in Bahir Dar. It was not yet light when I left the hotel, but Yishwas had assured me that crime was non-existent in Bahir Dar and so I had decided to walk the kilometre or so to the bus station. Actually I had no choice as there were no cabs outside the hotel and hardly any traffic on the road.

A handful of people were already walking in different directions at that early hour. I spotted two joggers doing what used to come naturally to me before I decided that the consumption of alcohol was an easier and better way to enjoy life than jogging. On the previous day, while shopping at the merkato, I had noticed that my foot was starting to bug me again. By the time I got to the bus station I was limping. Could it have been the wild dancing in Addis that, after all this time, had affected my Achilles tendon?

I had not expected so many people to be at the bus station so early in the morning. Not hawkers and people trying to sell their produce, as in Lilongwe, but people who were going somewhere else. A young guy who was going to take an Addis bus went out of his way to show me the bus to Gondar. Although it was 3 September 2005 according to the Gregorian calendar, it was the 29th day of the 12th month of the year 1997 according to my bus ticket.

Well, that ticket brought back good (and wild) memories. The year 1997 was a very good one for me. For starters, it was my second year working and I had already bought myself a flat and, at the beginning of the year, a car. When I turned 22, in June, I was convinced that I was going to be a playboy for the rest of my life. It's amazing how things change. At 30, I am no longer a playboy. I am just a boy who loves to play.

As we left the beautiful town of Bahir Dar, I could see people bathing in the lake just as the sun was rising. They were mostly men, but there were one or two women as well. That made me love Bahir Dar even more. It looked like paradise. I had thought I had seen green places before then, but Bahir Dar was the lushest, most verdant of them all. Whoever said the grass looks greener on the other side had obviously never lived in Bahir Dar. No place could be greener than this. To me, meanwhile, it looked as if the sun was rising in the west. I have always known and have made no secret of my lack of a sense of direction, confirmed once again by this new confusion.

There were quite a few hills on the winding road to Gondar and the seats in the bus were not the most comfortable. People would stand up now and then just to stretch their legs. I did not stand, not because I was comfortable but because I thought such an uncomfortable seat would be effective therapy for the flab on my bum.

On the way to Gondar we stopped at three permanent roadblocks. Unlike those on the Moyale–Shashamane road, these roadblocks were stop-and-go. The customs officials did not even get into the bus. It made me wonder why they bothered to be there at all.

To my surprise, we arrived within three and a half hours in Gondar, known as Africa's Camelot because of its abundance of monuments. As in Bahir Dar, the atmosphere was very relaxed. At the bus station I asked a youngster, who must have been about ten years old, for directions to the budget hotel I had found in my travel guide. He took me to a cab next to the bus rank because, according to him, the hotel was quite far off. Obviously, I had to tip him.

The taxi took me to the hotel, which was about one and a half kilometres from the bus station. As the cab pulled up at the hotel the youngster, who must have been running behind the cab, appeared from nowhere. When I asked what he wanted his answer, in fluent English, was: 'No, just nothing.' This young boy, whose name I learned was Doyt, remained at my elbow while I checked in and then followed me to my room. I am sure he knew that I would need him for one reason or another.

First of all, I had to find a restaurant since the hotel did not have an in-house restaurant. I explained to Doyt, who by then had become my shadow, that I needed a good restaurant. I felt like a real bimbo following a youngster who didn't bother to tell me when he was going to turn; he just did.

When we got to the restaurant I could not believe that Doyt had taken me on such a long walk to a mere shack. Surely, I thought, as a local he must know of better places. Not wanting to disappoint him, I walked in. I couldn't have been more surprised. The decor inside was world class: seats covered in cowhide, Ethiopian art on the walls and carvings galore. I was really impressed. In an instant I forgot that I was in what looked like a shack from the outside. I learned, again, that you must not judge a book by its cover.

Doyt was too shy to order initially, but I insisted. Although I had been helped by countless young people and had tipped almost all of them throughout the trip, this was the first time that I was having a meal with my guide (apart from when FK ate both his meal and mine in Moyale on the border). It seemed Doyt had a good appetite and he ordered a super-large lamb dish. I had spicy chicken curry.

As we were eating I was for some reason or other filled with contentment. You know those 'feel-good' moments that it takes months, years, decades even, for some people to feel again.

I couldn't judge whether Doyt was feeling the same contentment, but his stomach would no doubt have felt super satisfied. After helping me to buy a bus ticket to Mettema (Metema), which is on the Ethiopia/ Sudan border, Doyt accompanied me back to my hotel. When we entered the hotel premises, he stopped. I knew he had to go back to the bus station and look for more customers. I took his photo, shook hands and gave him a tip. As soon as he left, I felt a sudden sharp drop in emotional well-being. I thought to myself, Why must some kids have so much responsibility at such a young age? Why couldn't he be just a playful, irresponsible child? I really went on an emotional rollercoaster.

Only one thing was going to make me feel better. No, not alcohol but a cold shower. Truth be told, I had no choice. There was no warm water and no bar at the hotel.

Since it was a Sunday I could have gone to the merkato but I feared that after all these weeks on the road my female side was getting the better of me and would be tempted by buy some more stuff. I decided, instead, to visit the walled royal enclosure in the centre of town, with its connecting tunnels, raised walkways and six castles. The locals call the entire 70 000-square-metre complex after the most impressive of these, the castle of Fasilidas.

I found the richness of Ethiopia's history and the stories of the powerful kings and queens who reigned in the northern part of the country fascinating. It was intriguing why Emperor Fasilidas had chosen, in 1636, to build his castle in what must have been the middle of nowhere. By the time he died in 1667, however, Gondar had become the capital of his empire, and it remained the capital of Ethiopia for 250 years.

The two-storey castle with its three domed towers and two-metre-high fortified stone walls looked completely impenetrable. After touring the castle I repeated Resolution No. 10: to return to do Ethiopia's historical route – the ancient towns of Lalibela and Axum, and also Gondar. Athough I was right there, I did not have enough time to visit other 17th-century castles and palaces in Gondar (there are some out of town as well) or to view the fabulously decorated Debre Birhan Selassie ('trinity of the place of light') church, just a ten-minute walk from the city centre.

My plan for the next day was to travel from Gondar via Mettema to the border town of Galabat, in the hope of catching a bus there that would get me to Gedaref in Sudan before sunset. I went to bed thinking that the worst-case scenario would be to arrive too late in Mettema and thus not be able to catch the connecting bus from Galabat to Gedaref. To prevent this from happening meant my third early start in three consecutive days. On the previous two days I had travelled first from Addis to Bahir Dar, then from Bahir Dar to Gondar. One way or another, I knew that the next day was going to be my last in Ethiopia.

I left my hotel in the morning while it was still very dark and followed two ladies who looked as if they might also be heading for the bus station. Just one street before the station, there was Doyt waiting for me. Happy as I was to see him, I was saddened again by the heavy load of responsibility resting on a young kid like him who should have been at home in bed, asleep.

Ethiopians are real early risers. A crowd of people was already gathered outside the bus station, waiting for it to open. After about ten minutes the wire with which the gates were secured was loosened and for a moment I thought I would be trampled in the stampede that followed. Everyone wanted to be the first to go through. And that was just a practice run. Once we were through the gates the real struggle began. People on the left wanted to go to the right, those on the right wanted to go to the left. I was caught somewhere in the middle.

Given that my ticket was written in Amharic and that there was insufficient light, it proved to be far from easy to find the bus to Mettema. Doyt, luckily, was still shadowing me. Even with his Amharic, it was a major problem to locate the right bus. Everything was chaotic – buses and people rushing in different directions, all in a relatively small area. Most of the passengers, to judge by their tattered clothes, lived a nomadic life. They were certainly not city dwellers.

After being pointed left, right and left again, we finally found the white Mettema-bound bus. Whatever the reason, our bus seemed to be the worst in the rank. I chatted for a couple of minutes with Doyt, who had climbed into the bus with me to ensure that I found my seat. Travelling solo and not having a companion to talk to, I thought I had found a pal in Doyt. But after I gave him a tip for helping me, he stood up and left unceremoniously. I soon understood that to him I was just another customer.

In keeping with the law, we left town only at sunrise. Even before the bus left the rank, my seat had begun to feel uncomfortable.

On the outskirts of the town I noticed people standing in a very long queue. As the bus moved closer I saw that they were queuing at the Missionary Charity building, waiting for food rations. The length and snaking shape of that queue reminded me of South Africa's first democratic elections, even though the purpose of the two could not have been further apart.

We were one and a half hours into the journey when it was break-fast time. I had learned that in small towns like these along the way there was only one type of food on sale – injera. I did not even attempt to ask if there was anything else. I just stood around watching people enjoy their spongy, sour flatbreads.

Forty minutes later we were back on the road. Although I knew that there had been sporadic fighting on that route between Gondar and Mettema I did not expect such a strong military presence. There were no roadblocks, just soldiers guarding the road, so to speak. The road was even more winding than the one from Bahir Dar to Gondar. The landscape was pleasing to the eye, although not as green and moun-tainous as before.

Just outside the small town of Sishedi I saw a Western Cape-reg-istered vehicle with the number CCK 6173 parked outside the customs office. It bore the South African flag and Mbeki's and Mandela's faces on the sides of the vehicle. Without seeing the occupants, I knew they were white because we darkies, besides being obsessed with soccer and guzzling large volumes of alcohol, do not travel, and would never paste the faces of politicians – not even Madiba's – on our cars, and if we travelled would never travel like this through Africa.

After five and a half hours we arrived at the rural town of Mettema. Unlike other border towns I had been through, there were no has-slers in Mettema. People just carried on with their normal business. The Ethiopian immigration office was a hut tucked away from the road. After accepting my passport the official sitting on a low stool just inside the door said in an irritated tone of voice, 'Go sit outside.'

Well, that was another first for me. Normally, getting out of a coun-try was not a problem; the problem was getting in.

Mettema, which was founded in the 18th century, was once a rest-ing-place for pilgrims on their way to Mecca and back. Conveniently situated on the main trade route between the then capital Gondar and Sudan, it grew into an important trade centre over time and, in the 19th century, became a major marketplace and slave market. I did not see much of Mettema, but the old slave market in Zanzibar flashed through my mind as I sat outside the immigration office.

After ten minutes I was called back into the office and asked basic questions like where I had come from and where I was heading. After the official stamped my passport, he gave me an evaluation form. The first question on it was: *How will you rate the efficiency of my service?* My answer was simple: *The service was very efficient.*

The official was reading over my shoulder as I wrote my response. Talk about objective feedback.

Finally, I had to go through customs. A local guy showed me a khaki-clad customs official seated under a tree with a woman. The man searched my bag and asked if I had a camera. I said no because my camera was not in my bag but in the pocket of my trousers. By then I had figured out that they did not do body searches at borders. Why, I could not work out.

After that, it was only a short walk over the bridge and I was in the shantytown of Gallabat in Sudan.

The most beautiful women on the Cape to Cairo route are undoubtedly the exotic females in Addis Ababa. It must be their cosmopolitan looks.

Fatherless Sudan

A nation at war

The ancient kingdom of Nubia flourished in what is now northern Sudan, coming under Egyptian rule after 2600 BC. In more recent times, Egypt again conquered Sudan in 1874 and, after Britain occupied Egypt in 1898, the country was ruled by both Egypt and Britain. In effect a British colony, it was known until 1955 as Anglo-Egyptian Sudan.

Sudan became independent on 1 January 1956. Since then differences in language, religion, ethnicity and political power between the Arab north, the seat of government, and the black African animists and Christians in the south have erupted in unending civil war. Under John Garang de Mabior, the Sudan People's Liberation Army waged war for 20 years before a peace agreement was signed with the Khartoum government in 2005. The agreement granted Southern Sudan autonomy for six years, to be followed by a referendum. Sadly, Garang died in a mysterious air crash only 21 days after he was sworn in as Sudan's deputy president, as part of the power-sharing agreement. (I was in Zambia at the time.)

In the meantime, tribal clashes in the western region of Darfur marked the beginning of the Sudan–Chad conflict, the government of Chad having declared a state of war with Sudan in December 2005, accusing the Sudan government and militia of supporting Chadian rebels. (I was back home by then.)

Sudan is the largest country in Africa and the tenth largest country (in area) in the world. Since the military coup of 1989, President Omar Hassan Ahmad al-Bashir, a former paratrooper and minister of defence, has been in charge of the Khartoum government and the country.

There are three reasons why I hate crossing borders. One: having to exchange currency, especially when it means dealing with incutras who hassle you and, if you are not careful, may give you counterfeit money. Two: having to deal with bureaucracy, which ranges from filling in immigration forms to being asked endless questions by officials and having your bags searched. Three: having to communicate in another, totally different, language.

As soon as I had set foot in Sudanese territory an incutra approached me. I agreed to change 330 birr to Sudanese dinar (SDD). Based on my spending patterns, I had figured out that this would get me to Gedaref, about halfway to Khartoum, with about 400 kilometres still to go. Based on the birr-to-US dollar (US$1=9 birr approx.) as well as the dinar-to-US dollar exchange rate (US$1=SDD250 approx.), I had calculated the previous night how many dinars, on average, I was going to get for my Ethiopian birr. It turned out I was spot on. I was really mastering the art of dealing with incutras.

At Sudanese immigration I, like everybody else, had to leave my bag unattended outside the entrance. After filling in the form – from right to left again – I had to go to the cashier and pay SDD7 500. When I wanted to pay in US dollars the cashier called a youngster named David to take me across the road to what looked like a warehouse. There I exchanged US$100 with another incutra.

The rate was bad, but they knew that I was desperate. After I had paid the Sudanese dinars to the cashier, and handed in a photo, my passport was stamped. I then collected my bag and took it to the customs office. Although the queue there was very long, it was moving briskly because the official simply entered names on his list. Thank heaven, there was no searching of bags, which would have delayed the process by hours.

I thought I was clear of officialdom now, but David told me that I still had to go and register with security. About 50 metres from the customs office, hidden away from the main road, was a small security office with a corrugated-iron roof. Another form had to be filled out and handed in with another photo, plus a thumb print. Only then was I officially in Sudan.

At the security office I bumped into the white South African couple I had seen parked outside the Sishedi customs offices. They hailed from the Western Cape, as I had concluded earlier from their registration number, and were also doing the Cape to Cairo. More information than that they did not seem eager to share. Although I did not expect them to hug me or anything like that, it would have been nice to chat to other people from Mzansi so far from home. Meeting compatriots at a border post in Sudan, especially when you have been travelling on your own by public transport, was quite an emotional affair for me. After all, the last time I had met South Africans had been at Lake Malawi, more than a month ago.

Exiting Ethiopia and entering Sudan took me a total of one and a half hours. It was exciting to think that I was going to make the Gondar–Gedaref trip in one day and even the fact that I was going to do so in the back of an old battered bakkie which David led me to – called a 'boksie' by the locals – could not dampen my spirits.

I waited under a tree for the other boksie passengers. David and some locals were very nice to me but we could not communicate properly with one another because of the language problem. Basically they spoke only Arabic. One guy succeeded in asking me, through David, how much I had paid for my hiking boots. When I told him they cost slightly more than us$100 he almost fainted. That was the end of the conversation.

The Western Cape couple left me sitting under the tree with about ten Sudanese guys. Seeing white people drive by in a comfortable 4x4 while I was waiting for unreliable public transport reminded me of back home. Involuntarily I started thinking about how much things could have changed since we started living under a new dispensation, and how superficial the changes have been.

Yet, under that tree I had another of those feel-good moments, as on the previous day. There is something about sitting under a tree that makes me feel one with nature. That moment reminded me of the shower of rain at the spice plantation in Zanzibar.

After an hour and a half of waiting, enough luggage and people had accumulated for the boksie to set off on the gravel road to Gedaref.

It did not feel that long because David and his gang kept me entertained by discussing and describing beautiful Ethiopian women.

The passengers on the boksie turned out to be the same people as on the Gondar–Mettema bus. Instead of turning left and heading to Gedaref as I expected, the boksie turned right and headed straight back to the immigration offices. An immigration officer came out of the building and we all had to get off the vehicle and have our passports checked against the boksie driver's passenger list. Only then were we allowed to proceed.

Just when I thought we were finally on our way, we stopped at the customs offices and the same procedure was repeated. The same at a military checkpoint within a kilometre of Gallabat. Thus, in less than 30 minutes, we had gone through three checks: immigration, customs and military – only the first taste of Sudan's bureaucracy. I was not too worried despite all these delays because I could see from the map that Gedaref was not very far from Gallabat. According to David, only about 160 kilometres away.

From the back of the boksie the vegetation looked much the same as in northern Ethiopia – bright green grass and healthy shrubs. Judging by the soft look of the soil, it was the rainy season. What amazed me was how flat Sudan was, unlike the undulating hills in northern Ethiopia, especially from Bahir Dar to Gondar. While the boksie was struggling on through dongas and big potholes in the gravel road I sent my eyes across kilometres of vast plains.

There were 11 of us seated on top of our bags in the back of the boksie: seven Ethiopians, two Sudanese guys and one Sudanese girl. It made me think of 'Scatterlings of Africa', that classic song by Sipho Mchunu and Johnny Clegg's band Juluka, which revels in the fact that everyone –'both you and I' as the lyrics say – originated from Africa and then scattered to all the corners of the globe. There we were, born in different countries and of different backgrounds, brought together by circumstances, sitting in the back of a boksie under a dark African sky, trying to make the best of what life was throwing at us.

None of my fellow passengers could understand why I was doing this trip. One of the Ethiopians even thought I was an ambassador, though I still have to see an ambassador who takes a ride in the back of a boksie.

The Ethiopians were on their way to Khartoum to apply for a UK visa, which they told me was easier to get in Khartoum than in Addis. I wondered what had happened to my Somalian friend who had gone to Addis on a similar mission, believing it was easier there than anywhere else in the region.

Within an hour of leaving Gallabat we were again stopped by the military. This time it was not just for checking passports, but also for registration of particulars such as name, profession, where from, where to, for how long, etc. All this information was scribbled on a piece of paper. It was a very time-consuming affair because most of the soldiers spoke Arabic and little Amharic and most of the Ethiopians spoke Amharic and little Arabic, if any. My own situation – speaking neither Arabic nor Amharic – was worse, and even more difficult was an explanation of why was I doing the trip. I mumbled something like 'Africa very beautiful continent. Me just want to see.' My mumblings helped.

As the light mellowed we happened upon another registration point. The registration stations were beginning to grind on my nerves. Time and again we had to get off the vehicle and stand in a queue while giving our particulars to an Arabic-speaking soldier. Most frustrating was that I could see that these so-called registrations were not adding any value to anything. It was not as if they were punching our information into a live information technology system and would thus be able to track us if we ever got to Khartoum. No, the soldier was just scribbling our names on a piece of paper.

As if the registration stations were not enough of a pain, there was this Ethiopian guy who kept nudging me and saying, 'Speak, Mr South Africa, speak' whenever the boksie was back on the road. Initially it was nice being called Mr South Africa, but after a while it, too, started to irritate me, the nudging in particular. The other Ethiopians spoke little or no English. They spent most of their time pointing at me while chatting in Amharic. Although I could not tell what they were saying, I knew they were talking about me and, given their broad smiles, it was something good.

It was just before sunset and young boys were leading livestock home. Loads and loads of cattle. It amazed me how much livestock the Sudanese owned. Suddenly I remembered that I had left Richard Carlson's book *You Can Be Happy No Matter What* under the tree in Gallabat. I took that as a sign, firstly, that from that moment onwards I was not going to need a book telling me to be happy no matter what. Secondly, I felt that somebody who was going through a bad patch would find that book and, hopefully, it would put things in perspective in his/her life too.

A few kilometres after the third registration point, the boksie's front-right tyre burst. I didn't consider it such a big problem until I saw the spare tyre had a big slash in it and virtually no thread. Obviously it had a tube, but, considering the size of the slash and the condition of the road, it was a disturbing sight.

The sun was setting, lending urgency to the situation, but in no time we were on our way again. The Ethiopians, a bunch of really nice and friendly people, offered me biscuits and cracked wheat to eat. I had not eaten anything all day, so everything, as long as it was not injera, was welcome.

By the time we had stopped for our third – or was it fourth? – corrugated-iron registration shack, the surface of the road had started to improve. By then it was already dark, so each person who was being registered had to hold a torch for the registering official. Quite a tricky thing to do because when the official looked at your passport you had to shine the torch on the passport, and when he wrote you had to shine the light on the paper. It was even more tricky when he wanted to compare the photo on the passport with the real person. He would hold and turn your hand around to shine that bright, blinding light on your face.

No sooner were we settled back in the boksie than it started to rain. The problem for me was not so much the rain but the lightning and thunder. The sky rumbled and flashed and crackled and lit up. It made me feel unpleasantly exposed and helpless. Soon thereafter the heavens really opened up. It poured. I was getting soaking wet. The same Ethiopian guy who had been nudging me and saying, 'Speak, Mr South

Africa, speak' looked at me and said, 'This is good history,' while laughing hysterically. At this all the Ethiopians started laughing. I began to
see that, whereas for me it was an exceptional situation, for them it
was just another day. For two hours I had to sit shamefaced, the butt of
those guys' good-natured laughter. Meanwhile, it became clear to me
why – apart from the bad road, three or four registration points and
rainy weather – it had taken us almost six hours to cover less than 200
kilometres: the boksie was one-eyed.

From what I could see of it through the pouring rain, Gedaref was
a spread-out town. The boksie dropped us at a guesthouse and we
all rushed for cover, only to be confronted by a verandah full of occupied single beds. Most of the people, mainly women, were already in
dreamland.

After an exchange in Amharic the Ethiopian guys followed one of
the local women to another guesthouse. I ran after them. By then it
was really bucketing down and my backpack was getting heavier and
heavier. Trying to run with a heavy backpack on a slippery and muddy
surface is not everyone's cup of coffee. It certainly wasn't mine.

The other guesthouse consisted of three mud huts. We were given
two huts in which to sort ourselves out. Two kids, aged approximately
two and four, were woken up and told to go to another hut. At this
juncture the Ethiopians, who really seemed to like their injera asked
our host to make them some. He was still trying to light the fire when
I decided I had had enough. It was time to go to sleep – on a bed
that I was going to have to share with another guy. The bed boasted
a mosquito net. I was not too worried about suffocating from the
smoke from the fire because our hut had a permanently open door
(read 'no door').

I had a good night's sleep. It must have been the smoke from the
fire. I never even noticed when the others retired and my bed companion joined me on the worn-out mattress. On waking, however, I realised that not only had I shared the hut with five humans but that the
floor was crawling with earthworms as well. Thank God, I saw them
only in the morning or I would not have slept a wink.

That morning was my fourth early morning in a row, but I didn't mind because I was well on my way to Sudan's capital city, Khartoum. Another boksie picked all of us up at our guesthouse and took us to the bus rank, to continue the journey. Now that it was daylight, I could see that Gedaref was not such a small town after all. At the bus rank we got into a luxurious bus that was going all the way to Khartoum. Maybe my judgement was clouded; I suppose that after six hours on a boksie anything would look and feel luxurious.

At sunrise, just when I thought we were leaving, we were all asked to go and register at an office near the bus station. Given the large number of people who had to register, the process took two hours and, after leaving the town, we were stopped and checked several times again along the way. Something you should probably expect in a country that has been embroiled in prolonged civil war and ruled by military regimes for half a century.

Each time, the passports of all foreigners, who constituted about 80 per cent of the total number of passengers, had to be collected by the driver's assistant. The assistant would take our passports to a particular office and within a few minutes we would be on our way again.

Two hours after leaving Gedaref we stopped for breakfast – in Ethiopia, injera; in Sudan, a bean burger which was just a big bun stuffed with beans. Since I had been told that Khartoum was only three hours from Gedaref I thought I would wait to eat until we arrived there.

The road from Gedaref to Khartoum was the exact opposite of what we had experienced the previous day. It was tarred and we were now travelling in what appeared to be a desert: nothing but sand. Everything looked different, including the Arabic-speaking pitch-black men wearing long, white dresses, some of them passengers on the bus and some walking along the road. It was very hot, but at least our bus was air-conditioned.

Five hours after leaving Gedaref we did indeed arrive at the hot, dry and dusty city of Khartoum, located at the point where the White Nile, flowing north from Uganda, meets the Blue Nile, flowing west from Ethiopia. I couldn't see the resemblance, but in Arabic al-Khartoum means 'elephant trunk'. It was here that the Confederation of African

Football (CAF) was founded in 1957, the year after Sudan's independence. Ironically, Sudan's national football team has always been, and still remains, one of the weakest teams in Africa.

Because of the chaos at the bus station as people tried to locate their luggage, I could not get a group photo taken with my Ethiopian friends, as we had agreed the previous night in Gedaref. Under a scorching sun, with taxi touts screaming, people welcoming their friends and relatives and at the same time making sure that their bags were not taken by someone else, the Ethiopian guys disappeared before I knew it. The heat was excruciating, normally 40 degrees in the shade (of which there was not much) at that time of year. Just sitting in a cab on my way to a hotel was making me sweat.

Finding accommodation in Khartoum can be quite difficult because most signs are in Arabic. I was relieved when I eventually found a budget hotel, but when I stepped into my room I was so disappointed that I immediately went back to reception and asked for a refund. No questions were asked, so I did not have to explain that the bed was too small, with a hollow mattress and no bedding to talk of, and that both lights and air-conditioner were not working and, to crown it all, the walls and floors looked as if at least one pig spent at least one day per week in that room. I moved to the hotel next door.

The second hotel was only slightly better but much more expensive. The accommodation was definitely not worth the price, but I thought it would be easier to sleep there for one night and then try to find a better place the following day.

I had not checked emails for a number of days, so I decided to use the facility down the road from the hotel to find out how everyone was doing. In my disappointment with Khartoum I was thinking things could not get much worse, but then I opened an email from my fiancée informing me that she had resigned from her job because 'it was a job from hell'. That meant that, at the end of that month, both of us would be unemployed. Good news for people with a 20-month-old baby. Talk about family planning.

It got worse. There was another email from my fiancée. She was questioning me about a certain SMS she had found on my cellphone.

I had given her my cellphone when I left but had taken out the sim card. What I did not know was that cellphones sometimes store sent messages on their hard drive. I had to do some quick damage control over the internet.

When I am drunk I have this really bad habit of flirting with women. You know, typical man with an ego that has to be stroked all the time? There are some women that you SMS or phone only when you are motherlessly drunk. This was one of those SMS's.

Between a depressing hotel and a disappointed fiancée that night, there was no way I could enjoy my dinner although I was ravenously hungry. Back at the hotel I flushed the toilet and seepage appeared between the toilet bowl and the floor. Luckily, I had only pissed. I knew I had no choice but to find better accommodation, fast.

Before setting out to look for a hotel the next morning, I thought I would register – in keeping with the law, which required that, as a foreigner, you register within three days of arriving in Khartoum. On my way to the Aliens Registration Office I noticed the Dubai Hotel and thought I would enquire about their rates. At reception, a black gentleman told me that the hotel catered for the Chinese community only. As he told me that, I looked around and saw a Chinese family having what looked like a gourmet breakfast. I could not believe that in Africa I was unable to get a room because of my nationality and/or race.

Another bright idea was born in my mind – Business Idea Four: I should open the Bunjumbura Hotel in New York, or the Lubumbashi Hotel in London, for Africans only. How possible was that? I began to think that people were correct in saying that the Chinese are Africa's new colonisers.

I proceeded to the Aliens Registration Office because I was sure the process would not take long. The officer at the door to the office, which was on the second floor of an old but recently painted white building, had to fill in the form on my behalf because everything was written in Arabic. Once inside, I was told by a tall man in a blue uniform that the form needed to be signed and stamped at my hotel. I could not believe that I had to limp (my Achilles tendon was starting to act up again) all the way back to my scruffy hotel. To make things worse, the heat must have been above 40 degrees.

After checking in at another hotel, which was even more expensive but at least had an effective air-conditioner, TV and a clean bathroom, I got my form signed and stamped. It looked as if hotels were under clear instructions to check the passports and visas of their guests. Happy that all formalities were done, I walked briskly back to the Aliens Registration Office. Where the real bureaucracy started:

1. My completed form, photo and passport were taken to the back office.
2. After ten minutes I was called to the counter to collect the form from another counter.
3. More forms were filled in by other officials in blue uniforms.
4. The completed forms were transferred to an officer who put them in a folder.
5. Another officer stapled everything neatly into the folder.
6. Another officer then gave the folder a reference number.
7. I was then asked to pay at the cashier's desk.
8. Still more forms were filled in by an official at another counter.
9. I was instructed to take a seat while the entire folder was taken to the back office.

It was while waiting for my passport to be returned that I noticed that some registrations were handled by agents. I got talking to one of them, Ahmed Elsadig Ahmed – a strange name for a pitch-black man. He explained to me that the big chain hotels took care of their guests' registration. Since I was not staying at a top-end hotel, I did not enjoy that service.

Sitting on a hard bench, mesmerised by this merry-go-round, I noticed that the registration office doubled as police headquarters. The officials handling alien registrations were, in fact, policemen in blue uniforms. The thought of not registering had crossed my mind earlier. When I asked Ahmed whether the authorities would have found out, he told me that after registration my passport would carry a sticker and stamp that officials would look for when I left the country. Without that sticker and stamp, irrespective where you were, you would be asked to go back and register. By then there would be a fine because, in all probability, you would have stayed for more than three days without registering.

In just under four hours I had finished registering and I was officially in Khartoum. I had one more registration to do though: to register my camera at the Ministry of the Interior. That, I thought, could wait for the following day.

I was dreading checking my emails again. As expected, there was a long email from my fiancée about disappointment, trust, love, the future – you know, the same old story. A few days earlier, before I lost it, I had read in Richard Carlson's book that couples spend a lot of time fighting over trivial issues until tragedy strikes – the death of a child, for example, or if one partner is diagnosed with a terminal disease. That kind of tragedy makes people see things in perspective.

It was while staring at the computer screen that I decided to tell my fiancée about a terrible thing that had happened to me the previous night: I was knocked down by a bus. In Sudan, unlike us in South Africa, they drive on the wrong side of the road: the right side. As a result, I had looked on the wrong side before crossing. I had been to the local clinic, where they bandaged my left hand and knee.

I knew that fabricating this story was a risk because my fiancée might become suspicious about the sequence of events – a domestic squabble and, all of a sudden, I have an accident. But it was a risk worth taking.

Back in my hotel room, I had to monitor developments in Egypt, which was holding its first contested presidential elections. With the price I was paying for the hotel came channel television and I could tune in to CNN. Hosni Mubarak, who had been president for 24 years, was definitely going to win. These were the first multi-candidate presidential elections since he was elected in 1981. Hitherto, he had secured his position by having himself nominated by Parliament and then holding a referendum to confirm his nomination. I was interested to see how the Egyptians were going to react to Mubarak's fifth term in office.

As expected, Mubarak won by an overwhelming majority. There were isolated cases of protests by daredevils who dared to challenge him, but within a day or two the Egyptian police had squashed all the riots.

Naturally I was nervous but eager to check my emails next morning. When I checked my inbox I found that my fiancée had sent me five messages in 12 hours. My plan had worked like a bomb! As I had hoped, the focus had changed completely: she reminded me how much she loved me and even suggested that, maybe, I should fly back to Johannesburg as soon as possible. That was good news, for me at least. I could concentrate on the trip again.

Not quite. I read in another email that my niece Nontetho (it was she who had given me Richard Carlson's book) had suffered a mild stroke. We darkies, generally speaking, do not believe in a stroke as a medical condition. More often than not we see it as part of being bewitched. Hence, when someone suffers from a stroke we often say *'izinto zabantu'* – she has been bewitched. I was not surprised, therefore, when in the same email I learned that she would be taken that weekend to *ukhokhovu* – a traditional healer with really strong, effective, guaranteed, come-back-for-more-at-no-extra-charge-if-you-are-not-healed muti.

I fully endorsed that decision because it was baffling to me how an energetic 24-year-old party-animal who was always full of life could suffer a stroke. After I got back to South Africa, however, I learned that Nontetho was addicted to drugs, mainly cocaine and crack, which had caused a nervous collapse that seemed like a stroke. She was subsequently admitted into rehabilitation for a whole month and within six months of her release, she resigned from her job, and then fell pregnant too. It does not stop, hey.

With my domestic squabbles sorted out, at least in the short term, it was time to register my camera at the Ministry of the Interior. I had a rough idea where it was, but the armed guard outside the building that I thought housed the ministry didn't have a clue what I was talking about when I enquired.

A few metres down the road I asked another armed guard, even showing him my camera. His response was simple: 'I am just a policeman.'

That was it. I was not going to trouble myself further by looking for a camera registration office. Instead, I decided to take a scenic walk to the White Nile bridge and started out along the Nile road which for three and a half kilometres runs parallel to the river.

Being such a bargain hunter, I decided that I would, when passing a grand hotel, pop in to find out its rates. The first of a string of fancy hotels was called the Sudan Hotel. I was surprised when the guard prohibited me from entering the hotel's main entrance, telling me firmly, 'This hotel caters for the Chinese community only.'

I burst out laughing in disbelief. This was the second hotel in the same city that catered for Chinese only. It is often said that women have men by their balls. It seemed to me that the Chinese had the Sudanese government by the balls for it to allow such a practice.

I walked past other beautiful hotels, but by then I was not interested in being turned away by more For-Chinese-Only hotels. I carried on walking past the National Museum and the al-Mogran Family Park, an amusement park on the pie slice of land where the White Nile and Blue Nile meet. It was too hot to bother visiting either of the two attractions. It was so hot, in fact, it made me wonder how many Sudanese annually die of heat stroke/heat exhaustion – which could also be described as bewitchment or *izinto zabantu*.

Owing to what looked like road upgrading, traffic on the White Nile bridge was being redirected to the new bridge just south of it. There was a strong military presence in the area. As I walked towards the centre of the new bridge some men who were working on it came to me and said, 'You same as Okocha', referring to JJ Okocha, the former Nigerian captain and then Bolton Wanderers player, who also used to have his hair plaited. Being a mediocre soccer player I felt happy to be compared to one of the players who was holding high the African flag in Europe.

A few moments later I stood facing the view I had always wanted to see: the merging of the Blue Nile, whose source lies in Lake Tana in

Ethiopia (which I had visited) and the White Nile, which starts in Lake Victoria in Uganda and which John Hanning Speke claimed to have discovered in 1863. On the very day he was to defend his case against Sir Richard Burton, leader of the two expeditions to find the source of the Nile of which Speke was a member, Speke accidentally shot himself while shooting partridges.

The confluence of the two Niles was a breathtaking sight. I could see water of two colours, side by side, before the actual merging downstream into the Nile proper. Actually you do not have blue water on the right and white water on the left. What you see is very muddy water on the right and not very clear water on the left. But it still looked magnificent, especially from the bridge, which is high above the water and offers an uninterrupted view of the confluence. Standing before such a phenomenon you cannot help but feel that there is a God above or a supernatural power at work somewhere.

From their source, the Blue Nile and White Nile flow for about 1 600 and 3 700 kilometres, respectively, before meeting in Khartoum. From there the Nile flows almost another 3 000 kilometres northwards – the longest river on earth. From Khartoum it follows a winding course across the desert and, after Cairo and just before reaching the Mediterranean Sea, it separates into three branches to form the Nile Delta.

It's a pity I could not take pictures of this exceptional natural phenomenon, but I didn't dare. I had read stories of people getting arrested in Sudan, even though they had photo permits, for taking photos of bridges, slums, or anything that was considered a security risk or might paint a bad image of the country in the outside world. I did not even have a photo permit and the last thing I wanted to do was to visit, even for an hour, one of Khartoum's prisons.

After spending a while on the bridge I walked to Omdurman, which looked more modern than Khartoum itself. It was only then that I understood why Khartoum is called a three-in-one city – a 'Tripartite Capital'. On the southern bank of the Blue Nile and to the east of the White Nile lies Khartoum proper; north of the Blue Nile is Khartoum North, which was originally established as a railway terminus and river port (one of Sudan's largest oil refineries is located there, along with other industries); and on the west bank of the merged Nile lies Omdurman, the most popular of the three and throbbing with traditional markets and informal social life. It also happens to be the largest city in Sudan and the country's commercial centre.

I didn't walk as far as Omdurman, but I heard that the handicrafts *souq* (market) was enormous. I couldn't face getting lost in that heat, which would inevitably have happened.

Well, it was time to head back, on foot. To show respect to local Muslim culture, which prohibits the showing of flesh and skin, I did not wear shorts, even though it was a scorching day and I was sweating like a pig (not a good metaphor in a Muslim country). But it felt good to get a bit of exercise.

As I walked back to my hotel I was struck by all the development taking place in and around the area where the Blue Nile and White Nile meet. Many construction and earthmoving vehicles were parked on building sites and lots of scaffolding was either being put up or was up already. I was convinced that Khartoum – where there were no signs of war – was a city marching into the future.

It was a long way back to my hotel. It took me over two hours to cover the same three and a half kilometres along the Nile. Not bad for someone with a snapped Achilles tendon and a two-centimetre built-up right shoe who was suffering from extreme heat.

The next day was Friday, which in Khartoum is like Sunday in a staunchly Christian country. Khartoum becomes a ghost town: almost all businesses are closed and there is only a handful of people on the streets. There was not much to do except to go back to Omdurman and watch wrestling, a solid Nubian tradition. Since I hate wrestling I was not going to pretend, now that I was in Sudan, that I loved it. In fact, I have always believed that wrestling, like rugby, is for men who would never dream of doing anything like skydiving but are desperately trying to prove something to themselves.

I spent most of the day in my hotel room taking some time out. Lying on the bed and looking at a map of Africa, it felt good to see not only how much distance I had already covered but also that Cairo was just up the road. Practically.

Since Sudanese currency was very confusing for me I used that lei-
sure time to try to master it. On average, us$1 equals sDD250. Therefore,
anything above us$4 would cost over a thousand dinars. As in Zambia,
Zimbabwe and Tanzania, almost everything was quoted in thousands.
What compounded the problem in Sudan was that the locals still
quoted prices in Sudanese pounds (S£), one Sudanese dinar equalling
ten Sudanese pounds.

For instance, a cab driver would quote you S£30 000 when he meant
sDD3 000. More often than not I was told the price in pounds but paid
in dinars, pounds being no longer in circulation. The Sudanese pound
was replaced by the Sudanese dinar in 1992 and, as I recently discovered, was officially reintroduced as the currency of Southern Sudan in
January 2007. So, how about this scenario: sDD1=S£10 (original) but
S£1 (new)=sDD100. Therefore, if you can do sums, you will conclude
that S£1=S£1 000. If you happen to visit Sudan, please, *asseblief, ngi-
yakucela,* bring a calculator.

On another note (excuse the pun), Sudanese men are known to
have the longest middle leg in Africa. Obviously if they are indeed
African champions, it goes without saying that they are world champions too. It made me think of one of my handful of ex-girlfriends who
I knew would have been thrilled to visit Sudan. In general, however,
most women get involved in a relationship because they are focused on
one thing: marriage. Men, on the other hand, become involved in relationships for one thing and one thing only: sex. After a while a woman
will start asking herself, What type of a husband will this guy be?
A man will just be thinking of one thing: Is she still a great lay?

All my ex-girlfriends had one quirk in common – they would wake
me up in the middle of the night to ask, 'Where is this relationship going?' 'How am I supposed to know, I'm sleeping' was my usual answer.
A few days later the relationship would simply crumble.

Thinking about Sudanese men being better endowed than their
South African counterparts made me – for the first time – not feel good
about being a South African male. Not that it mattered much right
then. There were no beautiful women in Khartoum, at least that I could
see, because if you did see a woman, she was usually covered from top

to toe. But even if there were any I would not have tried my luck. Given what those women are used to.

Tickets for the weekly train from Khartoum to Wadi Halfa, Sudan's inland port on the Nile, are sold only two days in advance of your journey. Since I did not know how much demand there would be for train tickets, it was imperative for me to go to the train station early. In Dar es Salaam I complained that the bus station was as far from the city centre as the airport; in Khartoum it was the other way around. Passenger trains departed from Khartoum North while the airport was on the periphery of the city centre. To kill time I decided to tackle the three kilometres to the train station on foot. Because Friday had been a rest day, Saturday felt like Monday.

This time I was walking along the scenic Nile road in the opposite direction. As to be expected, most government ministries, including the Ministry of Council of Ministers (yes, that is what they called it) and the Presidential Palace, are located on the Nile road. I crossed the Blue Nile on the Blue Nile bridge, which separates Khartoum North from the city centre. The traffic on the bridge – one-way only – was heavy, with hundreds of people travelling to the city centre from the northern part of the city in cars and a few buses to snarl up the traffic even more. The terrible congestion reminded me of one of the reasons why I had (temporarily) left the corporate world. As on the White Nile bridge, there was a strong military presence – not that the populace seemed to react in any way to the men in uniform.

The queue at the train station consisted of seven people only and things were a lot better organised than at the station at Victoria Falls in Zimbabwe. The queue moved smoothly. Before leaving the hotel I had asked the receptionist to write my request for a train ticket (first class) from Khartoum to Wadi Halfa, and a ferry ticket from Wadi Halfa to the port of Aswan in Egypt, in Arabic on a piece of paper. When I presented the paper to the lady at the ticket counter, she wrote *SDD14 000* – which was exactly the amount of money I had budgeted for. Although it felt very strange that they would sell both ferry and train tickets from the same office, I was sure from the number of papers (read 'tickets')

I was handed that I had both tickets. In fact, there was a photo of a ferry on the biggest piece of paper.

After dawdling around the station, the tickets safely deposited in the side pocket of my cargo pants, I decided to explore the streets nearby. It was then that I observed for myself that Khartoum is built on/in a desert that stretches northwards as far as the eye can see, and beyond. I knew that the North was an arid desert, plagued by dust storms and suffering from a shortage of drinkable water, unlike the South with its tropical climate, but somehow I didn't expect to see desert sand seeping up into the suburbs.

Just after midday I decided to walk back to the city centre. As I crossed the bridge – the same Blue Nile bridge – something looked different: the one-way traffic was now flowing in the opposite direction, from the city centre to Khartoum North. Back at the hotel the waiter explained to me that everyone was used to this way of doing things. People used the bridge to travel from home to work in the mornings, at that time one-way in the direction of the city centre; in the afternoons they used the same bridge, one-way after 12:00 in the other direction, to return home. Traffic officials monitored the situation, he assured me, reminding me that there was a permanently two-way bridge, further east.

While crossing the bridge I could not let a good photo opportunity pass me by again. Although I could see police at the other end, I took out my camera and started clicking away as I was walking, hiding the camera inside my *Lonely Planet – Africa on a Shoestring*. I knew I was taking a huge risk; it could look like espionage. When I walked past the police I greeted them. It was only then that I realised that they were unlikely to have seen me taking photos; they were all busy reading newspapers. From back to front, left to right.

I was starting to love Khartoum. The only thing I could not get used to was the heat. It was so hot and dry that all I wanted to do was spend my time in my air-conditioned room. It being my last full day in Khartoum, I was tempted to go to see the merging of the Blue and White Nile again but was discouraged by the heat. Instead, it being Sunday, I thought I would surf the Net and find out what was cooking back home.

I was totally shocked to read that Gabriel Siyabonga Ndabandaba, one of the few black pilots in South Africa, had died in an air crash on 10 September during an aerobatic display at an airshow at Vereeniging near Johannesburg. Although I had never met him personally, the fact that he had piloted the fighter jet that flew over the Union Buildings during President Mbeki's inauguration and was a first officer in our national airline, meant he was living my dream. People like him who manage to overcome trying circumstances really motivate me.

The death of a person is always a tragic event, but if we accept death not as the end of life but as an end to the experience-gathering stage in our spiritual journey, I cannot think of a better way to die than while doing something you have a passion for. Gabriel took part in a sport that is by its nature risky, but it is those very risks, I have discovered, that attract people to adrenalin sports. He had a short but intense life, unlike most people, who live long and boring lives or even short and boring lives. People who die never having taken risks in their lifetime have never truly been alive.

Gabriel, because he lived, qualified to die.

> Thanks for being an inspiration, Gabriel, *mfowethu*,
> thanks for making us proud,
> thanks for being one of a kind.
> Hey, keep flying,
> fly even higher,
> soar like a bird.
> Flap those wings,
> make those holes in the sky,
> blue skies ...
> *Ngiyabonga, Siyabonga.*

Gabriel's death reminded me of something that used to worry me during my skydiving days: if I were to die while skydiving, white people would turn around and say I could not do it because I was black; and black people would turn around and say it served me right because I was a coconut who was trying too hard to be white.

It's not easy being black. Nor is it easy to be white: white people are for ever worrying about whether they will, again, receive above-average returns on their investments.

The day to leave Khartoum had finally arrived. I got to the station just as the train for Wadi Halfa was pulling in. Since the train is the best way of travelling in northern Sudan, I was not surprised to see so many people waiting on the platform.

As all the writing on my ticket was in Arabic, I asked the security guard for assistance. When I handed him the pile of papers I had been issued two days earlier he asked nonchalantly, 'Where is your train ticket?'

Thinking there was something wrong with him, I went to another guard and showed him my papers. He replied, 'No, my friend, this is a ferry ticket together with a meal and drink voucher.'

I almost fainted.

'So where can I buy a ticket?' I asked, pretending to be calm.

The man told me to follow him to the ticket office. By then the train had started to blow its whistle. I was cursing myself for having been so stupid and thoughtless. I knew I was supposed to double-check every-thing. I could not even start contemplating the possibility of spending another week in Khartoum. The worst was that I was running out of cash and in Khartoum there is only one way of settling your bills – with cash. If I end up with grey hair before turning 40, it'll be because of that moment in Khartoum. I was so mad at myself. I was a nervous wreck.

Five minutes later the ticket officer pitched up and issued me a first-class ticket. All this time I was standing, hoping that – by some miracle – if I remained standing in the office and did not sit down the train would not leave.

When I eventually found the right wagon, five other gentlemen had already occupied five of the six seats in the small compartment I was to share with them: three on one side, two on the other. I more or less collapsed into the only free seat.

It turned out that three of the men were also going to Cairo.

As the train pulled away from the platform the unthinkable happen-ed: many people, especially women, started crying. Those on the train as well as those on the platform were weeping uncontrollably. Being emotional when leaving your loved ones is fine. Having tears roll down your cheeks is also acceptable. But, in my book, lamenting so loudly when parting, as if someone has died, is totally unacceptable. To my great relief the crying subsided a few minutes after the train had left the station.

About an hour from Khartoum the train stopped for no apparent reason. People disembarked and started eating their rolls, eggs and other *padkos* or what we call *umphako* in Zulu. It must be breakfast time, I thought. After half an hour, just out of curiosity I asked one of the guys I was sharing a compartment with when the train was going to start moving again.

'This train is no good,' was his reply.

It seemed that the train's diesel tank was leaking. The driver was talking on a citizen-band (CB) radio, so I assumed we would be on our way in no time. Two hours went by without anything happening and, just to pass the time, I decided to see how far I could walk on the railway track without losing balance. I was bored stiff.

It amazed me that the Sudanese men did not think twice about stretching out on the sand in their white jalabiyas, just lying there relaxing. Time passed excruciatingly slowly. After midday the temperature started to climb even higher and still nothing happened. Since we were more or less stuck in the middle of the desert, the sand was getting uncomfortably hot and so was the train. Everyone looked relaxed. I seemed to be the only one who was worried.

I was under the impression that we were waiting for a repair man to arrive, but I discovered – five hours later – we had been waiting for another locomotive. Since the other locomotive came from behind, and as there was only one line, we had to be pulled back to Badaru on the outskirts of Khartoum. The unhooking of the faulty locomotive and the hooking up of a (hopefully) reliable locomotive took another hour. As we were about to leave another problem was discovered: the air-compression (braking) system of some wagons was not working. That took almost another hour to fix.

More than eight hours later we left Khartoum for the second time.

Although we had been delayed for such a long time, it felt good to be taking a ride on a train. There is something extremely relaxing and soothing about a train journey. As you pass through different places you feel as if you are part of the environment – unlike travel by car, not to mention flying.

In no time it began to get dark. Instead of remaining in the crammed compartment, I decided to sit on the steps of the wagon and enjoy the wind on my face. Sitting out there that night as the train gently headed north, I felt I was truly living my dream of travelling through different countries on my own, although at times under very difficult conditions. Northern Sudan may be a desert; at that moment it felt like a dust-borne dream.

It turned out to be a very long, hot, dry and dust-filled night. Imagine dust settling on your wet and sweaty skin, clogging your pores, creeping up your nostrils. That was exactly what was happening.

After midnight I returned to my compartment, only to find one of the men sleeping on the floor between the seats. I had to squeeze my self in between two of the others who were slumped in their seats, one of them snoring as if there were no tomorrow. The noise was hard to take. But the worst part for me was the sand dust. It was unbearable.

Fairly early the following morning the train stopped at a small station for the passengers to enjoy a breakfast of bean burgers. For more than 24 hours I had not consumed anything other than five litres of water I had bought in Khartoum. And dust. I did not feel like eating. At least, not bean burgers.

Except for that long break, we spent the day in the train, stopping only to pick up passengers who would have been waiting for eight hours and more at small stations in a desert with no sign of life. Throughout the entire day I drank cup after cup of very sweet tea offered to me by the other five passengers sharing the compartment with me. I had little choice: Sudanese do not take no for an answer when they offer you something.

The railway line ran parallel to the Nile for many kilometres. Here, the waters of the Nile were not choppy and dirty but calm and clean, sliding gently north to the Mediterranean. It was ironic to see the old train running parallel to the magnificent river. When I raised my eyes and looked beyond the water, all I could see was an endless desert. It was a splendid sight: a vast wide river cutting through and bringing life to otherwise uninhabitable terrain. I could not help but think of the business potential in running luxury trains in that part of Sudan, and I would not be surprised if the Chinese, in the foreseeable future, end up doing just that. (I have since discovered that more than 70 per cent of Sudan's export commodities – oil and petroleum products, cotton, sesame seed, livestock, groundnuts – go to China while more than 20 per cent of Sudan's imports come from China, mainly foodstuffs and manufactured goods.)

Just before sunset the braking system developed a problem, which caused another hold-up. By now we were in the Nubian Desert in the eastern part of the Sahara, by and large a sandstone plateau between the Nile and the Red Sea where there is virtually no rainfall, no oases, but lots of wadis (dry riverbeds) flowing towards the Nile. Most passengers disembarked and used the enforced break to pray (about 70 per cent of Sudan's population is Muslim). A red sun was setting, a beautiful sight that I could not appreciate because as it got darker and darker I could feel my blood pressure go up and up. Sitting on the hot sand looking at the Sudan Railway Corporation logo, I thought it would look and read so much better if they were to add FUCKED UP right above that red emblem.

After three hours we headed off northwards again. Not for long. Within 20 minutes or so we came to a dead stop. I was beginning to dream of air-conditioned offices, boardrooms and cars, as well as cold beers after work. The train had broken down again.

Sudanese are such nice people. Every time the train came to a standstill, someone would come to me and explain that I should not worry because eventually we'd get to Wadi Halfa. I was so *gatvol* of that shitty train I was seriously starting to doubt whether we would ever reach our destination. But each time they would get the train going again.

The second night on the train was even worse than the first. Although it was not as hot, the dust seemed to be getting worse by the minute and the snoring from the guys in the compartment even louder.

We must have been two hours from Wadi Halfa when it felt as if we had hit a sand bank. Suddenly the air was thick with sand as fine as dust. The fact that I could hardly breathe and was sitting on a very uncomfortable seat made that night the worst night of the whole Cape to Cairo trip. At one point the cloud of dust did not let up and almost everyone was coughing – we were probably travelling through one of the dreaded desert sand storms.

Just after sunrise, 46 hours after leaving Khartoum, we arrived at the inland port (read 'village') of Wadi Halfa. According to the train schedule we were supposed to have covered the 1 000-kilometre distance between Khartoum and Wadi Halfa in 30 hours. Wiping the sand from my eyes and looking at those locomotives, wagons, railway lines, I wondered whether the trains of the Sudan Railway Corporation ever ran according to schedule. Whether anything ever went as planned.

Like Khartoum – and Walvis Bay in Namibia – Wadi Halfa is built on sand. There is sand everywhere and everything looks dusty. I followed the men I shared the compartment with to the ferry check-in office. Afterwards I had to go to the immigration office, where it took more than an hour to process my documents. In one of the queues I had to pay a certain amount of money, but I could not tell how much because the official spoke Arabic only. The man behind me took my wallet from my hand and gave himself permission to take out the required amount. One thing about Africa, generally speaking: alongside poverty there is both innocence and honesty.

After passing through immigration I had to take a ten-minute trip on an open truck to the port of Wadi Halfa. Waiting for the truck, I used the opportunity to reflect on the past two days on the train. Only one word kept coming to mind: dust.

There were more immigration offices at the port where my passport had to be stamped. Having experienced Sudanese bureaucracy more than a few times, I thought it would be wise to get my passport stamped before most of the passengers on the ferry got to customs. It was not to be.

As per usual procedure, the immigration offices were opened only one hour before the departure of the ferry. New forms had to be filled in and I had to join a long queue for the actual stamping of the passport. Before my passport was stamped, however, an immigration officer wanted to see my yellow-fever vaccination certificate. Then I had to join another queue to have my bag checked and, once that was done, join another queue to have a blue sticker attached to it. Then I had to join the queue where they checked for the stickers. Only then could I leave the waiting hall, not to go to the ferry but to join another queue for the truck that was going to take us to the ferry one kilometre away.

It was another very hot day and the truck seemed to take forever to arrive while we waited in the baking-hot sun. Getting on the truck was chaotic as everyone was pushing hard to get a seat.

Getting off was equally so, as was embarking on the waiting ferry. I could not understand why things could not be done in a proper and systematic way.

I had been allocated a two-bed cabin on the ferry to share with a Sudanese man of Indian descent. Although small, it was air-conditioned and very comfortable. I gave a sigh of relief.

As the ferry chugged out of the port I thought to myself that it was a pity there was no academic course, as far as I knew, on bureaucracy. Had there been one, every Sudanese would hold a PhD in the subject because they are all such natural masters of that trade. In addition, the ability of the Sudanese to change what is supposed to be a simple and straightforward process into a highly complex one that ends up confusing everybody but themselves made me conclude that all women must originate from Sudan (not Ethiopia despite its candidacy for 'Cradle of Mankind' status).

Just before sunset, as the ferry moved along Lake Nasser, we had an awesome view of Abu Simbel, the temple built about 4 500 years ago by the greatest pharaoh of them all, Ramses II. After glimpsing these gigantic monuments I knew that as soon as I got to Aswan I would have to turn back to visit Abu Simbel.

Most people, especially those with third-class tickets, slept on the deck of the ferry. The smoothness of the lake and my having spent the two previous nights slouched on an uncomfortable seat in a dusty train made me sleep like a baby that night. Nevertheless, I awoke feeling very lethargic. Only then did I remember that I had not had a bath in more than 72 hours. What aggravated the situation was that 46 of those hours were spent in a sand-infiltrated train.

In order to have a better view of the lake and the desert I went to the upper deck, where I was joined by a young man named John. Judging by his fluency in English and his very tall stature and pitch-black skin colour, I thought he must be a Dinka from Southern Sudan. What made me even more sure that he came from these cattle-herding people were the linear markings on his forehead. Like Sothos and Xhosas, who go to the mountain for circumcision as part of their initiation rituals, Dinka boys have to endure the pain of being scarified on their foreheads with a sharp object to prove that they are ready for manhood.

Thanks to King Shaka, the founder of the Zulu nation, we Zulus do not have to go to the mountain.

Thanks to Shaka, again, I still have my foreskin and sex has never been better. (I do not use a condom because I sleep only with my partner, thank you very much.)

After some small talk, John and I began to talk politics. He looked very puzzled when I referred to myself as a black person. His response was: 'If you are black, then what am I?'

Another first. Nobody had ever before questioned my race. I tried explaining to him that some black people are light in complexion. He did not want to hear anything of the sort. To him being black meant exactly that: being black, like soot.

John turned out to be a very informative and friendly man. He explained to me that other black Sudanese considered themselves Arabs purely because Arabic is their first language, which further explained their commitment to Islam. (According to statistics I saw later, 52 per cent of Sudanese are black, 39 per cent Arab.)

We were still talking about politics, women, cars and life when

189

we were interrupted by the arrival of Egyptian immigration officials on board. A small boat had brought the five or so smartly uniformed gentlemen to our ferry.

Sudan is the only country where I did not see even one beautiful woman. I personally do not consider women like Alek Wek – Sudanese supermodel and MTV's 1997 Model of the Year, sometimes also referred to as the 'Face of Africa' – to be beautiful.

Nasser's Egypt

Father of the Nation

Of the African countries I visited, Egypt has the longest colonial history. The last Egyptian pharaoh was defeated as early as 343 BC by the Persians. Later, the Greeks and Romans invaded, leading to over 2 000 years of foreign rule. In 639 AD the Muslim Arabs invaded Egypt; they stayed for the next six centuries. Then, in 1250 AD, the Mamluk Turks took control and governed even after the Ottoman Turks conquered the country in 1517.

The history of modern Egypt is generally accepted as beginning in 1882, when Egypt became a de facto British colony. This situation persisted until 28 February 1922 when the country was officially granted independence; British troops, however, remained in Egypt and true self-rule did not occur until 1952 with the rise to power of Colonel Gamal Abdel Nasser. Nasser's one-party state has seen many changes but has remained in place under his successors.

Gamal Abdel Nasser was born in Alexandria in 1918, the son of a postal worker. As a schoolboy he attended his first political demonstration. He became so caught up in politics that he spent only 45 days of his last school year in school. When he was admitted to the Egyptian Military Academy at age 19 he abandoned his political activities for a while, but after the outbreak of World War II he resumed his active involvement in national affairs.

Regarded as the father of modern-day Egypt, Nasser was president for 14 years (1956–70). He is credited with Pan Arabism: the creation of strong, aggressive Arab states that are able to challenge the imperialist West and whose resources are used for the benefit of the Arab world and not for the West. When Nasser died in 1970 of a heart attack while still in office an estimated five million people attended his funeral – one of the largest funerals in world history.

Nasser was succeeded by his long-time friend and ally Anwar Sadat who led Egypt for eleven years (1970–81) before he was assassinated. He was succeeded by the then deputy president and former air chief, Marshal Muhammad Hosni Said Mubarak, the present head of state.

My first impression of Egyptians was that they were very efficient. We were still about two hours from the port of Aswan when officials came on board the ferry to begin processing our documents. An announcement was made on the loudspeaker, which John interpreted for me – the officials would process foreigners first, followed by the Egyptians and, lastly, the Sudanese. That was good news for me, but not for John.

The ferry's dining room served as the immigration office. I was the third person in the queue. Two guys from Brazil in front of me were stamped in without a problem. I thought that I would follow suit, but when my passport was given to an official he pointed me to another official, an elderly man seated on a chair behind a table in the corner. After asking me a few basic questions this official requested that I wait at another table.

It was a long wait. After about two hours there were ten of us who had been put aside like this. All the others were from Sudan. It so happened that two of the five men with whom I had shared a compartment on the Khartoum–Wadi Halfa train were also on the waiting list with me. Although happy to see each other again, circumstances were different now and we did not even talk to one another. The old man who had questioned me earlier left with all ten passports. I am not sure where he went.

The good news was that, although the ferry had docked, nobody was allowed to disembark until everyone had been processed. An hour later the first batch of passports came back, but mine was not among them. I started to panic and that is when I remembered the big sign I had seen at the Egyptian embassy in Addis Ababa: *Having a visa does not guarantee entry into Egypt. Officials at the point of entry have a final say.*

I began to think of what I would do if I were refused entry into Egypt. Going back to Sudan was out of the question because I had a single-entry visa only. While I was still weighing the few options open to me, my passport was returned – after almost four hours of sitting in the ferry's dining room. It had been stamped. From a bureaucratic point of view at least, Cairo was now a certainty.

Getting off the ferry was far worse than getting on beause of the rule that all passengers had to be cleared before any could leave the boat. It didn't take me all that long though, after some pushing and shoving. But once we were outside and on the quay we had to wait again, now in blistering heat, for the Egyptian military to accompany us to the customs and immigration offices. The same procedure ensued: foreigners, excluding Sudanese, had to go to the front of the queue. Security was very tight; all bags were scanned and then searched by hand. Passengers, too, had to go through the scanner and were then searched, just like the luggage.

As I exited, still considering whether or not to wait for the Sudanese guy, John, who was behind me somewhere, I was suddenly overwhelmed by taxi and bus touts, just when I least expected it. If I had thought that harassment was bad in Moyale in southern Ethiopia and at the Songwe border in Tanzania, I was totally mistaken. The Egyptian touts literally pulled me in different directions. Eventually, it came down to two guys, each pulling on an arm. After a lot of shouting at each other, and a bit of pushing and shoving, one finally gave up. I allowed nature to take its course and I took the winner's cab.

That youngster drove like a maniac and, in no time at all, we were in the very attractive town of Aswan. He dropped me off at the budget hotel on Corniche el-Nil Road, which had a beautiful view of the Nile.

Given my dislike of big cities (the rush, the concrete jungle, everyone trying to make a quick buck and looking at life mainly through material- istic eyes), I instantly fell in love with the relaxed atmosphere of Aswan. That afternoon I had a good meal of fish and chips at a picturesque riv- erside restaurant while watching feluccas, the traditional wooden sailing boats, sailing up and down the Nile. It was another of those 'life is good' moments. The Sudanese train was a distant memory; I did not envy the people who were now on their way from Wadi Halfa to Khartoum.

The following day I decided, in order to better understand Nubian history, to visit the Nubian Museum. At Aswan the desert closes in on the river and it is very hot in summer (average temperature 40 degrees). Still, I thought I would attempt the ten-minute walk down the road to the museum. The city itself runs in a strip along the Nile.

I have always wondered why there is a separate branch of study called Egyptology. My first few minutes in the Nubian Museum answered that question: it showed me how very long and complex Egypt's history is. I was amazed by the intelligence and achievements of the Egyptians in the BC era, revealed in facts that I had not encountered as yet in history books. To understand the role played by the different rulers in Egypt over the centuries, however, you needed a lot of time and mine was too limited.

The most disturbing events for me in Egypt's history were the building of the Aswan Dam and the High Dam by the British in 1898–1912 and by Nasser's government in 1960–1971, respectively. With more than 95 per cent of Egypt a desert, the authorities had to try and capture as much water as possible during the annual flooding of the Nile by building a dam and big reservoir. It came at a price.

After the Aswan Dam (sometimes referred to as the Old Dam) was built, it was found to hold insufficient water. Twice the wall was raised, making the dam the biggest in the world for a while. But, 50 years later, it became clear that the Aswan Dam could no longer satisfy Egypt's need for water. Work started on the High Dam, in the construction of which 451 people died and more than 40 000 Nubians, a people who are seemingly unrelated to the other desert tribes in the region, had to relocate.

Faced with the choice of either preventing the flooding of the Nile delta up north in years when it rained a lot (and famine when it didn't) or destroying an ancient culture, the Nasser government chose the latter. It built a wall that is a kilometre thick at the base, 3,6 kilometres long and 100 metres high, creating a 510-kilometre-long reservoir – Lake Nasser, the world's largest artificial lake. In the process, the Nubians were displaced and a way of life shattered that had existed unchanged for five millennia. Many ancient monuments had to be moved from the Nile Valley and reassembled on higher ground.

As I had promised myself on the ferry from Wadi Halfa, I did not leave Egypt without visiting Abu Simbel. The day after my arrival I joined an organised tour, supposedly the best way to visit the temple complex from Aswan.

It was another early start. On the outskirts of the town our group had to wait for other tour groups because tourists are obliged by law to travel in convoy. This is to ensure that they do not fall victim to some fundamentalist who would like nothing better than to blow up a few Westerners. In the end we were about five vehicles travelling in line.

The golden sunrise over the desert as we drove to Abu Simbel was the best I had seen on the trip. It must have had something to do with the very straight and flat road and the sense of infinity created by the unending desert on both sides of the road. With a couple seated next to me, however, who kept touching each other in very sensitive places, I could not concentrate on the magnificent rising sun, yellow like egg yolk, as much as I would have liked.

It took us just over three and a half hours to cover the approximately 300 kilometres to Abu Simbel. Judging from the number of visitors it appeared to be a major tourist attraction.

Just a short walk from the security gates at the entrance to the complex, I came face to face with four gigantic and majestic statues. Ybsambul, as Abu Simbel was called in ancient times, had long been forgotten when, on 22 May 1813, a Swiss explorer named Johann Ludwig Burckhardt noticed, by chance, the upper parts of four stone giants protruding from the sand. The temple, re-buried in sand after the initial clearing of its entrance, emerged only in the 20th century when the sand was finally cleared.

I could not believe that such a huge monument had to be moved from its original site in the Beka Valley in the 1960s in order to escape the rising waters of Lake Nasser – at a cool cost of us$40 million, a debt that, apparently, is still being repaid. The entire monument was hand-sawn into 1 050 blocks that weighed up to 30 tons apiece – after the sandstone, which was very brittle and starting to fall apart, was injected with synthetic resin.

The four 22-metre-high statues of the seated figure of Ramses II (1304–1237 bc) in the Sun Temple, each measuring over four metres from ear to ear, were carved from a single rock. The detail of the paintings on the walls of the temple, all depicting scenes of Ramses' victories over the Nubians, was mind-boggling. Right at the end of the temple is the most secret place, the sanctuary, again with four statues. One is of Ramses himself, the pharaoh-god who clearly liked his own image; the other three represent patron deities – Ptah, Amun-Re and Re-Herakhte.

What really blew my mind, however, was the miraculous penetration of the entire length of the temple twice a year – on 22 February and 22 October – by the rays of the sun, which then and only then, illuminate three of the four statues in the sanctuary. After about five minutes the light disappears. True to his name, Ptah, the god of darkness, is never touched by sunlight. How the ancient Egyptians worked that one out beats me.

A little further north of the Sun Temple stands the Temple of Hathor, which is decorated with six colossal, ten-metre-high statues – four of Ramses II and two of Nefertari, his wife (not to be confused with Nefertiti, the famous wife of Pharaoh Akhenaten c.1339–1362 BC). Each statue is accompanied by two smaller figures, standing knee-high in the shadows – their children.

Later, I sat with Lake Nasser at my back, gazing at the beauty in front of me. One of the disadvantages of being part of a guided tour is that everything is planned in advance. I would have loved to stay and feast my eyes on those statues for much longer, but we were scheduled to leave for the High Dam.

After stopping at the High Dam tower to see both the Aswan and High dams, we left for the the island of Philae, where the Temple of Isis once stood. Apparently, European travellers in the 18th century could marvel at it only from a distance because the islanders fought them off whenever they tried to land. With the construction of the Aswan Dam, the temple complex on Philae was submerged under water for half the year, in the rainy season. When the High Dam was planned, it became clear that the entire island would disappear forever under water once construction was completed. So a massive operation was undertaken between 1972 and 1980 to move the complex from its original site to nearby Aglika Island, which was landscaped to look just like Philae.

In Egypt you pay baksheesh for almost everything. Even a policeman insisted on baksheesh after he took a photo of me in front of one of the pillars of the temple. I spent an hour wandering around the island before heading back with the group to Aswan.

Since it was my last day in Aswan I decided to take a sunset cruise in a felucca moored next to the restaurant alongside the Nile embankment. It was most relaxing and since feluccas use only lateen sails and no motor we drifted gently on the waters of the Nile. I spent half an hour on the Island of the Plants (Geziret al-Nabatat), which is popularly known as Kitchener's Island. It is named after Lord Horatio Kitchener and was presented to him in recognition of his distinguished service as head of the Anglo-Egyptian Army after he crushed the Sudanese rebellion of 1898 and ensured British control over Sudan. (Yes, the same Omdurman that is now part of the three-in-one capital of Sudan.)

Kitchener, showing his human side, imported flowering plants from as far afield as Asia, in a variety of colours and fragrances, which turned the island into a lovely botanical garden and one of Aswan's main tourist attractions. Kitchener is the same guy who headed south from Egypt to sort out the Boers in the Anglo-Boer War (now called the South African War because darkies also took part in the war, on both sides).

On waking the following day I decided not to leave Aswan. It is amazing how things had changed. At one point I was obsessed with getting to Cairo as fast as possible, but now that I was in Aswan I could not care less about the rest of the trip. I really loved Aswan. Maybe it had to do with the fact that locals were calling me a Nubian, which to me sounded very exotic. Besides visiting an unfinished obelisk, I spent the day lazing around stalls and chatting.

I decided to take another sunset cruise. While having pre-cruise drinks I met three guys from Denmark who persuaded me to do the full-day tour of Luxor with them the next day. I gave them the name of my hotel and my room number. Early the next morning the receptionist knocked on my door to tell me that a tourist minibus was waiting for me downstairs.

Security is very tight in Egypt. On the outskirts of Aswan, we had to wait for other tour operators so that we could travel in convoy to Luxor. It took us three and a half hours to get to Luxor, just under 300 kilometres away. Like Khartoum, it is a three-in-one affair. On the east is Karnak village and the actual city of Luxor, on the west bank lies the Valley of the Kings.

Our first stop was the Colossi of Memnon with its two gigantic 20-metre-high enthroned statues with feet two metres long and one metre wide. The statues were built in 1400 BC and are thought to have stood at the entrance to the death temple of a pharaoh. The place was plundered for building material by later pharaohs until nothing but the two 'colossi' remained. Both lost their faces and crowns in a severe earthquake in 27 BC. To add insult to injury, one was also split to the waist.

In the Valley of the Queens, to which we then went, only two tombs were open to the public. Our guide, Mohamed, was very clued up on the process of mummification, which involves the removal of all internal organs from a corpse, including the brain. The organs were put in jars and placed next to the corpse in the burial chamber within the tomb. Only the heart was left because the ancient Egyptians believed that people are judged not by their deeds but by their heart.

No mummies, unfortunately, were on display, but the walls of the tombs had very detailed drawings and paintings of humans. I noticed the paintings were crawling with snakes as well as strange human beings with tails or an animal head. The Valley of the Queens is right in the middle of the desert and I was pouring with sweat. To make things worse, some small insects there were specialists in biting. And it looked as if those insects were more interested in Nubian than in European blood.

Just one and a half kilometres from the Valley of the Queens is the Valley of the Kings. Although only about 200 metres wide and 400 metres long, it houses more than 64 known tombs. The most famous is that of Tutankhamun, the boy-pharaoh who ascended to the Egyptian throne in 1361 BC when he was only nine. His tomb, probably the greatest tourist attraction on the west bank, was found by an archaeologist in 1922.

I did not visit King Tut's tomb – most of its treasures are in the Cairo Museum, anyway – and, instead, descended the steep stairways of the vast tomb of Ramses II into the actual burial chamber, to see his sarcophagus (stone coffin). Comparing modern graves to these ancient tombs is like comparing a shack to a multi-storey mansion. The ancient Egyptians must have had a lot of time on their hands. How else could they have constructed such big chambers in the sand in the middle of a desert? Surely the sand would have kept filling up the holes they dug?

Mohamed, although a very informative tour guide, would harass us by telling us repeatedly to 'buy this, buy that, this is good price', etc. He even lured us into a shop by promising us that we were going to get complimentary drinks, which in that very hot weather was most welcome. After the drinks, however, we realised that we were expected to buy some souvenirs before heading for the east bank.

Mohamed promised to take the Danes and me to a five-star hotel for lunch, for which we were going to have to pay ourselves. The tricky part of this arrangement was that we had to pay Mohamed beforehand. Even though someone was waiting for us when we entered the restaurant we were treated as if we had not paid. We were told to serve ourselves quickly and that if there were any questions we should give our room numbers as 303–305, as if we were hotel guests Although the Danes, like me, were not impressed, we had no choice but to oblige. The food was great, however. A full buffet of the quality you can expect in the restaurant of a five-star hotel.

After lunch Mohamed collected us from the hotel's lobby to take us to the Karnak temple complex. According to him, this massive archaeological site was built over a period of 2 000 years. Different pharaohs made their mark by extending the grandest of the three temples, the Temple of Amun, adding halls and chapels. The Hypostele Hall, which is regarded as one of the greatest pieces of ancient Egyptian art, is located in the temple. Mohamed boasted that, at 6 000 square metres, it was big enough to hold both St Peter's in Rome and St Paul's in London. The hall contains 134 gigantic, evenly spaced columns, some of which are more than 20 metres high.

Within the temple there is an area that worshippers in ancient times circled seven times before making a wish in the belief that everything they wished for would come true. Well, in the present, too, there are tourists going around and around, making their wishes. During our visit, while wondering whether I should join the circle, I overheard a girl saying, 'Well, if I don't get married in the next 12 months, I will definitely give up.' I decided not to join the circle.

After Karnak we visited Luxor Temple, right in centre of the city. The temple was built over a span of 250 years, mostly by Amenhotep III (who erected most of it around 1380 BC) and the great and powerful Ramses II. But other pharaohs also added bits and pieces.

Luxor Temple, I discovered later, was meant to serve as a love nest for the gods: once a year, during spring, the statues of Amun and his wife Mut would be brought here by sacred boat from Karnak Temple in a fertility festival that was famous for its public debauchery. The temple was modified by Alexander the Great after he conquered Egypt in 332 BC and, when Islam arrived in Egypt after 600 AD, two mosques were erected on top of it. One of these is still used for worship today. Of course, once the two mosques were put up it was the end of all the fun and games.

I was deeply impressed that most of the structures we saw that day were built more than 4 000 years ago. I had to agree that Luxor was the undisputed capital of the ancient world. The whole day was a case of information overload for me, however. It was too much to absorb in 24 hours.

Later that afternoon it was time to say goodbye to my Danish companions who, for no reason I could see, had been holding hands during the day and now and then touching each other's bum. They were heading back to Aswan and it was with a sigh of relief that I saw them disappear in the dust.

Sharm el-Sheik on the Red Sea, the popular resort town east of Luxor where 88 people were killed in a bomb attack two days before I set off from Durban, should have been next on my itinerary. Pondering my next move, I decided to check for emails from my fiancée. By this stage she was the only one still keeping in touch. In the email she sent me she poured her heart out about how much she was missing me and how much she was longing for me to come home. More than anything – besides requesting an update on my recovery from my Khartoum accident – she was concerned about my safety and well-being. The words that changed the course of the rest of my trip were: *Without you by our side Nala and I are losing our minds.* That was it – the decision was made. I would head straight for Cairo. And I would apologise to my fiancée about the SMS.

I emailed back that being knocked down by a bus in Khartoum was just my way of coping with such a demanding trip. It was not possible for me, I explained, to focus on the challenge ahead while at the same time being questioned about my imperfect behaviour. With Cairo in sight, I told her, I could now afford to speak the truth. Recklessly I signed off with *I love you.*

I went to the train station and, although there were a number of people buying tickets, things went in a very orderly fashion and, unlike at Victoria Falls, the queue moved very quickly. I bought a first-class ticket (as all tourists are required to do by law for security reasons). For once I was going to travel in style. While hanging around for more than an hour, waiting for the train to arrive, I bumped into a backpacker, Mark, from Australia. We chatted for a bit until I mentioned that I was on the home run on my Cape to Cairo trek. He looked at me for a few seconds without saying a word. Then he said, 'You? Please. A sissy like you did the Cape to Cairo?' With that he picked up his dirty backpack and disappeared down the platform among the other passengers.

The train heading for Cairo arrived at 20:00 on the dot. A twenty-something Japanese guy was already in my compartment when I got there. He was visiting Egypt for a month in order to study Arabic. When I told him I was from South Africa he immediately asked me, 'Is it true that Namibia means North India?' It had been a while since I laughed so hard that my stomach ached.

As we reached the first houses of Luxor I remembered that exactly a week earlier I had spent my first night on the Khartoum–Wadi Halfa train. I drank my whisky while enjoying a shwarma and thought about the people who, at that very moment, would be breathing in vast quantities of sand dust on the train. After a while I thought that maybe they were not breathing in any dust because the train had broken down again. Just before falling asleep that night I had another of those feel-good moments. I was very close to fulfilling my childhood dream and I could see that dreams do come true if you keep on keeping on.

The next morning we were woken up for a warm and delicious breakfast of eggs, tomato, toast and coffee that was served in the dining car of the train and soon afterwards stopped at Gaza station, the last station before Cairo. Eight and a half hours after leaving Luxor, we arrived at our destination.

I was in Cairo.

It was still early in the morning and I had to take a taxi to my Cairo budget hotel. On my way there it suddenly hit me that I had been travelling continuously for almost three months, although it felt more like five. I looked around me. I could not see much because the taxi (yes, in Egypt cabs are called taxis) seemed to be travelling through underground tunnels.

Getting to Cairo felt, firstly, like a huge relief and, secondly, like I had achieved something big with my life. I had never felt that sense of achievement before.

It felt better than the safe landing on my first parachuting adventure.

It felt better than crossing the Comrades finishing line.

It felt like scoring a winning goal during extra time in a World Cup final must feel.

The only difference was that when I got back to Mzansi no one, except for Lulu and my daughter, was going to welcome me at the airport.

During the trip I had been constantly aware that my failure to get to Cairo would make certain individuals very happy – for example, all those doomsayers who kept telling me, before I left Durban, how dark and dangerous the rest of Africa was. If for one reason or another I did not make it to Cairo, almost everyone would have said *sakutshela* – we told you so.

It felt good to have proved to myself that a small-town boy from rural Nqutu in northern KZN could travel more than 11 000 kilometres all by himself to see the sun rise over the largest and most populous city in Africa and the Middle East. On my own steam I had achieved my goal, which is more than Cecil John Rhodes could say about his heavily British Empire-sponsored, imperialist, painting-the-map-red dream.

It had always been my plan to spend a few days in an upmarket hotel and have buffets, cocktails, massages – the works – when I eventually got to Cairo. But here I was on my way to checking into a cheap place. The thing about us black people is that we curse everyone, especially the black government (these days), when we can't afford anything, but when we spend lots of money we feel guilty. Anyway, I checked into a very old and grubby hotel, dropped my bags and headed for the Nile, just in time for a sunrise cruise in a felucca.

Aswan, Luxor and Cairo are all built on the banks of the Nile. Cairo, with a population of more than 15 million, is by far the largest of the three. It was not as chaotic as I had been led to expect. The traffic was flowing freely. In fact, there was not really traffic to speak of at that hour of the morning. Most of shops were still closed and there were hardly any people walking on the streets.

Sailing down the Nile in a felucca simply has to be the highlight of my entire trip. I watched Cairo wake up, the sky turning brighter and brighter, traffic starting to accumulate on both the gigantic Tahrir and 6th of October bridges, the sun reflecting on the skyscrapers on the banks of the river. While drinking in these sights I thought how I could have flown directly from Johannesburg to Cairo but had decided, instead, to do the difficult thing just for the fun of it and push myself to the limit.

At that moment, with Cairo floating by, I felt as if I could do any-thing that I put my mind to. I felt that I was truly and honestly the master of my own destiny. I found myself thinking that:

> I could go one on one with Tiger Woods in a round of golf
> *and win.*
> I could go one on one with Lennox Lewis in a 12-round boxing
> contest *and win.*
> I could go one on one with Luciano Pavarotti in a music
> competition *and win.*

I could go one on one with Roland Schoeman in a 100-metre
freestyle race *and win.*
I could go one on one with Michael Jordan on a basketball
court *and win.*
I could go one on one with Serena Williams on the tennis court
and win.
I could go one on one with Michael Schumacher in a 25-lap
race *and win.*
I could take on Jennifer Lopez and Janet Jackson simultaneously
on the dance floor *and win.*

At that moment I felt – considering my good looks, natural charm,
not to mention adventurous spirit – that I stood a very good chance of
having J Lo and Janet literally fighting for my attention in the back seat
of a limousine.

That is what doing the Cape to Cairo does to your already messed
up mind: it pushes it over the edge. It was a very emotional moment
for me.

The felucca sailed on to Zamalek Island where the rich and famous
live. From the river I could see the posh hotels where I had thought I
was going to stay. Drifting downstream I wished only that Lulu and
Nala could be there with me. Still in the felucca, with the sun rising in
the east, I drew up this agreement with God:

*I, Sihle Khumalo, while fulfilling my spiritual needs, accumulating
material possessions, nurturing my mind through reading, keeping
physically fit and trying to be sane most of the time, will take time off
to, amongst other things:*
Smell the grass after it has been cut
Smell the soil after the rain
Listen to birds singing
Listen to water going down a stream
Kiss my daughter's plump cheeks
Hold the hand of a destitute and underprivileged child
Savour the abundant fresh and juicy fruits and vegetables of the earth

Appreciate nature's beauty on top of mountains and under the sea
and everywhere in between.

To which God responded:

I, God Almighty, will:
in a way
kind of
directly or indirectly
in one way or another
in the short, medium or long term,
overtly or covertly
single-handedly,
on my own terms without prejudice or favour
justifiably or otherwise
based on my own objective, fully informed judgement
after full consideration of past, present and future,
and also of the dead, living and yet-to-be-born
and without owing you or anyone any explanation
unreservedly allow you to do all of the above
and more if you so wish.
And always stand by my word.

After an hour or so of drifting on the Nile past a skyline of skyscrapers, including the 60-storey Cairo Tower commissioned by Nasser to mark the rise of industry in Egypt, it was time to visit the legendary Egyptian Museum, a brightly coloured building tucked behind the City Hall and the hotels that line the Nile.

I spent four hours at the museum, including more than half an hour in the royal mummies room. I would have spent more time there had it not been for the other tourists, who were giving me that 'what is wrong with you' look.

For people who died about 4 000 years ago, the mummies looked in very good shape. I spent most of the time looking at Ramses II, the self-loving pharaoh responsible for most of the monuments in Egypt, including those at Abu Simbel. He supposedly spent 66 years on the throne and had 67 wives and about 110 kids. It depends on whom you ask – one taxi driver told me that Ramses had more than 150 children.

Whatever the correct figure, it is not so high if you consider that our very own King Sobhuza of Swaziland was on the throne for 61 years and in that time had 70 wives (excluding mistresses) and 210 sons and daughters. A great achievement if you consider that the small blue pill had not been invented yet. But then, in Africa it has always been an open secret that the horn of a rhino – *uphondo lukabhejane* – is the best 'medicine' if you are looking for sexual vigour. That also explains why, irrespective of how African governments try to fight it, rhino poaching will never stop.

Another highlight of my visit to the Egyptian Museum was Tutankhamun's treasure room. I could not believe how much the ancient Egyptians had managed to do so long ago in the way of heavily decorated furniture, golden statues, jewellery, masks and weapons. Most of the stuff that had been removed from Tutankhamun's tomb in the Valley of the Kings was in the museum. For me, the most amazing thing was that his body was put in four coffins, one inside the other, the innermost one made of solid gold. King Tut, as he is affectionately known, reigned for only ten years and died at the age of 19. Clearly he made history not because of his political legacy but because of his burial treasures.

When I walked out of the museum I could not help but wonder what had happened to all the technology and expertise of ancient Egypt. As I left the brightly coloured building I was convinced that if the pharaohs and their subjects could do so much they must have had much more intelligence than we normally expect of people who lived so many centuries before us – as if true intelligence is a modern invention.

Later that afternoon, driving back to my hotel in a cab, I saw the real Cairo: continuous hooting, disorder, chaos, cars pushing into the traffic from the side, buses and trucks switching lanes. I was convinced we were going to have an accident. The cab driver told me that in Cairo accidents rarely happen and when there is an accident, it is usually just scratches, nothing major.

That evening I went to the hotel bar, which was dead quiet. I suspect this had something to do with Egypt being a Muslim country and with alcohol, although available, being so expensive. I decided it was time to go to bed.

There was one thing left to do while I was in Egypt, maybe two. One, anyway, was to see the only surviving wonder of the seven wonders of the ancient world: the Great Pyramid of Giza near the ancient city of Memphis. The others – the Hanging Gardens of Babylon on the banks of the Euphrates River; the Statue of Zeus at Olympia; the Temple of Artemis at Ephesus; the mausoleum for the Persian King Maussollos at Halicarnassus; the Colossus of Helios near the Greek harbour of Rhodos; and the Lighthouse of Alexandria on the island of Pharos – no longer exist. To be able to dictate my own tour pace and time, I decided not to join the guided tour but to travel by public transport to Giza.

I spent the whole morning downtown trying to get used to Cairo's chaos. Looking at the disorder on the roads, I arrived at Business Idea Five: to start a company devoted to defensive driving. There would be neither course nor instructor. My company would simply organise air travel to Cairo and, once there, hire cars for our trainees. If they could drive in Cairo for three consecutive days without an accident, they would pass. Trainees who had an accident would have to stay longer in Cairo – at their own expense, of course.

I caught a Giza-bound bus behind the Egyptian Museum. When I alighted in Giza, in front of a market consisting of only a few stalls, touts from the stables in the area were already waiting for people like me who wanted to explore the pyramids on the back of a camel or a horse. I chose Farouk – somehow I believed him when he promised me that he would take me to the 'best stable in Giza which will also give you a good price'. The stables offered short, medium and long tours, but the manager was quick to point out that I should take the long tour 'because you do not get the chance to see the pyramids every day'. After some administrative procedures (read 'payment') it was showtime. I was given a horse named Miriam who, I was told, was very docile.

Owing to the extremely hot weather I had stopped wearing underwear in Sudan. I had continued with that practice in Egypt and
had not regretted my decision until my first few seconds on the back
of Miriam. Almost at once I realised that my pyramid sightseeing
was going to be a good and moving story with a very painful ending.
Accompanied by a mounted guide, who spoke little English, I hit the
backstreets of Giza and then the desert. Miriam was proving to be a
very tame horse indeed. I could hardly get her to move.

The pyramids – there are two big ones, one medium-sized and
six small ones, built as tombs by the pharaohs – are raised on a kind
of plateau, almost on the fringes of Giza. For a good view we had
to climb the sand dunes on horseback. On our way to the dunes we
passed a young couple who were having a heated argument because
the woman had decided that she could not ride a horse and was insisting that she and her friend/husband should go on one horse. Whether
on a horse or a quadbike, women are clearly not made to ride in the
desert …

At a height of 135 metres, the Great Pyramid, the oldest as well as
largest of Giza's pyramids, also known as Khufu or Cheops, was far
bigger than I had ever imagined. Even after all the explaining by the
various guides, I could not understand how such a huge monument
could be built in the middle of the desert more than 4 500 years ago.
Khufu – made of 2 300 000 blocks averaging two and a half tons in
weight (some weighing almost 15 tons) – is supposed to weigh a total
of 6 000 000 tons.

When Miriam eventually reached the top of the plateau, I had an
awesome view of all nine pyramids. It was a moment I knew I would
cherish for the rest of my life. I wished I could just sit there on Miriam's
back and look and look.

On our way back the guide and I went past the mysterious Sphinx,
a 57-metre-long half-human statue carved out of limestone, with the
body of a lion and a man's face. I felt a sudden upsurge of energy and,
since this was my umpteenth time riding a horse, I thought I should
see how fast Miriam could run. I pushed my heels into her flanks
and the normally calm creature leapt forward. After almost falling off,

I decided to take it easy, like everybody else. Besides, the lack of underwear was not really conducive to racing.

The whole trip was over in two hours. Just as every Muslim should visit Mecca at least once in his or her lifetime, I wished as I took leave of my guide that every living human being would visit the pyramids at least once before departing this life. I had never before considered the possibility of living in a desert, but I now felt I could live there any time – the desert next to pyramids has, surely, to be the most sought-after real estate in the whole world.

Back in Cairo, and feeling spiritually very uplifted, I decided to have lunch at one of the upmarket hotels along the Nile. As I was enjoying a scrumptious buffet in the Hilton, one of Cairo's finest hotels, I began to feel guilty. Not because of how much I was going to pay, but because of the rich and fattening food I was consuming: a variety of fruits, yoghurt, seafood galore, roast vegetables and meat, desserts to pick and choose from. Especially since I had weighed myself in Aswan and discovered that, irrespective of the vast amounts of alcohol that I had consumed, I had managed to lose more than ten kilos in just more than two months. I had come to the conclusion that the most effective weight-loss programme was to do the Cape to Cairo by public transport.

I was about to ask for the bill when a tall, classy, sexy woman walked into the restaurant. She looked exactly like my fiancée, except that she was not as elegant and gorgeous. She was more like Desirée – a London-based artist of Jamaican origin who sang the hit songs 'You gotta be' and 'Life'. The Desirée look-alike must have been in her late thirties or early forties. I have always had a soft spot for older women because of their maturity, being comfortable in their own skin and accepting the women they have become. In fact, nothing turns me on like a mature sister who oozes confidence and elegance. Even my fiancée knows that, besides her, I honestly think that Angela Basset – of 'How Stella got her groove back' fame – is the sexiest woman alive.

Considering what happened in Nairobi when I approached somebody else's girlfriend/wife, I was very reluctant to approach this woman. I thought I would just hang around instead and get myself some more dessert. All the time I was thinking with both my heads, and my upper head – the rational one – was telling me to leave the restaurant. After all, I had abstained for more than two months and a few more days, until I got back to South Africa, were not going to kill me. My upper head insisted that I leave the restaurant immediately – I did not want to spoil my record of having been faithful to my fiancée. But my other head was saying, 'Oh man, that sister is so hot and sexy! Go for it, bru! Do not deny me.'

My dessert eaten, I was trying to analyse these conflicting thoughts and to decide whether to approach the Desirée look-alike or not. After more than half an hour, when I was sure that she was definitely on her own, I decided to pounce. I considered a variety of approaches, including: So, you also believe that the longest bone in a human body is the femur – the thigh bone? I have news for you, my sister. My longest bone is not my femur ...'

I was tempted to say this, but of course I could not bring myself to utter such words.

When I finally approached her, I discovered that Emily Williams was the owner of a travel agency in New York and that she was in Egypt to attend the Mediterranean Trade Fair to network with other stakeholders. She was a divorced mother of two boys and on a mission to expand her business. She made it quite clear she wanted to prove to her ex-husband that she could make it big on her own. To me, at least, that was a sure sign that she still adored her husband.

'My sister,' I said while looking at her cleavage, 'life has proved over and over again that if you still feel that you have a point to prove to your ex, it means you still have feelings for him. The only time you know you are done with your ex is when you have no emotions, either positive or negative, towards him and when you have no point to prove to him. Your ex-husband must be a nobody to you. That is when you know he is history.'

According to Emily, it was not that simple. 'We brought two beautiful boys into this world,' she told me with a very heavy sigh. 'And that will always somehow keep us connected.'

While we were talking she kindly remarked that, like her, I sported a dimple in the right cheek. It also turned out that she was booked into the very hotel where we were having lunch. After chatting for almost half an hour she invited me not to her room but to the hotel's terrace for a cup of coffee. We had a very good chat about a variety of topics, such as the state of Africa as a continent, George W Bush and racism in America. In the course of our conversation she mentioned that she was going to visit Luxor, Aswan and Hurghada, a lively city on the Red Sea. I told her that my plan was to go north to Alexandria, Egypt's second largest city, where a lighthouse considered one of the seven architectural wonders of the ancient world once stood.

After some more soulful talk, Emily and I prepared to go our separate ways. She paid for both our coffees and, as we were about to leave the table, she opened her arms to give me a hug. Naturally I could not refuse such a gesture; after all, I do not get hugs from stunning sisters like her every day. The problem was that because she was so tall – Tyra Banks's height, at least – I found my head right between her boobs and my full stomach right against her pelvic area. Have you ever been in a situation that you just wished, hoped and prayed would linger forever? Although I was almost suffocating, I did not want to let go. I was convinced that if I should die at that moment (from lack of oxygen) I would go straight to heaven.

One of my heads started getting bigger and I found myself thinking again that I should, maybe, have started the trip in Cairo and finished it in Cape Town. That way I would have spent a week at least with Emily in Luxor and Aswan. Wow!

My other head put the matter straight. But Sihle, it reminded me, if you had started in Cairo you would be in Cape Town by now. So there is no way you would have met Emily.

I was thinking all this while holding Emily very tight just above her bum. In no time it was time to let go. 'So how is the view of the Nile from your room?' I asked.

It's breathtaking. Do you want to come up and have a look?

I was hoping she would say something to that effect. Instead her response was, 'Don't spoil it. It was nice meeting you, my brother.'

I watched her from behind as she wiggled her humungous cellulite-inflated bum from side to side towards the lifts. Sour grapes – I know.

Considering Cairo's chaos and noise you would be forgiven for thinking that Cairo has a vibrant nightlife. It's actually quite the opposite. Bored later that night and dozing off, I had Business Idea Six: open a nightclub in Cairo and call it The Pyramid. The VIP section and the DJ's box of the nightclub I opened would be called The Tomb and The Sphinx, respectively, whereas the dance floor, for obvious reasons, would be The Desert. With so many tourists visiting Egypt, The Pyramid was bound to be a hit.

As I had explained to Emily the previous afternoon, Cairo was proving too chaotic for my liking. I decided to head further north (northwest, in fact) to Alexandria. The story of Alexander the Great, after whom the city is named, has always fascinated me. During his short 33 years on this planet Alexander the Great had conquered most of the known world. I was intrigued that the great Alexander, after grabbing Egypt from the Persians, instructed his architect to build a new Egyptian capital. He then travelled to Asia, where he died without ever having seen Alexandria.

I had been so impressed with the Luxor–Cairo overnight train that I decided to go by train to Alexandria. As usual, after buying my ticket I had to find someone to help me locate the right platform, train and compartment, everything on the ticket being written in Arabic. The man I found was an employee of the railways. Naturally he wanted baksheesh after helping me.

This time I travelled second class, but I was still impressed. It was a very comfortable ride, more so because the wagon was air-conditioned. The railway line sometimes ran parallel to the road. Observing the traffic on the road convinced me that rail was by far the best way to travel in Egypt; it was more comfortable and much faster than road transport.

I planned to spend the whole day in Alexandria and catch the last train back to Cairo at 22:00, allowing me just enough time to pick up my backpack from the hotel, take a cab to the airport and catch a flight that was due to leave in the early hours of the following day, non-stop to Johannesburg. I knew that the trip was technically over and the next time I went to bed it would be in my simplex (flat) back in Durban.

Relaxing in the almost empty train on the way to Alexandria, I started thinking that in a few days' time I was to return to reality and, like other real people, start worrying about real issues like:

> whether Kaizer Chiefs were going to beat Orlando Pirates, or vice versa
> whether the Blue Bulls were going to beat the Natal Sharks, or vice versa
> what would happen in the next episode of *Generations*
> who had the smallest cellphone with the most features
> who was driving the smartest car
> who had bought a new house
> who was dating who
> who was getting married
> who was getting divorced
> who was wearing the same clothes as at last year's end-of-year function

It was depressing to think that the vast majority of people – thanks to mainstream media – sweat the small stuff and not only worry but are obsessed about small, tiny, minute, useless little things.

In less than two and a half hours on the train I was in Alexandria. My first impression of the waterfront city with its old colonial buildings was that Alexandria's buildings urgently needed a very big scrubbing brush and a very powerful hosepipe.

I decided not to take a cab or tram from the train station but to walk to el-Corniche, the beachfront. I looked down at my feet: I was still wearing the same built-up boot. If it had carried me this far, I thought, it might as well carry me to el-Corniche. It was not the best decision, but after more than an hour of hit-and-miss and not asking for directions I finally made it to the beachfront, specifically 26 July Street.

Alexandria is not referred to as the waterfront city for nothing – el-Corniche stretches for 18 kilometres along the Mediterranean. It just goes on and on and on.

Within seconds of arriving at the beachfront I had fallen in love with the relaxed atmosphere of the place. After Cairo, any place would, without a doubt, seem relaxed, but I ended up liking even the very dirty colonial buildings in Alexandria. I sat for a few minutes at the water's edge, just gazing out at the Mediterranean Sea, and found myself making Resolution No. 11: when I finally get married I want my honeymoon to be a Mediterranean cruise.

It was a very good idea because, apart from other considerations, it was going to motivate me to go for swimming lessons (Resolution No. 4). It's not that I expected there to be an accident, but considering how much we'd be rocking that boat it would be better to come prepared for any eventuality.

I was walking from west to east along the waterfront when that noble piece of architecture, the Bibliotheca Alexandrina, suddenly appeared on my right. The new library was inspired by the Royal Library of Alexandria founded in 295 BC, once the largest collection of books in the world, which was mysteriously destroyed by fire around 3 AD. Legend has it that the original library held more than 500 000 scrolls. The idea of reviving the library was first mooted in 1974. The design was chosen in 1988, but construction began only in 1995 and the Bibliotheca was inaugurated on 16 October 2002 – US$220 000 000 later. I figured a visit to Alexandria would not be complete without a visit to the library.

There was a bit of a problem though: to get to the library I had to cross a three-lane highway. I failed to understand how there could be a six-lane freeway – three lanes in each direction, with cars speeding in opposite directions – without a pedestrian bridge to cross it. Imagine the irony of doing the Cape to Cairo on public transport and then being knocked down by a car in Alexandria.

I had no choice, however, but to risk my life and cross the highway.

The inside of the library has a gently sloping floor with many pillars supporting a glass roof. Being such a bookworm, I had to read a book or two. When the library was opened it only had 500 000 books, a very small number if you consider that it has shelf space for 8 000 000 volumes. That explains why, although there were books on the shelves, the library still looked empty-ish.

Instead of asking for help I, typical male, decided to find my own way through the 11 cascading levels. I was basically scanning the books and at the same time appreciating the grand architecture, in particular the pillars that support the sliding glass roof. While thus engaged, I made Resolution No. 12: to get a PhD in something. I was not sure in exactly what, but I knew it would definitely not be economics. After all, the biggest bullshit of our time, besides religion and politics, is economics. I wanted to do research that was going to improve people's lives.

I was still glancing over the rows of books when my attention was caught by two history books: *The History of the World* and *The Second World War*. There is something about books on history that makes me believe in my future. The more I read such books the more confident I feel. If we human beings have made it this far, given some of the leaders we've survived in the past, I believe we will make it to eternity.

My reading was interrupted by the announcement that the library was about to close. I had been there for more than four hours!

It was almost sunset when I left the building. I walked past the huge scripted and carved grey granite walls convinced that the Bibliotheca was one of the finest buildings in Africa, perhaps even in the world.

Moved by this idea, I decided to risk my life again by crossing the highway to the beachfront. I sat at the water's edge and watched couples strolling hand in hand, parents walking with their children. It was time for reflection.

Egyptian women are unattractive as well as very stuck-up and too serious about life. Hence Emily, who (in retrospect) was not so gorgeous, looked so very sexy and special.

Looking back

Travelling alone gives you a lot of time to think about things that you would not have thought about if you were travelling in a group – or stayed home.

Gazing at the Mediterranean I thought that one day I would get married, but not for the wrong reasons, which include but not limited to proving to my Zulu nation that I am no longer a boy. In my society, irrespective of what you have achieved with your life, as long as you are not married your family members, especially uncles, are bound to ask you: *Ushada nini mshana?* – When are you getting married, my nephew?

I also thought that, without being too selfish, I would spend more time with myself by myself and strive to be the person I want to be by not succumbing to any flavour-of-the-month pressures.

Furthermore – based on the number of Africans* I had met on my journey who had no financial resources but were very content with their lives – I thought that although money is important, given the capitalist society we live in, I must never sell my soul just to have purely material things.

Indigenous black people with hair that is coarse, frizzy and very thick when left in its natural state; with skin, whether dark or light, that does not contract cancer. Their males are known worldwide to be well endowed, obsessed with sex, soccer and substance abuse. Their females are said to have big bums riddled with cellulite. These people are born with rhythm in their bones and are eternally optimistic, irrespective of external circumstances. History has proved over and over again that their lives are cheaper and of less value than those of other nations on earth. These people fight, maim, kill and slaughter each other for no reason other than that they belong to different ethnic groups – Sihle Khumalo, private definition.

Thinking about the future, I was generally content with how my life had recently turned out. I was glad that I had

> bungee-jumped twice
> done the Comrades marathon (you don't run it, you do it)
> jumped off a fully functional airplane at 4 000 feet
> > (1 220 metres) above ground level just for the fun of it
> taken a ride on a Pitts plane doing aerobatic flying
> and that I was going to get married to the woman of my
> > dreams.

I was glad that I had left normal life in July and come on this journey. Otherwise I would not have

> quadbiked at Swakopmund in Namibia, kicking dust in a
> > German couple's eyes
> microlighted over Victoria Falls in Zambia with a Swede
> > between my knees
> visited Lake Malawi in the company of multiple guides
> > and touts
> had to shelter from pouring rain under shrubs next to a spice
> > plantation in Zanzibar in Tanzania
> taken a ride on a converted truck from Nairobi to Moyale on
> > the Kenyan border, half-buried under luggage
> done the pantsula at a club in Addis Ababa in Ethiopia –
> > which caused a few jealous stares from some wealthy
> > older guys
> discovered that the Blue Nile and the White Nile were not blue
> > and white where they merge in Khartoum in Sudan
> visited the Great Pyramid of Giza in Egypt – the only surving
> > wonder of the ancient world – on horseback.

With the bright red sun reflecting on the sea, a refreshing sea breeze touching my face and a great piece of architecture at my back, I had to try to answer the question that had been bugging me for the entire trip:

What went wrong on the African continent?

Before answering that question I had to accept two facts that had been glaring at me for the entire trip. One, the Boers, much as they treated their dogs better than us Africans, built South Africa's economy and infrastructure in such a way that nothing elsewhere in Africa can be compared to it; although it was sad for me as an African to admit it, were it not for the Boers South Africa would not be boasting about Africa's biggest economy and a world-class infrastructure, much as they used black labour to do the hard work.

Two, African leaders, both traditional and political, over a period of time have betrayed their people in a big way. For:

> I could not sit there and pretend that from Cape to Cairo I did
> not see malnourished people, because I did
> I could not sit there and pretend that I did not see starving
> people
> I could not sit there and pretend that I did not see sick people
> I could not sit there and pretend that I did not see dying people
> I could not sit there and pretend that I did not see people with
> absolutely nothing on; people living in dismal conditions,
> because I did.

What I could not work out was whether this state of affairs was the result of incompetence, naïvety, greed, a don't-care attitude – or a combination of some or of all of these on the part of our leaders. Or, could it be a combination of some or all these factors plus complicated and complex external factors too involved for a simple mind like mine to comprehend?

It was getting dark and the beachfront was emptying but, based on the suffering of my fellow Africans whom I had seen throughout the trip, I could not help but struggle to understand how

> so-called liberators had turned into dictators
> so-called liberators had ended up being president-for-life
> so-called liberators became heads of one-party states

so-called liberators allowed countries entrusted to them to
deteriorate so much
so-called liberators could neglect their people and ignore their
plight so completely.

I simply could not understand why Africa, the continent with so much abundance, is so abundantly poor.

It all boils down to the leadership we have had on this continent, I thought to myself. We are where we are as a continent – the poorest, least developed, without adequate infrastructure, politically unstable – because of the corrupt, inefficient bureaucrats who cannot see the big picture and thus make us the laughing stock of the whole world.

While our own Mandela spent 27 years in prison fighting for a free South Africa, both Kaunda and Banda spent exactly the same number of years in office. Their actions (or lack thereof) are still evident, even to-day, in Zambia and Malawi. Nyerere was not so bad. He stayed in power for only 24 years. Even better, by African standards, were Nujoma and Mengistu – only 15 and 17 years, respectively. God, thank goodness, now and then does intervene: Kenyatta and Nasser both died while in office, coincidentally also after 15 and 17 years, respectively.

And then, as that fiery ball disappeared behind the horizon, I some-how, against all logic and rational judgement, had this very deep, pro-found and unshakeable belief, based partly on the history of Egypt and partly on the triumph of the African spirit over all injustices and ad-versity, poverty, suffering and neglect – that the future of the world is not only in Africa but the future of this world is Africa. On the spot I decided that I would love to embark on other African expeditions.

It was then that I also decided that when everybody else ran away from Africa I would run to her. After all, I have no other home, but this cradle of humankind.

As I turned my back on the Mediterranean Sea, as if to look at the entire African continent all at once, I found myself thinking, There is something about this continent, there is something about Africa that makes me say:

Ngiyabonga, Africa
Asante sana, Mama Africa
Thank you

If you still think that this is a dark continent, notify Sihle on
sihle.khumalo@webmail.co.za

Acknowledgements

First and foremost I would like to thank my mother for literally praying twice a day throughout my trip. I guess God listens (sometimes).

I am also highly indebted to my wife – my fiancée then – for believing in my dream and standing by my side when almost everyone thought I was mad, crazy and nuts.

To my other family members and friends: I am not sure what I should thank you for. Thanks anyway for whatever ...

This book would not have materialised if it were not for Annari, my publisher, who saw the potential in my manuscript.

And Jeanne: although I sometimes felt you were unreasonable with all the due dates and additional information required, your patience and guidance are highly appreciated.

For companionship and friendship, thanks to all the backpackers and travellers I met along the way. I guess we share the same philosophy – the least we can do, in this ever expanding universe, is to travel extensively on our tiny blue planet Earth.

To all the Africans I met (and the ones that I did not meet) on this journey: you are full proof that the human spirit still triumphs over injustice and profound adversity against all odds. In my eyes, all of you are heroes and heroines.

Last, but not least, how can I forget Leonie, a Dutch gal from Amsterdam who refused to share a room with me in Dar es Salaam? Thanks for nothing, Leonie.